Greening Libraries

Greening Libraries

Edited by Monika Antonelli
and Mark McCullough

Library Juice Press
Los Angeles, CA

Published by Library Juice Press in 2012.

Library Juice Press
PO Box 25322
Los Angeles, CA 90025

http://libraryjuicepress.com/

This book was printed on acid-free, sustainably-sourced paper.

The layout is by Martin Wallace.

The cover was designed by Jana Vukovic.

Library of Congress Cataloging-in-Publication Data

Greening libraries / edited by Monika Antonelli and Mark McCullough.
    pages cm
  Includes bibliographical references and index.
  ISBN 978-1-936117-08-6 (alk. paper)
  1. Libraries--Enviromental aspects. 2. Libraries and community. 3. Library buildings--Environmental aspects. 4. Environmentalism. 5. Libraries--United States--Case studies. 6. Libraries--Canada--Case studies. I. Antonelli, Monika. II. McCullough, Mark.
    Z716.4G75 2012
    027--dc23
            2012020036

Table of Contents

Introduction

In the fall of 2008 my article, "The Green Library Movement: An Overview and Beyond," appeared in *The Electronic Green Journal*. It has since been accessed online over 5000 times. The article presented a snapshot of green, environmental and sustainable practices occurring in the library profession at that time. Many of the projects explored in my article, like seed lending libraries, have since taken root in the public arena and have even received national media attention.

This book, *Greening Libraries,* revisits and expands on the trends that appeared in the original article. In this volume the reader will be introduced to innovative examples of librarians and libraries working to grow and sustain environmentally friendly developments in their home institutions and in the library profession. Some professionals are creating green library buildings while others are providing green programs and offering green services. Some of the articles document what librarians have done while others show us how to green future activities.

The book is divided into three sections: "Green Buildings;" "Green Committees, Services and Programs;" and "Green Resources and Reflections." In "Green Buildings" the reader will explore the construction of Leadership in Energy and Environmental Design (LEED) libraries being built in the United States. This section examines two specific library projects, the LEED Silver George R. White Library and Learning Center on the Concordia University campus in Portland,

Oregon, and the LEED Gold Santa Monica Public Library in Santa Monica, California. Samantha Jane Alberts investigates sustainable library design in Long Island, New York in her research article. The process of making historic buildings green is examined in Rebekkah Smith Aldrich's article, "Greening Libraries in Historic Buildings." Adrianne Ralph explains in her article why every green library does not need to be LEED certified to be environmentally friendly. The innovative green construction being done by the city of Chicago is explored in Greta Bever's article, "Chicago Standard Operating Procedure," which documents how a major urban center can build numerous affordable green libraries.

In the second section of the book, "Green Committees, Services and Programs" a variety of articles examine what dedicated librarians are doing to create beneficial environmental practices within their institutions. The work of a green academic committee is explored in "From Grass Roots to Vital Player: Michigan State University's Library Environmental Committee." In "Tending the Garden: Growing Your Own Green Library Committee" readers get a look at the accomplishments of the Green Task Force at East Carolina University's Joyner Library. In two articles public libraries in Canada demonstrate they are actively green, "West Vancouver Memorial Library: Green by Nature" by Julie Backer and "Greening a Library, Greening a Community: The Calgary Public Library's Eco-Action Plan" by Rosemary Griebel.

Readers will also discover how libraries take their green programs and services out into the community. In Kate Lawrence's article "Library-Sponsored Sustainable Living Outreach in Denver," we learn about a Transition Libraries Committee's work to increase sustainability within the Denver Public Library while at the same time developing green partnerships with the City of Denver and their local Transition Denver Initiative. Robbie Sittel shares her successes and challenges in offering green programming at the Tulsa City County Library in her article "Going Green @ Your Library: One Librarian's Lessons in Programming." In the final article in this section, readers will discover how bookmobiles can run on biodiesel fuel and how solar panels can be used to power in-bus computers and lights in Kathryn Totten's "Bookmobiles are Going Green."

In the third section of the book, "Green Resources and Reflections," readers will discover the challenges of greening a national library conference in "Going Green at the 2009 ACRL 14th National Conference in Seattle." Beth Filar Williams shares her experiences writing as a green librarian in "Green Librarians Blogging." Laura L. Barnes in "Resources for Greening Libraries" provides an extensive annotated bibliography intended as a starting point for librarians who want information to help them green their institutions. Dave Hudson ruminates on the environmental problems of conference swag and the sustainability challenges of library giveaways in his article "Beyond Swag: Reflections on

Libraries, Pencils and the Limits of Green Consumerism." In "Environmental Programs and Green Practices," Maria J. Jankowska provides a valuable timeline of green and environmental activities within the American Library Association and other library organizations. Audrey and Brett Barbakoff explore the idea of greening the library by taking it to where people congregate in "Building on Green: Sustainable Thinking Goes beyond Green to Unite Library Space and Community." The concluding article in the final section, "The Public Library's Role in the Transition Towns Movement" explores how Transition Towns and public libraries can work together to help people access information and provide programs to assist their communities in transitioning to a lower energy future.

In closing the editors would again like to thank everyone involved for their efforts and hard work to make this book a reality. As can be seen from the range of topics, there is something for everyone to explore. The editors hope the information will prove useful to readers and that others will take what they learn here and expand on it.

~Monika Antonelli

Section One

Green Buildings

Chicago Standard Operating Procedure

Greta Bever

The Chicago Standard is a set of construction standards for public buildings in the city of Chicago. Adopted in 2004, the Chicago Standard was developed to guide the design, construction and renovation of municipal facilities in a manner that reduces operating costs and conserves energy and resources while providing healthier indoor environments. It also addresses the sustainable outfitting, operating and maintaining of those facilities.

Starting at the Top

Mayor Richard M. Daley returned to Chicago from a 1997 trip to Hamburg, Germany, intrigued by the concept of rooftop gardens.[1] Chicago's motto, adopted in 1837, is "the City in a Garden", with *Urbs in Horto* actually included on the City Seal. "Urban Heat Island" might have become a more appropriate description in recent years, however, given decades of traditional development and construction with materials which absorb the heat of the sun during the day and retain it, creating a metropolitan area significantly hotter than its surroundings. Taking the lead in the city's progress toward more sustainable practices, the Mayor turned the roof of City Hall into a rooftop garden designed for maximum environmental and educational impact. The garden on the City Hall roof,

---

1. Shelly Banjo, "Up on the Roof", *Wall Street Journal*, October 6, 2008, p. R5.

completed in 2001, now cools the building in the summer, cuts energy costs and prevents rainwater runoff into the sewer system.[2] In ten years Chicago has progressed from a garden on the roof of City Hall to a green roof as standard for new library branches.

The Richard M. Daley, Greater Grand Crossing, Dunning and Little Village branches of the Chicago Public Library system each feature a rooftop garden as will subsequent branches built by Chicago's Public Building Commission. Each library design comes from the same flexible prototype.[3]

These four new branches will bring the number of LEED certified branches of the Chicago Public Library to a total of fourteen, all completed within an eight year span. In addition to the primary function, each green branch serves as an educational and environmental example for the community. Chicago's commitment to the building of green libraries reflects a new standard operating procedure in a governing approach to environment.

The Road to Budlong Woods: The Environmental Scan

The Chicago Public Library operates as a department of the City of Chicago and serves all its residents. Comprised of the Harold Washington Library Center, two regional libraries and more than 70 branches, the Chicago Public Library system is engaged in a major capital program, aggressively pursued since 1995, resulting in 53 new or renovated branches since 1989.[4] Once they identify the need for services or a new building in a particular neighborhood, Commissioner Mary Dempsey and her team begin the process of site selection. The collaboration with other city agencies begins with securing the funding for the property. The Public Building Commission of Chicago builds the branch and the Department of General Services maintains the branch. A flexible prototype design, developed jointly by the Library, the Public Building Commission of Chicago and the Department of General Services and then constructed by design firm Antunovich & Associates, was used for a series of new library branches beginning with the Rogers Park Branch dedicated in June of 1999. Given the expressed desire of the Mayor to make green building the norm, the Public Building Commission brought this approach to the Chicago Public Li-

---

2. City of Chicago, Mayor's Office. "Daley Remarks at Massachusetts Institute of Technology" (April 7, 2005).

3. Chicago Public Library, 2008 Year End Review, http://www.chipublib.org/ dir_documents/ar_2008review.pdf.

4. Chicago Public Library, Press Release, "Mayor Daley Dedicates New Beverly Branch Library," June 27, 2009. http://www.chipublib.org/aboutcpl/cplpr/2009/beverly.php.

The Richard M. Daley Branch, dedicated on July 28, 2011 by Mayor Rahm
Emanuel, achieved LEED gold certification. The branch was called West Humboldt
during planning and was renamed for the former Mayor just before the dedication.

brary in redesigning the flexible prototype for the remaining new branches, the
first of which was Budlong Woods Branch. According to Kevin Hall, Deputy
Director for Municipal Design at the Public Building Commission of Chicago,
"The library was the early adopter. That's why there are so many LEED certified
branches already. They embraced it earlier than other institutions."[5]

The experience of Chicago's Department of Environment and the Public
Building Commission in renovating and opening the Chicago Center for Green
Technology facilitated the incorporation of LEED points into the Budlong
Woods Branch design. Featuring solar and geothermal power, a rooftop garden,
recycled finishing products and a habitat area that filters storm water, the Center
opened in 2002 and was awarded a Platinum LEED rating. LEED, or Leadership in Energy and Environmental Design, was developed by the U. S. Green
Building Council as an internationally recognized green building certification
system, providing third-party verification. The Chicago Center for Green Technology was the third building in the country to receive this certification and
the first government owned structure to do so. Located on the site of a former
brownfield, or land previously used for industrial purposes, the Chicago Center
for Green Technology became, as intended, a model of environmentally friendly
design.[6]

5. Telephone interview with author, December 29, 2009.
6. The Public Building Commission of Chicago, Department of Environment Projects,
    Center for Green Technology. http://www.pbcchicago.com/content/
    projects/project_detail.asp?pID=CS-044.

Budlong Woods Branch opened in 2003 was the Chicago Public Library's first LEED certified building.

In February 2003, Budlong Woods, built under the auspices of the Public Building Commission of Chicago, opened as the Chicago Public Library's first LEED Certified branch. Like the Chicago Center for Green Technology, the Budlong Woods branch also features environmental remediation or treatment of a former industrial or contaminated site and the use of solar power. A sixteen kilowatt photovoltaic system uses solar panels to convert sunlight into electricity, which provides seven percent of the building's energy. Highly reflective, energy star compliant materials work together on the white roof to reduce the heat island effect by absorbing less heat from the sun.[7] The use of concrete pavement for the parking lot instead of black asphalt has resulted in lower cooling costs for the building in the summer as well and has become a standard feature for new branches.

The project overview for both buildings benefited from the expertise of Helen Kessler, then of Sieben Energy Associates, who was a member of the design team and designed the state-of-the-art lighting system for the Center for Green Technology. She also analyzed the feasibility of adapting the library's

7. The Public Building Commission of Chicago, PBC Projects, Chicago Public Library Projects, Budlong Woods Branch Library. http://www.pbcchicago.com/content/projects/project_detail.asp?pID=CPL-20.

flexible prototypes to achieve LEED certification, heading the sustainable design and energy modeling, or simulation, process. Budlong Woods branch, like the West Englewood branch, the Chicago Public Library's second LEED certified branch which opened just six months later, resulted from adjusting the flexible prototype to include opportunities to attain LEED points. Kessler targeted specific criteria for LEED within existing designs, materials and furnishings for one-story and two-story branches. Each building site already included ready access to public transportation as well as the available space to incorporate Reading Gardens. The design changes suggested by Kessler were incorporated into future branches already in planning.

Cracking the Code

In December 2003, the Assistant to the Mayor for Green Initiatives, Sadhu Johnston and the Director of the Development Center for Appropriate Technology, David Eisenberg, led a sustainable building processes workshop aimed at identifying the parts of Chicago Building Code that inhibited LEED construction in the city.[8] This all-day session led to specific recommendations for code changes as well as incentives for the private sector to construct sustainable buildings. The results included expedited permits for green projects, a higher profile for sustainable building processes and, ultimately, a wider pool of expertise in green building throughout the area. The City's prior LEED experiences helped to inform this project and the subsequent projects profited from the more streamlined processes as a result.

Setting the Standard

On June 10, 2004 Mayor Richard M. Daley, in his welcoming remarks to the national convention of the American Institute for Architects, announced the adoption of the Chicago Standard, explaining, "I want City Government to lead by example. While these standards apply only to public buildings, I hope the private sector will adopt many of these same strategies."[9] Based on a selection of points outlined in the LEED rating system, this sustainable policy led to

---

8. Kelly Jon Andereck, "Evolving Codes in Chicago," *Building Safety Journal,* June 2005, p.33.

9. City of Chicago, Department of Environment. Initiatives and Programs, The Chicago Standard, "Remarks of Richard M. Daley to AIA (6/10/04)". http://egov.cityofchicago.org/webportal/COCWebPortal/COC_ATTACH/ AIA_remarks.PDF.

the directive that all new municipally funded buildings in the City of Chicago be designed and constructed to qualify for LEED certification. Later that same month Mayor Daley opened Oriole Park branch, the Chicago Public Library's third green branch.

Climate Change

Between June 2005 and July 2006 the Chicago Public Library celebrated the opening of five more LEED certified branches: West Pullman, Logan Square, Avalon, West Chicago and Bucktown/Wicker Park.

Operations throughout the library system evolved to more environmentally-friendly practices during this time as well. Older library locations participated in energy efficiency upgrades conducted through the Department of General Services. In cooperation with the Department of Environment, library locations city-wide were established as regular battery recycling drop off points for the public. This partnership also resulted in a one-time long-life light bulb distribution at branch libraries with an outreach campaign explaining their benefit to the environment.

The Chicago Public Library also instituted a policy to replace its conventional vehicles with hybrids as parts of the fleet pool were decommissioned. Two-thirds of the pool, including the car used by the Director of the Library Buildings Program, is now hybrid. The library discontinued providing plastic bags to the public for their books but sells, instead, reusable bags at cost. Requirements in procurement contracts for library supplies were updated to include 30% post-consumer recycled content for paper, construction paper, hanging file folders and boxes, as well as for Post-it Notes, name labels and multipurpose labels with 100% recycled paper and 30% post-consumer recycled content. Packaging for the inkjet cartridges used in the library are 100% recycled paperboard. The Marketing Department emails the monthly calendar of events to any members of the public who will provide an email address, but even those patrons who prefer a hard copy now receive a document printed with vegetable-based inks on recycled paper with 30% post-consumer waste.

Silver, the New Green

By the time the Library Commissioner Mary Dempsey welcomed colleagues to Library Journal's 2nd Design Institute in December 2007, the Chicago Public Library, which hosted the event, boasted six LEED Certified branches and one LEED silver branch, with two more already under construction. The program-

The Bucktown/Wicker Park Branch is an example of the Chicago Public Library's
two-story prototype.

ming and practices of the library had incorporated green design and operation
into a public education piece. In addition, the bar had been set even higher
now as all new buildings receiving city financial assistance would be required to
achieve at least silver status in the LEED rating system and to include a green
roof.

The Vodak/Eastside branch, which opened in October 2006, became the
first for the Chicago Public Library to achieve silver status in 2008. Public
Building Commission Executive Director Erin Lavin Cabonargi joined Mary
Dempsey in a press release issued on Earth Day announcing the receipt of the
silver status plaque and detailing the accomplishments of both departments in
achieving their seventh branch library to attain LEED certification.[10]

This news helped to kick off the 2008 Summer Reading Program theme for
children and adults, *Read Green, Live Green.* Partners included power company
ComEd, the Chicago Department of Environment, the Chicago Park District,

---

10. The Public Building Commission of Chicago and the Chicago Public Library. "Earth
Day is Every Day at Chicago Public Library Branches and Other Facilities Built by
Public Building Commission." April 21, 2008.
http://www.pbcchicago.com/content/about/press_detail.asp?pID=206.

and the Garfield Park Conservatory Alliance. Other sponsors like the publication *TimeOut Chicago* and the Chicago Tribune Printer's Row Book Fair helped to spread the word, while the Macy's Foundation and the Chicago Public Library Foundation provided funding for key programs on how to make daily life greener. An example of such programming was *Green Cleaning* presented at four different branch libraries where the public learned how to incorporate natural and home-made cleaners into their regular cleaning routines. *Vermicomposting for City Slickers* also introduced Chicagoans to the joys of having worms turn organic food waste into rich soil. Five branches hosted Andrew Comens with his *Vegetarian Cooking & Baking Demonstrations* for teens to learn to make healthy, environmentally-friendly and sustainable meals. The *Read Green, Live Green* resource guide for adults informed the public of changes even at the mammoth central library built in 1991: "Resource-saving features at Harold Washington Library Center include: replacement of metal halide and normal fluorescent light fixtures with energy-saving compact fluorescent light fixtures, . . . recycling of paper, light bulbs and monitors, restroom upgrades to water-saving auto-flushing fixtures and sensor faucets."[11]

With the new Beverly branch, the Chicago Public Library's tenth green branch, poised to open in June of 2009, it was time to reexamine the flexible prototypes. The Public Building Commission of Chicago held a series of *Lessons Learned* workshops in late 2008, with Chicago Public Library staff, the Department of General Services and their building engineers, plumbers and electricians to discuss what worked and what did not with the existing prototype. While the initial flexible prototype had to be adapted to achieve LEED certification, the modified flexible prototypes, designed by the architectural firm Lohan Anderson, based in Chicago, are a result of integrated design. Integrated design allows for a different perspective from the beginning: according to Kevin Hall, "You start with the idea of sustainability rather than focusing on the checklist. You start with the goals, rather than chasing the points."[12]

The new flexible prototypes include a large one-story branch, a smaller one-story branch and a two-story branch. In addition to the rooftop garden, new standard features include "smart building" concepts such as lighting and irrigation systems on timers and remote monitoring of the heating, ventilation and air-conditioning system. Storm water management systems and the purchase of green power appear as standard operational requirements for LEED silver status. The new branches feature attractive and durable furnishings and materials with post consumer recycled content such as rubber flooring. Geothermal energy was

---

11. Chicago Public Library, *Read Green, Live Green*, 2008, p. 5, 9, 33–34.

12. Telephone interview with author, December 29, 2009.

Greater Grand Crossing, dedicated April 23, 2011, achieved LEED Gold
certification.

featured for the first time in the branches opening in 2011, allowing the use of
sustainable power throughout the life of a building.

Four new library branches based on the new flexible prototype started construction at the end of 2009 and opened in 2010 and 2011. At the time of
publication land acquisition was in process to build several additional branches
from this prototype as well. All new branches will meet the goals of the Chicago
Standard. The Chicago Standard was not created to attract attention to unique
architectural achievement—the point has been to elevate our expectations for
what we consider the usual, the ordinary. As Executive Director Cabonargi of
the Public Building Commission of Chicago indicated in her presentation at the
Library Journal Design Institute in 2007, the goal is "making green routine."[13]
For the Chicago Public Library dedicating new library buildings with silver
ratings has become standard. What is regarded as standard in Chicago construction, informed by best environmental practices and the leadership of city
government, will continue to evolve. On June 14, 2011, newly elected Mayor
Rahm Emanuel pledged to double the number of municipally-owned LEED
certified buildings within four years.[14] So while library branches represent the

13. Erin Lavin Cabonargi, Public Building Commission of Chicago, Director of Planning
    and Design, "Making Green Routine" presented at Library Journal Design Institute,
    Chicago, Illinois, December 11, 2007. http://www.pbcchicago.com/pdf/
    green_routine.pdf.

14. The Public Building Commission of Chicago, "Mayor Emanuel Announces Commit-
    ment To Double The Number of LEED Certified Buildings In Four Years." June 14,
    2011. http://www.pbcchicago.com/content/about/press_detail.asp?pID=322.

majority of the city's existing LEED buildings many others will join the list. It seems appropriate that with a history of providing the public a model of sharing resources, the Library led the way in sustainable building. The Chicago Public Library's construction of an unparalleled number of green branches in the last decade results from the recognition of a unique window of opportunity to provide not only information but an example as well and become, more than ever, a reference point for the community.

Building a Green Community at the Concordia University Library

Krista M. Reynolds

Walk into the newly constructed library on the Concordia University campus and you might witness the following:

- A teacher from a neighboring school leading a class of 6th graders to the Northwest Center for Children's Literature to explore the latest publications for children;
- A theology professor instructing students on the finer points of Latin grammar in the reading area;
- University Writing Center tutors critiquing fellow students' work in Café 1905.

These mentor-student interactions reinforce the idea of the academic library as a community learning space. As students and faculty increasingly access resources for their work online, independent of the physical library, librarians have had the opportunity to reinvent the concept of the library—to create a vibrant and attractive resource that meets evolving user needs. As noted by Buschman and Leckie and many others, the library as place is not merely a repository of printed knowledge; it is an entity with a "particular place-based character" (2007, 3), a unique gathering place for people to connect with others to ponder, wrestle with, and produce knowledge. But students must want to be there; a welcoming space is necessary to facilitate students' information behaviors and scholarly endeavors (Given 2007). Thus, how libraries are designed to support social interaction and intellectual exploration is critical. How has the library's design and construction been an extension of the library's and, indeed, the university's philosophy regarding building community?

In this chapter, I will explore the connections between green libraries and community building by examining Concordia's unique construction experience and institutional worldview. Specifically, I will explore the convergence of green architectural design and design of a community-friendly space in an academic environment. Through discussion with the building architect, contractor and examination of the LEED (Leadership in Energy and Environmental Design) certification checklist, I will share how the university earned LEED credits and describe the relationships developed within the community through this process. I will reflect on the implications of building a multipurpose space and the opportunities this offers our students. Finally, I will elaborate on the library's involvement in other green institutional initiatives.

Concordia University, a Lutheran liberal arts institution located in Portland, Oregon, was founded in 1905 as a four-year academy to train pastors and teachers. By 2009, it had evolved into a dynamic campus of undergraduate and graduate students preparing for work in nursing, education, business, and social work. The university is charged with "preparing leaders for the transformation of society"—a challenging task (Concordia University 2005, 7). In support of that mission, Concordia espouses the following core values: Christian principles, community involvement, excellence, learning and teaching, and service. These values grew out of the university's early focus on training individuals for positions affiliated with the Lutheran Church Missouri Synod and also the recognition that a liberal arts education provides students a broader understanding of the world and their roles within it. Concordia strives to "sensitize students to humanity's strengths and weaknesses, and to take initial steps in bringing solutions to the mass of perplexing problems which confront humankind and society" (Concordia University 2005, 7). Concordia is grounded in the idea that service to others is transformative: it can have a profound impact on the life of the student performing the service, as well as on the lives of the beneficiaries of the service. Service learning is integrated with the undergraduate and graduate curriculum, and faculty members are expected to volunteer in the community to advance in rank.

The university administration leads by example to accomplish this mission. It has worked diligently to build relationships locally, working with organizations such as the Concordia Neighborhood Association, Black Parent Initiative, and the Portland Public Schools Day and Residential Treatment (DART) Program. The results have been positive. Tom Potter, former Mayor of Portland, recognized that "Concordia University is at the head of the class for community engagement. Concordia connects campus and community like no other. It's a place where students serve the community and, in the process, become servant leaders" (Concordia University n.d., 2).

Within the last five years, the student body has grown tremendously, from 1,243 to 1,718 student FTEs; as a result, the physical facilities no longer adequately supported the student population. Classrooms were at capacity, and the nursing program was relegated to two modular units located far from other campus facilities. Measuring approximately 10,000 square feet, the library was cramped with shelving that held more than 90,000 volumes and housed only one group study room. Poorly lit, with its mismatched 1970s era furniture, the library had a dated feel. Students often complained to library staff about the lack of enclosed group study spaces and quiet areas for individual study. The university, with the assistance of a contractor, had developed a Campus Master Plan in the 1990s. With the rapid growth of the student body, it was clear the university would need to act on this plan to accommodate the burgeoning need for instructional space and a more serviceable library.

In September 2005, when the university began working with the architectural firm Group Mackenzie on the construction of a new library and classroom facility, it was not surprising that the idea of an environmentally-friendly design was introduced. Group Mackenzie is experienced at integrating green features into their designs; in 1999 they created a distribution and training facility for American Honda in Gresham, Oregon which earned LEED Gold certification (Group Mackenzie 2009). Since then, Group Mackenzie has worked on more than twenty LEED projects. In addition, many of their non-LEED projects also have incorporated sustainable systems, as they have become more economically viable options (Brett Hanson pers. comm.).

Why was a green design appealing to the university? By going the green route, the university could demonstrate its commitment to serve the community in a new way. In 2007, University President Chuck Schlimpert had signed the American College and University Presidents' Climate Commitment, which asks campuses to adopt strategies to go "climate neutral" in an effort to reverse global warming. This set the stage for further campus-wide environmental initiatives. At its core, environmental stewardship is an expression of community engagement. By acting in an environmentally-responsible way, the university could not only benefit the global climate, it could also be a good neighbor: by leaving attractive green spaces, by not taxing the local waste water system, and by maintaining a compact footprint in its residential setting. In addition, the university could demonstrate a respect for the well-being of its employees and students by creating a healthy, hospitable working and learning environment.

Why is green building design important? According to the U.S. Department of Energy (DOE), the building sector consumed 39% of U.S. primary energy in 2006. "Electricity made up the overwhelming majority of consumption, representing 74% of all primary energy used" (D&R International, Ltd. 2009, 1–1). Commercial buildings were responsible for consuming 36% of all electricity used in the United States (Energy Efficiency and Renewable Energy 2009). The DOE has estimated buildings in the U.S. emitted 2,318 million metric tons of carbon dioxide in 2005 (Energy Efficiency and Renewable Energy 2009). To compare, the DOE estimated the United States contributed a total of 5,982 million metric tons of human generated carbon dioxide to the atmosphere that year. This accounted for 21% of human generated carbon dioxide emissions worldwide (Energy Efficiency and Renewable Energy 2009). If, through their design, green buildings can reduce energy consumption and carbon dioxide production, they can have a significant impact on reducing the negative environmental effects of commercial properties.

The George R. White Library and Learning Center (GRWLLC) was designed according to the Leadership in Energy and Environmental Design for New Construction (LEED-NC) standards, version 2.1. Why use LEED and not another certification system? According to Yudelson, "More than 98% of certified green buildings come from the LEED system" (2008, 13), and the system now has widespread name recognition. LEED is based on points earned in the following six categories of green design: sustainable sites, water efficiency, energy and atmosphere, materials and resources, indoor environmental quality, and innovation and design process. Certified, the lowest certification level, is obtained by earning 26 to 32 points; Platinum, the highest level, is obtained by earning 52 or more points (U.S. Green Building Council 2003, 6). Library planners selected the Silver rating as the certification goal; however, at the end of construction the project had accrued enough points to be within reach of a Gold rating.

In the fall of 2009 Group Mackenzie submitted the LEED application for the GRWLLC to the Green Building Certification Institute (GBCI) for review. In March 2010 library staff learned the LEED review team had awarded the project 36 of 41 credits, earning enough for a Silver level rating (the project goal). The five credits not awarded were in the "optimize energy performance" section which relates to maximizing efficiencies in heating and ventilation systems, pumps, service hot water, and interior lighting; these fall within the "energy and atmosphere" category. Group Mackenzie appealed this decision, as allowed by GBCI guidelines, and library staff learned in July 2010 the appeal was successful, and the building achieved a Gold rating. Appendix A summarizes attempted credits; in the text, I will elaborate on how various credits were obtained, focusing on those that relate to building community.

George R. White Library & Learning Center

The U.S. Green Building Council, the organization responsible for the LEED Green Building Rating System, recognizes the importance of community in environmental sustainability. "Green building design strives to balance environmental responsibility, resource efficiency, occupant comfort and well-being, and community sensitivity" (U.S. Green Building Council 2003, 1). This community-focused perspective aligns with the university's philosophy, as discussed earlier.

Sustainable Sites: Credit 1: Site Selection

Site selection is focused on minimizing impact on biologically sensitive habitats. It also relates to designing a project thoughtfully so that a building is integrated into the surrounding area, is representative of neighborhood features, and allows room for green spaces. To earn this credit, construction must not take place on prime farmland, flood-prone areas (determined by land elevation), land within 100 feet of a wetland, or areas that were previously public parkland (with exceptions) (U.S. Green Building Council 2003, 13).

Because the Concordia University campus is located in a residential neighborhood and is surrounded by privately-owned houses, the siting options for the

GRWLLC in the immediate vicinity were limited. The most obvious choice and final decision was to locate the building on the baseball/soccer field at the north end of the campus. Because the land was owned by CU and had already been developed as an athletic field, no natural area was disturbed. However, one environmental effect, the aesthetic impact of the building on the surrounding area, was an important consideration. Visitors have noted how the campus, with its low brick buildings and compact 10.15 acre footprint, is tucked unobtrusively into the residential neighborhood. It was important to Concordia administrators to maintain positive relations with the University's neighbors; one way they could do this was to create a facility consistent with the design of other campus buildings and that fit the character of the environs. A much taller building had been approved during the zoning process, but this plan was rejected in order to maintain a consistent campus design and environmental fit. At three stories tall, the GRWLLC is no taller than other campus structures and thus maintains a relatively low profile in the surrounding neighborhood. In addition, the building's placement allowed space for construction of an amphitheater and lawn which created an attractive park-like setting which students and visitors alike could use for casual recreation.

There was significant community outreach while the university was updating the Campus Master Plan. University administrators met several times with the Concordia Neighborhood Association and invited comments from area residents before construction on the new library began (Brent Mai, pers. comm.).

One other facet of green design that falls under the Sustainable Sites category is stormwater management. In a natural environment, the majority of precipitation is absorbed by the ground, and only a small percentage runs off into waterways (U.S. Green Building Council 2003). This "stormwater runoff" increases in an urban development because surface permeability is reduced; sewer systems typically handle the excess and convey stormwater to larger bodies of water, often lakes or rivers. Stormwater from urban areas is frequently polluted and contains sediments which reduce water clarity; for example, water runoff from a parking area likely contains oil, fuel, chemicals from worn tires, and other road debris (U.S. Green Building Council 2003). Shallow ditches called swales, also known as bioswales when planted with vegetation, can be a "cost-effective method for controlling runoff pollution from land surfaces" (Yu et al. 2001, 168). Bioswales act as natural filters; they contain porous soil that collects runoff and traps sediments (Plaster 2003). In Yu et al.'s study of swales planted with grass, "Average pollutant removal efficiencies reported for the test swales vary from 14 to 99% for total suspended solids (TSS), chemical oxygen demand (COD), total nitrogen (TN), and total phosphorus (TP)" (2001, 168).

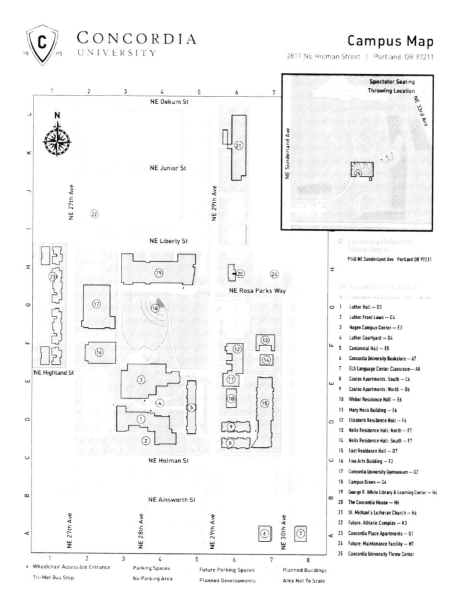

Campus Facilities, Departments, & Offices

Building Number, Building Name, Grid Coordinate

1. **Luther Hall — D3**
   - Admission Office
   - Business Services Office
   - Financial Aid Office
   - International Studies Office
   - Registrar's Office

2. **Luther Front Lawn — C4**

3. **Hagen Campus Center — E3**
   - ASCU/Student Government Office
   - ATM
   - Brandes Dining Room
   - Public Safety
   - Cavalier Café
   - Center for Service Leadership
   - Christian Life Ministries Office
   - Computing Center
   - Concordia University Foundation
     - Alumni & Parent Relations
     - Church Relations
     - Development
     - Marketing & Communications
   - Dining Services
   - Information & Service Center
     - Mail and Shipping Services
     - Printing and Duplicating Services
   - Information Technology Services (ITS)
     - Technology Help Desk
   - Physical Plant Services
   - Student Involvement Center
   - Student Lounge

4. **Luther Courtyard — D4**

5. **Centennial Hall — E5**
   - Counseling Services
   - College of Education
     - Undergraduate Education & Christian Ministries Program
     - Graduate Education Program
     - Director of Christian Education Program (DCE)
     - Education Placement Office
   - ELS Language Center
   - Health Services/Campus Nurse
   - School of Management
     - BA Business Administration
     - BS Business Degree Completion
     - Master of Business Administration (MBA)

6. **Concordia University Bookstore — A7**

7. **ELS Language Center Classroom — A8**

8. **Coates Apartments South — C6**

9. **Coates Apartments: North — D6**

10. **Weber Residence Hall — E6**

11. **Mary Neils Building — E6**
    - Student Services
      - Career Resources Center
      - Housing & Residence Life Office
      - Tutoring & Learning Services

12. **Elizabeth Residence Hall — F6**

13. **Neils Residence Hall: North — F7**

14. **Neils Residence Hall: South — F7**

15. **East Residence Hall — D7**

16. **Fine Arts Building — F2**

17. **Concordia University Gymnasium — G2**
    - Department of Athletics
    - Fitness Center/Weight Room

18. **Campus Green — G4**

19. **George R. White Library & Learning Center — H4**
    - FWJ Sylwester Library
      - Art & Carol Wahlers Center for Applied Lutheran Leadership (CALL)
      - Jody Thurston Northwest Center for Children's Literature (NWCCL)
      - Robert & Virginia Hilken Family Nursing Center
      - Center for Volga German Studies (CVGS)
      - Shakespeare Authorship Research Centre (SARC)
      - Center for Excellence in Learning & Teaching (CELT)
    - Cafe 1905
    - College of Health & Human Services
      - Exercise and Sport Science Program
      - Health Care Administration Program
      - Nursing Program
      - Social Work Program
    - College of Theology, Arts, & Sciences
      - Department of Humanities
      - Department of Social Sciences
      - Department of Math-Sciences
      - Department of International Studies
      - Department of Performing and Visual Arts
      - Division of Theology

20. **The Concordia House — H6**
    - Executive Offices
    - Office of the President

21. **St. Michael's Lutheran Church — K6**

22. **Future: Athletic Complex — K3**

23. **Concordia Place Apartments — G1**

24. **Future: Maintenance Facility — H7**

25. **Concordia University Throw Center**

Directions from campus to Concordia University Throw Center:

9140 NE Sunderland Ave   Portland, OR 97211

Drive: 1.9 mi – about 6 mins

1.	Head east on NE Holman St toward NE 33rd Ave	0.3 mi
2.	Turn left at NE 33rd Ave	
3.	Take the Col. Blvd W ramp to Marine Dr	0.2 mi
4.	Slight right at NE 33rd Dr	1.1 mi
5.	Turn left at NE Sunderland Ave	151 ft

At Concordia, two bioswales were constructed to reduce stormwater runoff, control pollution, and mitigate effects on the natural water flow around campus. The bioswales contain native vegetation and were designed to collect and treat all building and site stormwater (Brett Hanson pers. comm.). From a community perspective, the addition of bioswales means less water and fewer pollutants are entering the Willamette River and Columbia Slough, resulting in healthier waterways. The reduced water flow from campus also lessens the burden on the city to maintain sewer infrastructure. In addition, they are an attractive natural feature adjacent to the east entrance of the GRWLLC. The bioswales, surrounded by walls which provide outdoor seating, invite passersby to linger outside the building and enjoy the natural environment.

Materials and Resources: Prerequisite 1: Storage and Collection of Recyclables

One of the most visible indications of Concordia University's commitment to environmental stewardship is the placement of recycling receptacles throughout the GRWLLC. To satisfy this LEED requirement, CU must "provide an easily accessible area that serves the entire building and is dedicated to the separation, collection and storage of materials for recycling" (U.S. Green Building Council 2003, 187). While recycling has become a cultural norm in many cities throughout the United States and the City of Portland has an especially progressive recycling program, the importance of this activity cannot be overstated from a community perspective. Participation in the program encourages the city to continue its recycling efforts, and the city may use Concordia as an example for other institutions. It may also have significant economic impacts. According to the U.S. Green Building Council (USGBC), "Recycling efforts return valuable resources to the production process and provide more jobs versus landfilling. . . . Higher recycling rates also result in more stable markets for recycled materials" (2003, 189). By distributing more than thirty recycling containers in areas where students congregate, the odds increase that patrons will take notice and use them.

At Concordia, one environmentally-conscious decision inspired another. Sisters Coffee Company, the business responsible for running Café 1905 in the GRWLLC, had been providing beverages in compostable containers since the library's opening in August 2009. However, when the library opened, there were no facilities for the separation of compostable items in the building. As a result, biodegradable containers ended up in the regular trash. Taking note, facilities managers were inspired to expand on the campus recycling program, and

Bioswale at George R. White Library & Learning Center

in November 2009 they added more than ten containers for the collection of compostable materials to classrooms and public areas of the GRWLLC (Doug Meyer, pers. comm.). Thus, less waste will be destined for a landfill. This ongoing and highly visible project will continue to promote CU's commitment to environmental initiatives.

Materials and Resources: Credit 2: Construction Waste Management

Building construction has a considerable impact on the environment. In the United States builders produce 30–35 million tons of construction, renovation, and demolition waste each year (Energy Efficiency and Renewable Energy 2009, table 1.4.12). Approximately 24% of the municipal waste stream comes from construction and demolition debris annually. However, for many construction projects, "as much as 95% of buildings-related construction waste is recyclable" (Energy Efficiency and Renewable Energy 2009, table 1.4.12). By reducing construction waste, contractors can mitigate environmental impact in a significant way.

To earn credit under LEED standard 2.1, at least 50% of construction waste (including demolition and land clearing debris) must be diverted from the landfill. Institutions may redirect recyclable materials back to the manufacturing process and/or "redirect reusable materials to appropriate sites" (U.S. Green Building Council 2003, 199). To earn a second point under credit 2.2, institutions must divert 75% or more of construction waste from the landfill. The contractor, Union Corner Construction, was able to prevent an astounding 95% of construction refuse from entering the waste stream. At the site 600.51 tons of material, including concrete and cement, scrap metal, wood, brick, cardboard, and sheetrock, were diverted, and 25.81 tons were sent to the landfill (626.32 tons total) (Matt Rush, pers. comm.). How was this possible? Very little site preparation was necessary before construction began, as the site had been used previously as an athletic field and was primarily open. A contractor specializing in demolition was hired to dismantle the only building on site, an athletics storage unit, and these materials were sent to reuse facilities.

What community infrastructure facilitated this process? The Metro Regional Government (Metro), which serves Clackamas, Washington, and Multnomah counties, of which Portland is a part, has worked within the tri-counties to promote construction waste recycling as one facet of its recycling program. On their website, Metro provides links to publications which give those in the industry tools for maximizing their construction recycling and provides a list of more than 100 local recyclers. The "Succeed with LEED: Recycling and Salvage

Recycling & composting at George R. White Library & Learning Center

Tracking Form" provided by Metro makes it easier for businesses to document their practices (Metro Regional Government 2010).

By recycling construction waste, Concordia has reduced demand for virgin resources, reduced environmental impacts of resource extraction, and reduced the need for additional landfill space in the community (U.S. Green Building Council 2003). Consequently, CU is supporting Metro's recycling programs and local processing facilities such as Portland area recyclers Porter W. Yett Co., Inc., Metro Metals Northwest, Inc., and AGG Enterprises, Inc.

The USGBC (2003) suggests reuse of materials on site may reduce the need for debris removal and thus decrease potentially disruptive traffic in the community. However, because few, if any, materials were reused at Concordia, there was probably no reduction in hauling traffic. To the contrary, the contractor speculated traffic in the area might have increased due to the need for multiple recycling containers required to sort materials on site (Matt Rush, pers. comm.). This is one factor that institutions planning LEED construction projects might want to plan for in advance.

Materials and Resources: Credit 5: Regional Materials

Transportation accounted for 28.6% of energy consumption in the United States in 2007 (Davis, Diegel, and Boundy 2009, 2–3). Of the energy used for transportation, 27.4% was used to fuel light trucks and 18.8% was used by medium/heavy trucks; presumably these vehicles were used for the transport of goods (Davis, Diegel, and Boundy 2009, 2–1). Through buying goods from locally owned and operated businesses, transportation costs and associated environmental impacts are minimized. In addition, money is invested back into the local economy, in both the labor force and capital for community members (U.S. Green Building Council 2003). To obtain LEED credit 5.1, the project must use a minimum of 20% of building materials and products that are manufactured within a 500-mile radius (U.S. Green Building Council 2003, 221).

Items manufactured locally included the vapor barrier beneath the concrete slab (from Stego Industries, LLC in Yakima, WA), concrete reinforcement rebar (bent and cut to length by Farwest Steel Corp. in Vancouver, WA), and concrete mix (from Glacier Northwest, Portland, OR). Credit 5.2 specifies that "Of the regionally manufactured materials documented for MR Credit 5.1", a minimum of 50% of building materials and products that are extracted, harvested or recovered (as well as manufactured) should come from within 500 miles of the project site (U.S. Green Building Council 2003, 222). Brick and concrete pavers, provided by Mutual Materials, were made from materials extracted in

Tacoma (approximately 140 miles from CU) and Lacey, Washington (approximately 114 miles from CU), respectively (Matt Rush, pers. comm.).

Materials and Resources: Credit 7: Certified Wood

Credit 7 was developed by the USGBC "to encourage environmentally responsible forest management" (2003, 231). To obtain this credit, at least 50% of wood products used in the construction and furnishing of the building must be certified by the Forest Stewardship Council's (FSC) Principles and Criteria program (U.S. Green Building Council 2003, 231). The FSC not only considers the direct environmental effects of forest management, it also considers indigenous people's rights and involves community stakeholders in forest management decisions. Again, this practice parallels Concordia University's own view of it neighbors as important stakeholders in campus decision-making.

Products at the GRWLLC which contain certified wood include the suspended linear wood ceiling above the reading area and grand staircase and approximately one-third of the cabinetry and millwork by materials cost (Matt Rush, pers. comm.). Milled materials include the façade covering large concrete planters placed beneath the staircase on the first and second floors and panels which line the balcony soffits above the reading area. Certified wood products were also used for structural features in the roof and above classrooms. The cabinetry in the Center for Applied Lutheran Leadership is stunning, as it lines every wall, creating an elegant and functional showcase.

A builder can foster a sense of rootedness to place by choosing regional materials and incorporating them to create visually stimulating features in a building. Wood paneling was a quintessential choice to highlight the building's Pacific Northwest location, as the region is known for its forests and wood products industry. The wood paneling in the GRWLLC ceiling and other areas adds warmth and an artistic touch to a space dominated by open expanses and metal fixtures. These green features not only have environmental benefits derived from their production and manufacture, they benefit library patrons by creating a striking environment, an inspirational space to which people are naturally drawn.

Indoor Environmental Quality (IEQ)

U.S. Environmental Protection Agency (EPA) studies have shown that indoor pollution levels can exceed pollution levels outside (U.S. Environmental Protection Agency 2007). Because Americans spend an average of 90% of their

Wood ceiling in George R. White Library & Learning Center

day indoors, indoor air quality has the potential to significantly impact health (U.S. Environmental Protection Agency 2007). Poor indoor air quality may result in eye, nose, or throat irritation, headaches, and fatigue, and, over the long term, may lead to respiratory illnesses, heart disease, and cancer. The "EPA estimates that poor indoor air may cost the nation tens of billions of dollars each year in lost productivity and medical care" (U.S. Environmental Protection Agency 2007). The USGBC recognizes the impacts of air quality on health and incorporates several measures in the LEED standards to improve air quality for building inhabitants. From the building owner's perspective, incorporating these designs may not result in an immediate economic gain, but if occupants know they are in an environment that promotes well-being, their satisfaction with and loyalty to the institution are likely improved. This also presents a positive image to the public; Concordia is perceived as a worker-friendly employer.

Concordia University adopted several strategies under the IEQ heading to earn credits. Prerequisite 2 specifies that building occupants are not exposed to environmental tobacco smoke. CU achieved this by prohibiting smoking within the building and designated one outdoor smoking area at the southwest corner of the building, away from doors, windows, air intake vents, and away from areas of significant pedestrian traffic. Other campus smoking areas are at least 100 feet from the GRWLLC.

CU earned LEED credit 1 by installing a permanent carbon dioxide monitoring system. With a conventional ventilation system, ventilation rates are determined using standards for a particular building design (U.S. Green Building Council 2003, 250). For example, a space designed for a maximum occupancy of 24 people is continuously ventilated under the assumption 24 people are present, even if there are long periods it is not fully occupied. Thus, energy is wasted due to unnecessary ventilation. A more effective way to maintain healthy air quality is to monitor carbon dioxide concentrations. With a "Demand Control Ventilation" system, facilities managers can keep carbon dioxide levels inside a building similar to outdoor levels, based on occupant demand. Whenever carbon dioxide levels in a particular space in the GRWLLC rise above 1,000 parts per million, the associated air handling unit opens to allow more fresh air in to reduce carbon dioxide levels. After levels fall below 1,000 parts per million, the Demand Control Ventilation mode is disabled until needed again. As a result of this cyclic system, energy required to operate the air handling equipment is conserved (Nick Marcyan, pers. comm.).

Conventional materials used in the interior of buildings, including paints, adhesives, and sealants often contain volatile organic compounds (VOCs) such as formaldehyde and styrene that can be irritating to installers and occupants (U.S. Green Building Council 2003). VOCs can cause chemical sensitivities and affect outdoor air quality, sometimes contributing to smog (U.S. Green Building Council 2003). To prevent this source of pollution, low emitting materials, including low VOC paint, carpet, coatings, wood, carpet adhesives and sealants were used in the interior of the building. It is interesting to note this credit applies only to interior spaces; exterior spaces are excluded from the LEED standards.

Credit 5 relates to indoor chemical and pollutant source control. The intent of this credit is to minimize the impact of chemicals and other pollutants in the building on air quality. To obtain this credit, "walk off" mats, fiber mats designed to trap debris from foot traffic and limit dust and dirt entering a building, were installed at each outside entry. Janitor rooms are ventilated separately from the rest of the building and have full height walls to prevent the spread of chemical fumes. Even the staff room, which contains a food preparation area, was designed as a segregated space with a separate exhaust system to prevent food smells from traveling and bothering other building occupants.

Community benefits of implementing indoor environmental quality measures are improved occupant productivity and reduced absenteeism (U.S. Green

Building Council 2003, 255). On a larger scale, health care costs and insurance costs could be reduced due to improved health of building occupants. It would be interesting to track absenteeism of building occupants before and after construction to determine whether these benefits are being realized at Concordia.

Credit 8.2 relates to daylight and views; one point may be earned if building occupants can achieve a direct line of sight to the outdoors from 90% of regularly occupied spaces. The savings that can be reaped from smart design are significant; energy costs due to lighting may be reduced 50–80% in buildings constructed to maximize natural lighting (U.S. Green Building Council 2003, 303).

To earn this credit, the GRWLLC was designed with a relatively open floor plan with a high percentage of wall space dedicated to windows on the north and south sides of the building. Most faculty and staff offices are located on the building perimeter and have exterior windows, and all group study rooms, while located in the interior of the building, have one wall of floor-to-ceiling windows with views outside. The 170 by 22 foot wall of windows lining one side of the reading area takes full advantage of the southern exposure and provides views to the amphitheatre and campus green, campanile, and most university buildings. Because the GRWLLC is relatively distant from other classroom and academic spaces, this visual connection, which fosters cohesiveness, is important. Connectivity is not limited to campus but also extends to the neighborhood. From the second and third floors of the GRWLLC one can see adjacent residences, suburban flora, and on a clear day, Mt. St. Helens. From the library service desk, which faces south toward the expansive wall of windows, the sky comprises half of the view—providing a dynamic backdrop and a pleasant view during the work day. When asked what qualities make a welcoming space, library patrons at the University of Alberta most commonly mentioned "bright, natural light" and "comfortable" (Given 2007, 180). The brightly lit space at the GRWLLC is particularly inviting in the winter months, when the sky is often obscured by clouds.

In addition to energy savings, there is a less intuitive reason for providing natural light in a building; according to the USGBC, "Studies have demonstrated that productivity increases dramatically for those building occupants working in daylit areas" (2003, 303). However, productivity isn't the only gain; there are physiological and psychological benefits of experiencing daylight in indoor spaces (Kahn et al. 2008). A study conducted by Kahn et al. (2008) demonstrated that the heart rate recovery of office workers exposed to low-level stress was better when they had views of a natural scene compared to workers with no outside view. In his seminal study, Ulrich (1984) examined the effect of natural views on the recovery of surgical patients in a hospital and found those

Exterior corridor of George R. White Library & Learning Center

patients with views of trees outside required shorter hospital stays after surgery and took fewer moderate and strong doses of painkillers compared with those patients whose windows looked onto a brick wall. Views of nature may simply "promote recovery from mental fatigue" (Kahn 2008, 198). Without a formal study, it would be imprudent to extrapolate these observed effects to the Concordia population; however, from informal observation and verbal feedback, it is clear that students and faculty enjoy using the large, open reading room and study spaces near windows. And judging from the awed looks of first-time visitors, there is a keen positive emotional response to this place.

When the library opened in August 2009, expectations were high, from the campus community and neighbors, that this multi-faceted space would be able to fulfill the needs of divergent user groups. Students need spaces that promote academic success and that are flexible enough to accommodate their diverse study requirements and information seeking: ergonomic workstations and facilities that support technology, space to spread out, space to be quiet and alone, space to work in a noisy group, social spaces to eat and drink, and private, semi-public and public spaces (Given 2007). In a "collaborative educational model", which typifies the current collegiate experience, students need to feel socially connected in their educational setting and require conversation with classmates

Reading room in George R. White Library & Learning Center

as part of the learning process (Given 2007, 182–183). When they emerge from classrooms at the GRWLLC, where their academic pursuits and information needs blossom, they are immediately surrounded by spaces designed to meet all of those needs—individual study tables, group study rooms, moveable furniture, large tables, wireless connections, and laptops available for check out.

At the GRWLLC, students are not only able to thrive in a space that was designed for their physical health and comfort, but are able to take advantage of the cross-pollination of ideas that happens in a space shared by multiple disciplines. With faculty from nursing, psychology, English, and history inhabiting the GRWLLC, students from these disciplines also congregate in the building, at spacious group study tables and at informal groupings of couches.

Community members have long lamented the lack of a public library branch in the immediate vicinity; the two closest branches of the Multnomah County Library System (North Portland and Albina) are both 2.1 miles away. Again, in line with its service ethic and community focus, the university promised neighbors access to library resources and a community meeting room in the GRWLLC. The response has been remarkable. As of January 2010, library staff had issued more than 650 library cards to community members, and some in the neighborhood have adopted it as their home library. Stay-at-home moms find the children's collection just as useful as students working toward a teaching degree. Boisterous neighborhood kids using computers near study areas can be distracting to CU students, but most students seem tolerant. They understand that children who see the benefits of libraries and witness higher education at work may grow up to become university students themselves. CU students become role models and may themselves benefit from this multi-generational interaction and added diversity. They see that the university is also a role model in providing resources to a broader group of patrons.

Being green isn't just an environmental choice; it's a social choice with economic ramifications. Construction of the physical space embodies respect for the community, both the immediate and regional environment and its human constituents. CU is sending the message that it values the health of its community, in an environmental sense and an economic sense. And in transforming the campus, CU has transformed the ability of its students to achieve academic success.

While many academic librarians have wondered about the future of the library in the era of Google, smart phones, and ebook readers, it's reassuring to know the library "as place" is thriving. As Given states, "By listening to students' academic and information needs, and designing spaces to meet those needs, librarians and campus administrators can ensure that the academic library remains at the heart of the university" (2007, 186). Because it combines traditional library spaces (individual study carrels, group study rooms, and areas for relaxation) with classrooms, offices, and a café, the GRWLLC naturally forms a hub for formal and informal intellectual engagement between faculty and students. Student "loyalty is determined largely by the quality of student relationships on campus" (Waxman 2007, 426). To develop loyalty and an emotional commitment to the university, students need to feel a sense of ownership. "Part of this loyalty to the university is determined by the quality of the experience a student has with university services such as the library and computer labs." (Waxman 2007, 426) The students have made this space their own. This is the community space—where people feel connected. And while students and other library visitors may not know their space contributes to the health of the community, the university has become a good steward of the community: by doing business with green and local companies, reducing the environmental impact of its new building, and participating in government sponsored environmental initiatives.

Appendix A

LEED Credits Earned by Concordia University, Portland

Credit Category & Number	Title of Credit	Points Earned
Sustainable Sites		
Prerequisite 1	Erosion & Sedimentation Control	0
Credit 1	Site Selection	1
Credit 4.1	Alternative Transportation, Public Transportation Access	1
Credit 4.2	Alternative Transportation, Bicycle Storage & Changing Rooms	1
Credit 5.2	Reduced Site Disturbance, Development Footprint	1
Credit 6.1	Stormwater Management, Rate or Quantity	1
Credit 6.2	Stormwater Management, Treatment	1
Credit 7.1	Landscape & Exterior Design to Reduce Heat Islands, Non-Roof	1
Credit 7.2	Landscape and Exterior Design to Reduce Heat Islands, Roof	1
Water Efficiency		
Credit 3.1–3.2	Water Use Reduction	2
Energy and Atmosphere		
Prerequisite 1	Fundamental Building Systems Commissioning	0
Prerequisite 2	Minimum Energy Performance	0
Prerequisite 3	CFC Reduction in HVAC&R Equipment	0
Credit 1.1–1.10	Optimize Energy Performance	5
Credit 3	Additional Commissioning	1
Credit 4	Ozone Depletion	1
Credit 6	Green Power	1

Credit Category & Number	Title of Credit	Points Earned
Materials & Resources		
Prerequisite 1	Storage & Collection of Recyclables	0
Credit 2.1–2.2	Construction Waste Management	2
Credit 4.1–4.2	Recycled Content	2
Credit 5.1–5.2	Local/Regional Materials	2
Credit 7	Certified Wood	1
Indoor Environmental Quality		
Prerequisite 1	Minimum IAQ Performance	0
Prerequisite 2	Environmental Tobacco Smoke (ETS) Control	0
Credit 1	Carbon Dioxide (CO2) Monitoring	1
Credit 3.1	Construction IAQ Management Plan, During Construction	1
Credit 3.2	Construction IAQ Management Plan, Before Occupancy	1
Credit 4.1–4.4	Low Emitting Materials	4
Credit 5	Indoor Chemical & Pollutant Source Control	1
Credit 7.1	Thermal Comfort, Comply with ASHRAE 55-1992	1
Credit 7.2	Thermal Comfort, Permanent Monitoring System	1
Credit 8.2	Daylight Views, Views for 90% of Spaces	1
Innovation & Design Process		
Credit 1	Innovation in Design 1.1: Water Reduction	1
Credit 1	Innovation in Design 1.2: Construction Waste Management	1
Credit 1	Innovation in Design 1.3: Regional Materials	1
Credit 1	Innovation in Design 1.4: Green Power	1
Credit 2	LEED Accredited Professional	1
TOTAL		41

References

Buschman, John E. and Gloria J. Leckie, eds. 2007. *The library as place: History, community, and culture.* Westport, CT: Libraries Unlimited.

Concordia University. 2005. *2005–06 faculty handbook.* Portland, OR: Concordia University.

———. n.d. In a nutshell . . . Portland, OR: Concordia University. http://www.cu-portland.edu/documents/concordia_in_a_nutshell.pdf.

Davis, Stacy C., Susan W. Diegel, and Robert G. Boundy. 2009. Transportation energy data book: Edition 28. Oak Ridge, TN: Oak Ridge National Laboratory. http://www-cta.ornl.gov/data/tedb28/Edition28_Full_Doc.pdf.

D&R International, Ltd. 2009. 2009 buildings energy data book. Washington, D.C.: U.S. Department of Energy. http://buildingsdatabook.eere.energy.gov/docs%5CDataBooks%5C2009_BEDB_Updated.pdf

Energy Efficiency and Renewable Energy. 2009. Buildings energy data book table 1.1.9 Buildings share of U.S. electricity consumption (percent). Washington, D.C.: U.S. Department of Energy. http://buildingsdatabook.eere.energy.gov/TableView.aspx?table=1.1.9.

Energy Efficiency and Renewable Energy. 2009. Buildings energy data book table 1.4.1 Carbon dioxide emissions for U.S. buildings, by year (million metric tons). Washington, D.C.: U.S. Department of Energy. http://buildingsdatabook.eere.energy.gov/TableView.aspx?table=1.4.1.

Energy Efficiency and Renewable Energy. 2009. Buildings energy data book table 1.4.6 World carbon dioxide emissions. Washington, D.C.: U.S. Department of Energy. http://buildingsdatabook.eere.energy.gov/TableView.aspx?table=1.4.6.

Energy Efficiency and Renewable Energy. 2009. Buildings energy data book table 1.4.12 Characteristics of U.S. construction waste. Washington, D.C.: U.S. Department of Energy. http://buildingsdatabook.eere.energy.gov/TableView.aspx?table=1.4.12.

Given, Lisa M. 2007. "Setting the stage for undergraduates' information behaviors: Faculty and librarians' perspectives on academic space." In *The library as place: History, community, and culture,* edited by John E. Buschman and Gloria J. Leckie, 177–189. Westport, CT: Libraries Unlimited.

Group Mackenzie. 2009. American Honda. Portland, OR: Group Mackenzie. http://www.groupmackenzie.com/honda.html.

Kahn, Peter H. Jr., Batya Friedman, Brian Gill, Jennifer Hagman, Rachel L. Severson, Nathan G. Freier, Erika N. Feldman, Sybil Carrere, and Anna Stolyar. 2008. A plasma display window?—The shifting baseline problem in a technologically mediated natural world. *Journal of Environmental Psychology* 28 (2): 192–199.

Metro Regional Government. 2010. Construction salvage and recycling. Portland, OR: Metro Regional Government. http://www.oregonmetro.gov/index.cfm/go/by.web/id=24684/level=3.

Plaster, Edward J. 2003. "Chapter 19: Urban soil." In *Soil science and management*, 318–329. New York: Delmar Learning.

Ulrich, Roger S. 1984, April 24. View through a window may influence recovery from surgery. *Science* 224: 420–421. http://find.galegroup.com/gtx/infomark.do?&contentSet=IAC-Documents&type=retrieve&tabID=T002&prodId=AONE&docId=A3238205&source=gale&userGroupName=conu&version=1.0.

U.S. Environmental Protection Agency. 2007. An office building occupant's guide to indoor air quality. Washington, D.C.: Environmental Protection Agency. http://www.epa.gov/iaq/pubs/occupgd.html.

U.S. Green Building Council. 2003. *LEED reference guide for new construction and major renovations (LEED-NC) version 2.1.* 2nd ed. Washington, D.C.: U.S. Green Building Council.

Waxman, Lisa, Stephanie Clemons, Jim Banning, and David McKelfresh. 2007. The library as place: Providing students with opportunities for socialization, relaxation, and restoration. *New Library World* 108 (9/10): 424–434. http://proquest.umi.com/pqdweb?did=1341235681&sid=2&Fmt=3&clientID=11269&RQT=309&VName=PQD.

Yu, Shaw L., Jan-Tai Kuo, Members, ASCE, Elizabeth A. Fassman, and Henry Pan. 2001. Field test of grassed-swale performance in removing runoff pollution. *Journal of Water Resources Planning and Management* 127 (3): 168–171.

Yudelson, Jerry. 2008. *The green building revolution*. Washington, D.C.: Island Press.

Santa Monica Public Library Collaborates with City Department to Create a Sustainability Destination

Nancy Bender

Santa Monica Public Library (SMPL) is a sustainable destination because of its unique combination of library programs, materials, and green architecture. An important part of the sustainability initiative is the collaboration that the Library enjoys with the City of Santa Monica's Office of Sustainability and the Environment. This relationship has allowed both departments, and by extension the City of Santa Monica, to further their goal of creating a sustainable community. Sustainability is defined by the City of Santa Monica Sustainable City Plan as "meeting current needs—environmental, economic and social—without compromising the ability of future generations to do the same."[1]

The LEED Gold certified Main Library, which opened in January 2006, provides the foundation for the Library's goal as a sustainability center. The building is 104,000 square feet of light-filled, open-air space, with an additional 20,000 square feet of sustainably landscaped space. The two-story building contains over 300,000 circulating items and includes three rentable meeting spaces—an auditorium, multipurpose room, and community room—as well as study rooms, a central courtyard with a café, and three levels of underground parking.

---

1. Office of Sustainability and the Environment, "Sustainable City Progress Report," City of Santa Monica, http://www.smgov.net/Departments/OSE/Categories/Sustainability/Sustainable_City_Progress_Report/Sustainable_City_Progress_Report.aspx.

The central courtyard features a café, water feature, and sustainable landscaping.

The Library began working with Santa Monica's Office of Sustainability and the Environment (OSE) in 2003 to discern how best to promote the new green facility, coordinate educational and entertaining sustainability programs, and develop a sustainability collection suitable for the novice and the scholar. Andrew Basmajian, Environmental Outreach Specialist, and his colleague, OSE Manager Dean Kubani, met with Library staff to discuss the collaboration, "we knew early on that, to be successful in promoting the program and the message of sustainability, we needed stakeholders in the community . . . speaking to the subject in their own voice." Basmajian's enthusiasm for the collaboration is evident; referring to the Library he explains, "they are experts in governmental outreach and leaders in the community. It was a no brainer."[2]

Kubani views the collaboration as another step in reaching out to the broader community of Santa Monica. By the late-1990s, OSE had transitioned to expanding its focus beyond city operations to comprehensively address sustainability throughout the community, including issues such as economic and social sustainability.[3] Today OSE collaborates with other City departments as well,

2. Andrew Basmajian, email message to author, December 28, 2009.

3. Dean Kubani, email message to author, December 24, 2009.

including the local bus system, Big Blue Bus, and the Farmers' Market. But it's the Library that Kubani singles out, "I think the Library wins the prize for taking sustainability and making it their own."[4]

Today Santa Monica is recognized as a leader in the sustainable communities movement. Since building its first LEED certified structure, the Public Safety Facility, in 2003, the City of Santa Monica has required that all new governmental buildings be LEED certified. Perhaps one of the most striking examples of this policy is Virginia Avenue Park, which expanded and reopened in 2005; it is the first park in the nation to receive the LEED Silver Rating. Santa Monica is one of the first cities to establish a Sustainable City Plan, with performance-based indicators outlined in a yearly Sustainable City Report Card.[5] Shannon Parry, Senior Environmental Programs Analyst at OSE, feels that the City's greatest strengths are its commitment to sustainability, the ability to track performance, success in engaging the government and community, and its outreach efforts.

The collaboration has resulted in programming such as panel discussions on sustainable issues, the establishment of the annual Green Prize for Sustainable Literature, several Sustainable Cinema film series, and ongoing quarterly programs with farmers and chefs on local and sustainable eating. OSE funding for materials has led to a substantial sustainability collection, ranging from the most basic 'how to be green' guides to LEED certification manuals. The Library features the collection on a permanent lobby display, and includes take-away outreach materials on sustainable City initiatives and services, such as green building and sustainable landscaping rebates. Library Director Greg Mullen feels that the collaboration with OSE has been successful because it "brings staff focused on sustainability (an explicit community priority defined by City Council) together with library staff who are expert at organizing and promoting programs, building and managing collections, and matching patrons with the tools they need—all in a building that embodies green design."[6]

Concurrent with sustainable collection development and program planning were arrangements for the Main Library's grand opening celebration in January 2006. A variety of events were organized and methods to highlight the importance of sustainability were explored. The idea was to kick off a succession of programs that would effectively highlight the features of the building and collection. The building houses a Stanton Macdonald-Wright mural, originally unveiled in 1935 and currently on loan from the Smithsonian American Art

---

4. Dean Kubani, email message to author, December 24, 2009.

5. Shannon Parry, email message to author, December 22, 2009.

6. Greg Mullen, email message to author, January 20, 2009.

Museum. Painted on plywood panels rather than in the traditional mural style of fresco (painting in wet plaster that becomes a permanent part of the wall), the portable mural originally covered the reading room walls of an earlier Santa Monica Main Library building. At the new Main Library, the restored mural has been given a second life. The California Collection at SMPL is a non-circulating research collection of approximately 4,000 items. The specialized selection of primary and secondary resources chronicles the history of the Santa Monica Bay region and the rest of California. The Collection is housed in a semi-enclosed room behind the Reference Desk, allowing for private and assisted research.

A series of panel discussions was planned, each highlighting a different topic related to sustainability and featuring experts in the field. OSE became an invaluable resource in coordinating the series, as they provided many contacts as possible panelists. Their experience working with local specialists and professionals provided the Library with not just a list of names, but an 'in' with the community. The programs took place quarterly throughout 2006, with a Green Building program in February, a Watershed program in April, an Organic Gardening and Sustainable Landscaping program in July, and a Living Sustainably program in October. Each program consisted of a three-to-five member panel. All panelists had a specific area of expertise and the discussions that followed were educational and entertaining.

Another program opportunity that arose shortly after the opening of the Main Library was a collaboration with the Santa Monica Farmers' Market. Renowned for its variety of seasonal produce and support of local farmers, the Farmers' Market approached the Library about presenting a series of panel discussions featuring farmers, chefs, and food writers from the *Los Angeles Times*. Programs would end with a sampling of food prepared by the chef panelist, using Farmers' Market ingredients. A quarterly series was coordinated with Market Manager Laura Avery. The series, with each program featuring a different topic and selection of panelists, has proved to be such a hit that it is still going strong five years later. The Farmers' Market has expanded its reach by including Library programs for children and teens as well.

SMPL's Sustainable Cinema series was developed in 2007, primarily as a less labor-intensive way to present sustainability programming. The Library had screened films in the past with a fair amount of success, and around this time many films were being released on sustainability topics. A monthly series of films allowed the Library to educate the public on these important issues, with a limited amount of staff time required. The first series, in 2007, featured four films, all recent theatrical releases. It ran from March to May, and featured the films *Who Killed the Electric Car?*, *Super Size Me*, *An Inconvenient Truth*, and *Fast Food Nation*. The film series averaged 100 people per screening.

The success of the first series led to a 2008 cycle of sustainability screenings. The focus remained on varied topics, but the films selected were less well known. The idea was to draw fans of the 2007 series, as well as a new audience, and screen films that may have been difficult to find in regular theaters. The film topics ranged from Cuba's agricultural reaction to the collapse of the Soviet Union in 1990 (*The Power of Community*), the rise of genetically modified foods and the reaction of alternative agriculture (*The Future of Food*), commercialization and over consumption (*What Would Jesus Buy?*), and the unsustainable American dream of suburban living (*The End of Suburbia*). Additional Sustainable Cinema series are planned for future years.

Within months of the Main Library opening, the idea of sustainable book awards was broached. It was suggested to Andrew Basmajian, Environmental Outreach Specialist, by a member of the local sustainable community, James Bassett. It was decided that the project would be the perfect fit for SMPL, a way to highlight the growing sustainability collection, and an additional way to emphasize Santa Monica's commitment to sustainability. The announcement of the Award stated that, "the Green Prize was created to encourage and commend authors, illustrators, and publishers who produce quality books that make significant contributions to, and broaden public awareness of, sustainability."

James Bassett conceived the idea of the award when encountering a number of professionals at a sustainability conference who revealed that reading *The Lorax* was the first moment of inspiration that led them to careers in sustainability. He was inspired by the idea of a piece of literature having such a profound impact on one's path in life. As a child, James' librarian father introduced him to Newberry and Caldecott books. He "grew up reading at the Santa Monica Public Library and knowing first-hand what a valuable and inspiring community resource the library was."[8] James felt that the Library's commitment to sustainability made it the ideal organization for a sustainable book award.

The first awards presentation was held in October 2007, which allowed for ten months of preparation. That first year provided a deep learning curve as to what it takes to develop an award, coordinate a committee, and produce an awards presentation. The Green Prize committee has evolved over the course of four years, but initially consisted of four SMPL librarians, including the author, a reference librarian, and two Youth Services librarians; two city employees with sustainability backgrounds and positions; and Bassett, a professor at California State University and University of California Los Angeles.

7. James Bassett, email message to author, December 18, 2009.

8. James Bassett, email message to author, December 18, 2009.

The criteria for the Green Prize includes: titles should be future and long-term oriented, have an awareness of ecological and resource limits, be regional as well as global in scope, be cognizant that everything is interconnected, be concerned with creating diverse and balanced communities, be inclusive of social equality and well-being, be supportive of public involvement in community decisions, promote environmental, economic or social equity ideals, and be published using sustainable practices. Evaluation is also based on the effective presentation of material, distinctive literary quality, and originality of scholarship. Youth titles must have potential for classroom use and be appropriate for students in grades K–12. Titles published in the United States during the previous calendar year are considered.[9]

Titles for Green Prize consideration are gathered in a number of ways. A press release is sent early each year to local media, and to library, literary, and sustainably-themed periodicals. Authors, illustrators, and publishers are encouraged to submit titles for consideration. Many of the books considered, however, are simply titles pulled from the Library's collection. Each year, the submissions have determined the categories of winners and some variation has occurred over the years. For example, the committee has yet to find an adult fiction title that warranted consideration. Green Prize guidelines and winners are posted on the web page, http://smpl.org/Green_Prize.aspx.

Over the years, the Green Prize has garnered recognition and accolades. As word of the Green Prize has spread, publishers and authors have expressed their gratitude and encouragement in a number of ways. The 2007 winner of the Green Prize Adult Reference Award, *Worldchanging: A User's Guide for the 21st Century*, edited by Alex Steffen, and published by Harry N. Abrams, added a seal indicating that the title had won the Award to the paperback release of the book. The 2008 Adult Nonfiction winner for *Blessed Unrest: How the Largest Social Movement in the World Came into Being and Why No One Saw it Coming*, Paul Hawken, recently added mention of the award to the biography page of his website. In 2009, two high-profile writers received Green Prize Awards: Ed Begley, Jr. won the Adult Reference Award for *Living Like Ed: A Guide to the Eco-Friendly Life*, and Jane Goodall won the Pioneer Award, given each year to a writer who paved the way for sustainable discourse. Both were unable to attend the Awards Presentation, but each provided a video acceptance for the ceremony. Their enthusiastic and gracious words were a highlight of the 2009 Awards.

Development of the sustainability collection at SMPL garnered a huge boost when OSE began contributing funds to the Library in 2005. Approximately

---

9. "The Green Prize for Sustainable Literature," Santa Monica Public Library, http://smpl.org/Green_Prize.aspx.

two-thirds of the yearly $10,000 contribution has gone to collection development. While the Santa Monica Public Library had been purchasing items on sustainable issues for some time, the additional funding has allowed the Library to augment the collection considerably. The additional funds have allowed the collection to broaden in both breadth and depth in all areas, including youth titles and audiovisual materials.

The focus of the sustainability collection has evolved over the years, but initially the goal was to purchase the most up-to-date materials on the broadest subjects, essentially building a foundation for the collection. The expertise of OSE staff Basmajian and Kubani was invaluable for determining essential collection titles. This allowed librarians to read reviews for and select the newest items, go to backlists to make sure classics in the subject area were also accounted for, and then additionally utilize the OSE knowledge to build the collection.

Each year, as the title output has grown, publishing trends of sustainable titles have become apparent. Initially the bulk of available titles were on broad environmental issues, and often academic or technical in nature. Over the years, however, the number of titles appealing to the lay person and budding environmentalist has grown. Topics such as organic gardening, mixed-use housing, recycling primers, creating a green home, living off the grid, the relationship between the economy and sustainable practices, and others are all represented on the shelves. Titles purchased are dispersed throughout the collection, and are cataloged and shelved normally. However, each catalog record is tagged "Sustainable Santa Monica Collection" for those interested in searching broadly. SMPL has kept up with the trends by regularly purchasing titles with the most up-to-date information on these subjects and others.

A recent focus of collection development has been on materials related to green building and interior design. The local Green Building Resource Center (GBRC), part of Global Green and partially funded by the City of Santa Monica, recently closed its Santa Monica location, causing a gap in the availability of books on sustainable building. OSE provided the Library with the stock list from the GBRC to develop the sustainability collection further in this area, and also donated copies of the U.S. Green Building Council's LEED certification manuals for reference use.

The extensive and flexible merchandising space in the new Main Library allows the Library collection to be featured in the lobby and other high traffic points in the building. Movable merchandising units can be reconfigured numerous ways, and display themes are changed monthly. The sustainably-themed display is a constant. The location changes and newer materials are consistently added, but merchandising of green materials is always present. In addition to books and DVDs, the display includes take-away materials for Library patrons.

The lobby features open space for displays and merchandising.

OSE, and other City departments, provide materials such as the Sustainable City Report Card, the Sustainable Directory, sustainable landscaping grant applications, and fliers on drought and water saving. Including these materials in the display effectively ties the collection, and the Library generally, into community activities and concerns. It is another way to emphasize the Library as a community center, but also as a one-stop center for information on sustainability.

The Santa Monica Public Library building and services come together to make a sustainable workspace, educational space, learning center, and entertainment venue. As a City of Santa Monica structure, it aims to create an educational and enjoyable green space for the public, while serving as an example of the value of such spaces. Together, library programs, the collection, the building and the services highlight sustainable ideas and actions.

Policies in place upon the opening of the Main Library, and ones implemented since, set an example to the public and suggest ideas on how they can participate. Battery recycling receptacles, in eye-catching 3 foot high clear tubes, encourage patrons to dispose of batteries at the Library. In 2008, the Library switched from offering plastic bags to $1.00 reusable cloth bags to patrons checking out. Behind the scenes, nontoxic cleaners are de rigueur and sink water

The main reading room features south-facing windows, providing light to both floors.

filters recently replaced water coolers in staff areas. Trained volunteers offer sustainability tours to the public by appointment.

OSE has developed a series of large vertical banners highlighting the green features of the Main Library. Currently the Library offers handouts on the building's sustainable features, as well as comprehensive information on the website. The idea of offering some kind of informational display on the Library's sustainable features had been discussed among OSE and Library staff for some time. The challenge was to develop a display that does not clutter the public space or provide information overload to the patron. The banners are moveable, allowing for maximum flexibility, and highlight the building's energy efficiency, the water efficient landscaping, and healthy indoor spaces.

Santa Monica Public Library staff use their experience and expertise each day to assist patrons, and provide a dynamic environment for learning and entertainment. The contribution of Santa Monica's Office of Sustainability and the Environment has allowed SMPL to excel in educating the public on sustainable issues. Dean Kubani describes the collaboration, "out of a very modest start with OSE contributing some funding to purchase books, the library has created a really comprehensive sustainability library and resource. . . . I think that the library is a great ally for OSE because you have such great resources to get the sustainability message out to the community in ways that are interesting and accessible to the public."[10] Funding by OSE has allowed the Library to develop one of the most comprehensive sustainability collections in the area, continually produce high quality educational and entertaining programs, and reward authors and publishers of sustainable titles with the Green Prize Award. Together, the Library and OSE continue to strive in creating an increasingly relevant sustainability destination, a place where patrons are surrounded by resources, enlightened by their environment, and encouraged to learn about and participate in creating a healthier world.

10. Dean Kubani, email message to author, December 18, 2009.

Not Every Green Library Needs to be Gold or Platinum

Adrianne Ralph

It is an amazing experience to stand in the parking lot at the new King County Library System (KCLS) in Sammamish, Washington during a typical pacific northwestern winter rainstorm and hear—very little. No rain splashing off asphalt. No children jumping in puddles on their way to story time. Instead, the rain passes through pervious paving.

The pervious paving is just one piece of the sustainability strategy for this particular library.

KCLS believes in incorporating sustainability in all aspects of its service, including construction. In 2004 KCLS embarked on a 172 million dollar capital building program. Since then, ten new buildings and six additions have been completed. Twenty projects remain. Prior to beginning the capital projects, KCLS formed a policy infrastructure to ensure that sustainability remains a focus. The Board of Trustees passed a site selection policy and approved design guidelines that include sustainability as a key component. LEED certification was not mandated.

Unfortunately, 2004 was the start of a period of significant escalation in construction costs. The historic four to five percent increases jumped to over ten percent.[1] The KCLS capital budget is finite. It quickly became apparent that

---

1. http://www.data360.org/dataset.aspx?Data_Set_Id=3629.

something would have to give. LEED certification for every project was one of the things let go early on.

KCLS certified one building LEED Gold. It will likely certify a few other projects, but has decided to incorporate green building practices without completing the formal LEED certification process.

While the cost of certification has been reduced, there is still a cost. By avoiding that expense, KCLS has been able to afford some of the upfront costs to install sustainable infrastructure in the capital budget that will pay off in the operation budget for years to come. This enables the Sammamish Library building to meet the sustainable expectations.

The Sammamish Library is a great example of how KCLS looks at and adopts sustainable building techniques at every phase of the project.

In site acquisition, instead of developing on a raw piece of land, the library is co-located on a site occupied by the Sammamish City Hall, a city park, and a skateboard park. This allows some infrastructure like parking and stormwater to be shared or augmented rather than constructed from scratch, resulting in less total infrastructure. It also puts the library in close proximity to public transportation to help reduce vehicle trips and resulting pollution. Bike parking and staff showers are provided to encourage patrons to bike to the library and staff to commute without a car.

On the site, to further reduce the impervious surface and stormwater runoff, the library has a partial green roof made from multi-coloured sedum. Due to the topography of the site, patrons can see the sedums from the adjacent roadway year round. The majority of parking is structured parking under the building. The limited surface parking is created with pervious paving, allowing for decreased storm water detention. The bulk of the storm detention that is not handled via the pervious paving and green roof is handled via bioswales rather than more traditional vaults.

The rest of the site landscape is sustainable as well. The plantings are native and draught tolerant. The 18 boulders incorporated into the landscape are actually rocks that were buried on site and unearthed during construction. This reduced the cost of excavation and transportation. It also minimized the environmental impact and reinforced the sustainable narrative that the building and site tell.

Along with the infrastructure benefits, the colocation of this building has significant social benefits. Patrons can combine a trip to the farmers market with dropping off their library materials. A trip to the skate park can become an opportunity to pick up a few DVDs. Paying a utility bill can be mixed with attending a story time. Through all these activities patrons get a chance to participate in, and learn about, the environmental and sustainable story that this complex creates. Whether it is through reading the signage about the pervious paving, taking a volunteer led tour, or simply enjoying the landscaping, patrons get to see and feel how beautiful, enjoyable and practical a sustainable building can be.

Moving into the building, the sustainable design continues. The heating and cooling system is geothermal. Water cycles through an underground piping loop and is warmed or cooled by the soil temperature. The system is sophisticated and is topped with a radiant floor slab. This infrastructure is visible to patrons. To make the system as effective as possible, large expanses of the concrete topping slab are left exposed to allow for the heating or cooling to easily radiate from the floor. This ensures that the area where patrons gather is kept at a comfortable, consistent temperature. The geothermal system is augmented with a ventilation system that includes operable windows.

From infrastructure to the building envelope, the sustainable strategy continues. The building itself is oriented in an East–West direction to maximize daylighting and minimize solar heat gain. Fixed sunshades on the western façade, and automatic operable sunshades, further minimize heat gain while allowing for daylighting. Skylights with translucent enclosures create a one hundred percent naturally daylit reading room for the bulk of the library's open hours. High performance glazing, with custom ceramic frit, maximizes daylight and minimizes heat gain.

The interior building details provide another layer to utilize sustainable design. There are waterless urinals and low flow toilets in the washrooms. The carpet has a high post-consumer recycled content. The carpet is also tiled so individual pieces can be replaced instead of vast expanses. The paint has low volatile organic compounds. The countertops and some of the benches throughout the space are made locally from hyper-local reclaimed and milled wood. The end panels of the book stacks are made from rapidly renewable bamboo. There are manual operable windows in the staff room. All the light fixtures are either compact fluorescents or LEDs.

The Sammamish Library is a great example of green sustainable design. While it has not been formally certified via the LEED process, it tells a compelling story about how a public agency can be a great steward of the environment and public funds. It invites library patrons to learn about how a building can fit into a landscape gently, while creating a beautiful, great place to spend time— even on a rainy northwestern winter day.

Sustainable Library Design: A Case Study of Library Construction on the East End of Long Island, N.Y. from 2007 to 2009

Samantha Jane Alberts

The terms "sustainable libraries" and "green libraries" are often used interchangeably in the context of library construction that is environmentally responsible. While the environmental component is an important aspect of sustainable libraries, the green element is only one part of what makes a sustainable library. In addition, LEED certification, which stands for Leadership in Energy and Environmental Design, developed by the U.S. Green Building Council (USGBC), provides certification by an independent third-party which verifies that a building project meets green building and performance measures. In some cases this is a limited and incomplete measure of overall sustainability because of its focus on green building.

This study relied on LEED Certification v2.[1] LEED certification has different rating systems for different projects. A building is awarded LEED Platinum (the highest), LEED Gold, LEED Silver or LEED certified. Certification is based on a point system. This paper focuses on the LEED certification for New Construction, which is what is meant when discussing LEED certification and does not include a recertification requirement. (LEED for Existing Buildings: Operations & Maintenance does maintain a recertification element.) LEED,

---

1. The revised list of criteria for LEED certification is now available and is referred to as LEED v3. The new rules do contain an energy use reporting mechanism which requires LEED certified building owners to report usage of energy and water for up to five years to the USGBC.

while arguably is a useful tool in monitoring green aspects of a building project as well as in creating positive public approval, does not necessarily represent the most efficient mechanism for measuring broad sustainability or even a more narrowly defined green building.

The case study referred to in this article examined three Suffolk County, New York libraries located on the East End of Long Island at different stages of the building process. These libraries were selected because of their similarities in location, demographics, type of library and relative stage reached in the library construction process. The directors of all three libraries were interviewed and filled out surveys for the original research paper that this article is based on. Although the sample is small and select, it provides a concise snapshot in time of each phase of that process from which information and guidelines pertinent to other projects may be extrapolated.

The three libraries were: John Jermain Memorial Library (JJML) in Sag Harbor, which has a service population of 6,631 and was in the beginning stages of a building project under Director Catherine Creedon; the Hampton Library (HL) in Bridgehampton, which has a service population of 1,186 and was in the middle stages of a building project under Director Susan LaVista; and Cutchogue New Suffolk Library (CNSL) with a service population of 3,392 and which had completed an entire building renovation under Director Elizabeth Burns.

These libraries provided a window into the three stages in the process of creating a sustainable library as follows: Planning (JJML); Breaking Ground (HL); and Moving In (CNSL). Planning (JJML) examines the intersection of the political and the pragmatic in formulating plans and implementing design in the context of community input, library needs and director and board response. Breaking Ground compares the initial plans with the final design, keeping in mind the inherent flexibility (or lack thereof) in the plans. Moving In looks at how well the library achieved the goal of building a sustainable library based on initial concepts, final plans, community response to the finished product and the real and perceived success in terms of sustainability.

What is a Sustainable Library? Most literature discusses sustainable libraries based almost entirely on environmental concepts. However, a sustainable library building also includes elements that allow the building to function in ways that will meet future demands of security, technology, and flexible work and public spaces. Libraries that rely on LEED certification as the standard for success in achieving sustainability may fail in creating a true sustainable facility. The building process needs to balance the concept of sustainability with that of staff and community needs. This balancing act can often inhibit the ability to follow through on sustainable library criteria. If libraries choose to focus on green

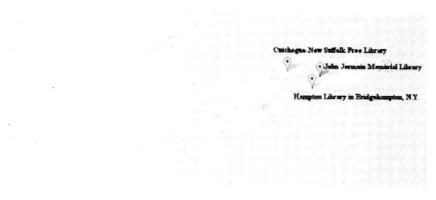

Figure1: Geographical location of libraries studied

concepts and technology, while discarding the other elements like security and flexibility, the building may not truly be a sustainable facility. Focus on green elements in LEED certification while the other elements of sustainable design, technology, flexibility and security are ignored or given minimal consideration may create a green building but in fact may be less sustainable overall. Therefore libraries which may be represented as sustainable are often only reflecting the environmental ideal described in the current literature with its bias toward green elements and LEED certification as the primary yardstick.

To infer what the true state of sustainable construction is on the East End of Long Island, three library directors were initially asked six questions through an online survey.[2] The questions and answers are as follows:

1. How would you define a sustainable library?

CNSL, Liz Burns: "I would say a sustainable library is one that meets the current and future needs of the community. In terms of future needs, I'd say the time frame would [be] minimally 10 years, but optimally 20."

HL, Susan LaVista: "A sustainable library, like any other sustainable building, has the least possible impact on the surrounding environment and on the people who use it. A sustainable library should be well planned to meet future needs for collection growth, changes in technology, and changes in use."

---

2. Survey completed by Directors for Samantha Alberts, "Sustainable Library Design: A case study of library construction on the East End of Long Island, New York," (unpublished paper, 2009).

JJER, Catherine Creedon: "Well, I've always thought libraries are the ultimate in sustainability: all those books being shared over and over again, and when at last the bindings are gone and the pages fly free, they can be recycled—or used for kindling! And, of course, librarians, especially those that manage buildings, look at sustainability in the more current usage of the word—energy sustainability—as we try to make sure to conserve heat, water and electricity, and when we create new buildings with geothermal heat, water reuse toilets, and green roofs (my dream library has these things). I am also mindful as director to watch not just the natural resources used by my library, but also our financial and personnel resources: how successfully am I avoiding waste in managing these areas?"

2. Which of the following are reasons that you and your library are or will be considering a building project? (Please choose all that apply)

Table1. Reasons for Libraries Considering a Building Project

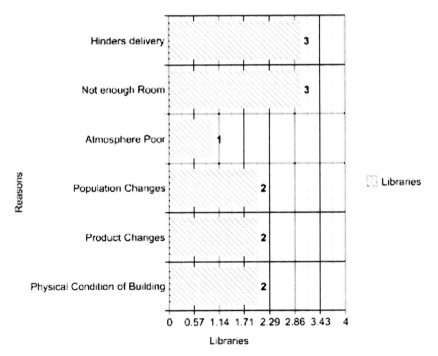

*Libraries refer to survey sample of CNSL, HL and JJER
Source: Survey Sustainable Libraries Research Paper 2009 (unpublished)

Each director was asked to add extra comments to Question 2. Ms. Burns explained that the Cutchogue library project focused on a community room, space for technology, ADA compliance, YA (Young Adult) and quiet spaces. According to Ms. Burns, "All these needs resulted from changing services and programs that did not exist when the library was renovated in the 1980's. Back then there was no media collection, no PCs, limited programs with no community groups needing to use space. The library was overall quiet and now is more of a community center. I don't know why the YAs never had their own area, perhaps just a space issue but we knew that was a definite need in the current project." The focus of the building would include three elements of sustainability: green, flexible spaces and technology. Since the project did not increase the footprint of the building and reused building materials the green element was implemented automatically with practical focus on space and technology.

Bridgehampton Director Susan LaVista said, "Our building was over 130 years old and in very poor condition. It was not accessible, not energy efficient, not built for technology. The library board chose to renovate and expand rather than demolish and build new. They accepted that this could cost more than a new building, but they felt it was important to reuse as much as possible, both for environmental reasons and aesthetics." Flexibility, technology and green elements were considered in varying degrees

John Jermain Director, Cathy Creedon, had concerns focused on the facility's space. She stated, "John Jermain Memorial Library is a beautiful and welcoming building, which first opened for service in 1910. We have an outdated HVAC system, inefficient plumbing, and cramped quarters—and, most importantly, only one floor of our three-story building is handicapped-accessible. Still, the building is welcoming and well-used. And, truly, I do not think the emphasis on the core services has changed that much in the last century: I am often moved by the reports of the earliest librarians and stewards of John Jermain; their concerns are very, very similar to my own."

3. How did you go about the needs assessment for the building project?

CNSL Director Burns "spoke to all the staff and had them write down what they thought were the needs of the project. To no one's surprise the staff lists closely matched the needs I had come up with. Overall the needs assessment was not too difficult. We have a very limited amount of land to use and had to stick to the very important and obvious needs."

In terms of needs assessment, HL Director LaVista's said, "The library board, along with input from staff and patrons, started with a list of all the things they felt was needed in a new library. There were many meetings with architects to learn about their building philosophies before one was selected. The library director consulted with colleagues who have gone through building projects, and she and the board attended several workshops on library buildings, including green building."

JJER Director Creedon used assessments gathered from two previous years, "I am a relatively new director; the needs assessment documents (one from 2003 and a second from 2006) were created before I arrived; the first by a library consultant hired by an independent citizen group, the second by an ad-hoc committee formed by the Board and consisting of Board members and community members. Information was gathered from surveys, analysis of circulation records, traffic studies, etc."

4. Which of the below did you find a need for?

Table 2. Needs Assessment

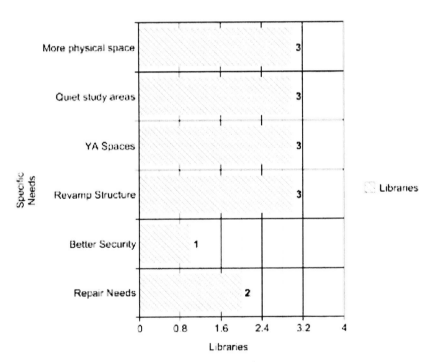

*Libraries refer to survey sample of CNSL, HL and JJER
Source: Survey Sustainable Libraries Research Paper 2009 (unpublished)

5. How important was/is creating a "green building" in your library building project?

CNSL Director Burns said, "Unfortunately, this concept was not very important in our project, due primarily to cost."

HL Director LaVista noted that "The library trustees felt it is very important to include as many green concepts in our project as possible. That being said however, we found that in many cases, green building is more costly—at least up front."

JJER Director Creedon said that being green was/is "Very important. But, in some sense we already are a 'green building'; I think it's axiomatic that an existing 100-year-old building represents sustainable use, especially in terms of the building materials: bricks, glass, wooden furniture, natural flooring surfaces."

6. Please select three of the following characteristics that were most important items in your libraries' building project.

Table 3. Characteristics of Building Projects

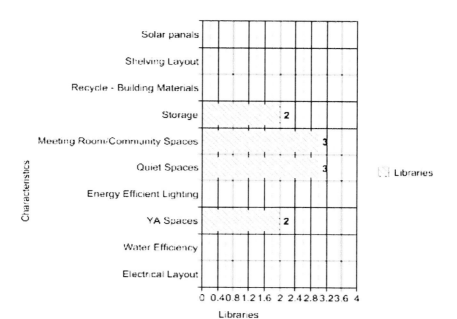

*Libraries refer to survey sample of CNSL, HL and JJER
Source: Survey Sustainable Libraries Research Paper 2009 (unpublished)

Subsequent tours and meeting with the directors provided three major insights. First, all of these libraries in their own way are sustainable. They either maintained the building's existing footprint (or choose to alter slightly) and/or used existing materials such as windows and shelving, thus demonstrating a sustained commitment to green building.

Second, while LEED certification provides only a limited measure of "being green" it is a valuable public relations tool to generate goodwill. Libraries can use the process of LEED certification for political purposes to gain access for funding a new building project. At the 2009 Long Island Library Conference, Mathew Bollerman, Director of the Westhampton Free Library, another East End library that was going through the process of construction and LEED certification, said:

> *Depending on your community, LEED certification can be an especially useful tool with respect to garnering some support for your construction project. Our community in Westhampton already had a LEED certified building, which established a precedent for LEED certified building in the community. There was an expectation of any new building being LEED certified (Bollerman, 2009).*[3]

Bollerman admitted that the process of going green "can be initially . . . somewhat more expensive" but as the architect for the Westhampton project, Pansy Cheng of Ward Associates pointed out during the conference presentation the new facility expects to save 25% more water and 40% of the energy used in the old building. "It's a lot of P.R.; we got a lot of tax payer support" (Cheng, 2009).[4] Bollerman wanted to make it clear that the project was not predicated on "point chasing" instead by properly starting the LEED process Westhampton expects to gain a Gold rating in the LEED certification process. When queried regarding LEED New Construction's lifetime certification of the building Bollerman agreed that "yes, that is one of the problems with LEED certification" and expressed the hope that the upcoming LEED 3v[5] guidelines will address this

---

3. Director of the Westhampton Free Library at the 2009 Long Island Library Conference Q & A *Lunch and Learn: Green Building.*

4. The Architect of the Westhampton Building renovation, Pansy Cheng (Ward Associates) speaking at the 2009 Long Island Library Conference *Lunch and Learn: Green Building.*

5. The revised list of criteria for LEED certification is now available and is referred to as LEED v3. The new rules do contain an energy use reporting mechanism which requires LEED certified building owners to report usage of energy and water for up to five years to the USGBC.

issue. But it's important to remember that, "this is the USGB Council not the USGB Police" (Bollerman, 2009).[6]

Third, LEED certification for building projects (still under the old LEED v2 rules) is just the beginning. The optional LEED for Existing Building: Operations & Maintenance buildings does offer a chance for a building to be re-certified. This is an optional element and if a building project does not take part the facility can still count on the cachet of being LEED certified for new construction if they are grandfathered in under the old rules. The commitment to maintain green sustainability can be addressed by voluntary LEED recertification every year. The new LEED 3v which requires owners to make available the facility's energy and water consumption for five years, comes close to a required recertification but seems to stop short. Either way green sustainability will always require an ongoing commitment of staff and administration, especially in light of the new reporting requirements for LEED3v which still may be found to be a costly measure for some entities.

The conclusions of this paper support the cost-saving benefits of green building, but do not equate green building with LEED certification, especially in view of the limitations inherent in such certification. Buildings that rely on LEED certification alone may be green, but not necessarily sustainable. Buildings that rely on LEED certification in conjunction with the elements of sustainability are both greener and provide for more sustainability.

LEED certification is effective primarily as a tool for garnering community support of a construction project such as a library. Otherwise, its usefulness has an "emperor's new clothes" quality. Many of the point categories are not necessarily the most appropriate way to go green. Although a facility may save money by meeting the LEED standards such as those for energy and water use, (critics of LEED are debating these cost savings),[7] the cost for LEED certification is an additional cost, and the facility may still pursue green/sustainable building goals without LEED certification if it does not need the public relations polish offered by LEED certification. In addition, a major weakness of LEED certification is the lack of review and reappraisal once a building has been certified. The effectiveness of new LEED 3v still needs to be measured. Absent required monitoring, LEED certified facilities have no incentive to maintain those LEED specified green elements that appear to make them energy efficient. Finally, the LEED focus on green elements to the exclusion of the broader sustainable con-

---

6. Director of the Westhampton Free Library at the 2009 Long Island Library Conference Q & A *Lunch and Learn: Green Building*.

7. "Some Buildings Not Living Up To Green Label," New York Times, 30 August 2009, http://www.nytimes.com/2009/08/31/science/earth/31leed.html.

cerns of security, technology and flexibility of work and public space means that LEED certified buildings could well in fact be less green. The need to address those concerns later may ultimately necessitate environmentally and financially expensive renovations, additions or new construction.

Concerns for the security of the staff and patrons as well as for the property and materials within and on the grounds of the library is an important sustainable library element. Libraries should give the issue of security added emphasis, especially in conjunction with technology. In the future public libraries may be increasingly called upon to provide not only information literacy for new technologies but will need to provide patrons the opportunity to interface with those technologies. The influx and growth of potentially expensive technology hardware and component software means that the need for appropriate security measures will also increase. These measures will need to balance ease of access with property protection. Libraries that have not implemented the four elements of sustainability may be unable to meet such demands and may face environmentally and financially expensive renovations, additions or new construction in that context as well.

As of July 2009 Cutchogue Library has a new library director. Liz Burns who was the director in charge of Cutchogue's building project is now director at Rogers Memorial Library in Southampton, New York. In January 2010 the Hampton Library completed the building project and moved into the new facility in 2011. Susan LaVista, the director in charge of the Hampton Library building project became director of the Hampton Bays Public Library. The John Jermain Library in Sag Harbor has received funding approval from the community of Sag Harbor for the construction project and will be applying for LEED certification. The Library in the summer 2011 is at a temporary location. The Westhampton Free Library building project was completed and opened to the public in late spring 2010. Westhampton was certified LEED gold and unveiled a LEED Gold Plaque April 22, 2011.

References

Alberts, Samantha Jane. (2009). *Sustainable Libraries Research Paper.* Unpublished.

Antonelli, M. "The Green Library Movement: An Overview and Beyond" *Electronic Green Journal* December, 2008. Academic Search Premier database (accessed May 14, 2009).

Brown, William M. "Future-Proof Design" *Library Journal,* September 16, 2008. MasterFILE Premier database (accessed September 30, 2009).

Davis Langdon (2007), The Cost of Going Green Revisited. http://www.davislangdon.com/USA/Research/ResearchFinder/2007-The-Cost-of-Green-Revisited/ (accessed April 26, 2009).

Rocky Mountain Institute (October 17, 2005) Why Build Green? http://www.rmi.org/ (accessed April 26, 2009).

Survey Monkey (copyright 1999–2009) [web program] . Available from: http://www.surveymonkey.com/.

U.S. Green Building Council, http://www.usgbc.org/ (accessed January 21, 2010).

Ward Associates. *Lunch and Learn: Green Building.* Long Island Library Conference. Crest Hollow Country Club, Melville NY. May 7, 2009.

Weiner, J., & Boyden, L. "Creating Sustainable Libraries "(2001, December 2). *Library Journal, 126* (20),8. December 2, 2001. Academic Search Premier database (accessed August 2, 2008).

Greening Libraries in Historic Buildings

Rebekkah Smith Aldrich

When buildings are abandoned both our environment and our cultural legacy suffer. Historic preservation and the green building movement have much in common. Both strive to preserve what we already have, to respect the future and to educate people through the built environment.

Libraries in historic buildings have already been green for decades if not centuries. Many historic buildings were designed to be sustainable from the outset and are already actually quite green in some ways.

Historic buildings are those of particular architectural, historic or local interest. Some may appear on state and national historic registers and others simply carry on an unrecognized, yet dignified existence within their communities. A good example of libraries in historic buildings are the more than 2,500 Carnegie Libraries—built between 1883 and 1929. It is relevant to note that just because a building is old, that does not make it historically relevant or worthy of rehabilitation or renovation as a library building.

A building designed as a library in the 18th or 19th century does not always make for a good library building in the 21st century. That being said, many libraries have made a commitment to their beloved facilities and have worked to upgrade, renovate and expand them, preserving the past while providing quality library service in the present.

Historic buildings may demand a more technically complicated approach when being greened. Awareness of a building as a system, a sum of parts that work together, is critical to greening any library building. Greening a historic library building follows many of the same paths as greening a contemporary structure, but requires more attention to historic building practices and materials used during the initial construction of the building. Library buildings that are on the National Register of Historic Places, embarking on a greening project that will impact the interior or exterior of the building, must also consider the Secretary of the Interior's *Standards for Rehabilitation.*

Greening a building means more than just reducing annual energy costs, although energy efficiency is a large characteristic of being green. Historic buildings speak to sustainability very clearly as they contain a large amount of embodied energy: they are existing buildings—they have already been built, materials have already been expended during their construction. There are opportunities to make these buildings more energy efficient and healthier for building occupants just as there are when building new, however, special care and attention should be given to the uniqueness of each historic building.

One of the earliest steps in greening a historic building is to first understand the building. Construction methods from previous centuries were often more solid than construction in the 20th century and therefore the life of a historic building may be longer than one built in the 1970s. Studies by the U.S. Department of Energy show that buildings with the poorest energy efficiency were built between 1940 and 1975. Historic buildings were often designed to be quite energy efficient due to the lack of reliance on mechanized climate control—wall thickness, reliance on natural ventilation, clerestories or skylights, exterior paint color—all work together to regulate interior conditions. Changing one of these passive features without giving consideration to their impact on the climate within the building would be a mistake.

When making a building more energy efficient learn about its history, construction methods, materials used to build the structure, amount of insulation present and the way features of the building work together so that it's clear how impacting one area of the building may compromise another area. For example, many older buildings are wood frame construction. If new insulation is introduced to the structure and the vapor barrier is installed facing in the wrong direction, moisture problems could arise and cause rot in the frame of the building. Inappropriate paint on cast iron radiators can reduce the energy efficiency of the radiator as the paint acts as an insulator. Leveling pipes leading from that radiator may prevent condensation from draining and compromise the heating system. Greening any building is a balancing act of energy efficiency, cost, aesthetics and preservation.

Green Options Exist on a Continuum

Going green involves *reducing* consumption (for example: energy, water, wood and other natural resources); *reusing* resources (for example: repurposing existing buildings and using construction materials from a deconstructed building in a new project); and *recycling* materials so that their useful life is maximized (for example: plastic bottles recycled into carpeting and bathroom stall dividers). Going green also includes options related to air quality, thermal comfort, visual comfort, physical comfort, water usage, light pollution, and noise pollution.

There are small, easy tweaks that increase your green quotient without impacting historic preservation issues and then there are expansive, potentially expensive options that can drastically increase your green quotient but may wreck havoc with historic preservation goals. For example, here are some relatively easy options:

- Utilize the energy saving setting on computers;
- Recycle paper, plastic and cardboard;
- Switch to compact fluorescent light bulbs (CFLs) as current bulbs burn out;
- Implement a green cleaning program;
- Routinely maintain heating and cooling equipment;
- Use only native plantings in your landscaping to reduce the need for irrigation;
- Collect rainwater for landscape irrigation;
- Seek environmentally friendly products for maintenance projects (low VOC paint, finishes, carpeting).

All of the above are relatively simple and have little-to-no impact on historic preservation concerns.

As we move through the continuum of choices, many projects that have a larger overall payoff from a green perspective require a larger upfront investment and begin to impact the structure in ways which could negatively impact historic characteristics of a building if care is not taken. Following are seven more complex green updates.

Addressing the Building Envelope (Attic, Roof, Walls and Basement)

The building envelope often contains some of the most unique historic fabric in the building, for example, roofing materials, old growth wood framing, stone foundations and plaster walls. Energy efficiency experts will start a project off by sealing up a building to reduce air infiltration through caulking joints and weather-stripping. While this is still the desired first step in an energy efficiency project for a historic building, special attention should be paid that infiltration is not reduced to the point that the building is air tight. If the building is completely sealed there will be moisture problems due to condensation. Moisture problems can lead to rot, mold and mildew problems.

Insulation is a logical project as many older buildings are not insulated throughout or have insulation that has degraded to the point of being almost useless. Installing insulation improperly can lead to moisture problems. Baird M. Smith, AIA, the author of the "Conserving Energy in Historic Buildings Brief," for the Technical Preservation Services division of the National Park Service provides clear tips for the application of insulation in various areas of historic buildings. Starting at the top with attic insulation there is the opportunity to upgrade insulation either between floor joists, or depending on the configuration of the attic, between roof rafters. There are multiple insulation options, some more green than others—fiberglass, closed or open cell cellulose, spray foam. When using an insulation material with a vapor barrier to prevent moisture infiltration it is important to install it correctly. Between floor joists the vapor barrier should face down. Between roof rafters the vapor barrier should face up. Smith notes that adequate ventilation in the attic must exist to avoid problems: net area of ventilation (free area or louver or vents) should equal approximately 1/300 of the attic floor area.

Moving lower in the building there are occasionally opportunities to address insulation in the interior walls, although it depends heavily on the materials used in original construction. This speaks to the thoughtful design of some historic buildings. For a wood frame structure augmenting insulation is usually not recommended and should only be attempted if the exterior siding can be removed without causing serious damage. If using blown or injected insulation the interior wall surface should be covered with an impermeable paint layer (According to Smith: two layers of oil base paint or one layer of impermeable latex pain.)

For masonry cavity walls augmenting insulation is not recommended as it is usually unnecessary. Masonry walls usually already have acceptable thermal performance. Introducing insulation could cause significant moisture problems.

As you consider the lowest points in the building, the basement and crawl spaces, Smith recommends different approaches depending on whether or not the space is heated. If unheated, insulation could be installed between the 1st floor joists (the ceiling of the basement). In this case the vapor barrier would be facing up. In heated basements Smith recommends batt or rigid insulation installed against basement walls within the 1st floor joists down to 3 feet below the exterior ground level with the vapor barrier facing in.

Addressing Air Infiltration Around Windows and Doors

Windows are a primary aesthetic focal point, as well as a source of contro-versy in many historic renovation projects. Anyone who has applied to a State Historic Preservation Office (SHPO) for project approval knows that one of the very first things considered is the condition of the windows. Windows in historic buildings should be routinely maintained, stabilized, and repaired. The old growth wood used in window construction for historic buildings is often far better than modern wood used in replacements. Replacement should only be an option if the wood frame has significant rot or their repair would be cost prohibitive. There are opportunities to weatherize historic windows including weather stripping, although it is advisable to avoid historic weatherstripping—felt—as it can introduce moisture to the frame, and sash locks to tighten seals. When replacing or introducing exterior storm windows, wood, aluminum, vinyl or plastic storm windows may be used although unfinished aluminum should be avoided. Use colors that match existing trim color to mitigate this visual ad-dition to the façade. Interior storm windows are not recommended as there is a high risk of damage to wood frames due to condensation. Windows should still be operable for ventilation in warmer months.

Historic wooden doors are another defining characteristic of historic build-ing facades. Check that the frame and door sit tightly to avoid air infiltration. Routine maintenance—sealing or painting—should help keep the door in good repair. Repair and restoration are preferable to replacement. Adding storm doors is a possibility for colder climates and should complement the architectural char-acter of the building.

Installing Energy Efficient Lighting Solutions

Adequate and appropriate lighting is critical in any library setting. Historic buildings are often at extremes—some were designed to maximize day lighting potential, while others minimized windows to such a degree that there is very little daylight. Seeking the expertise of a lighting specialist is advised; not only to insure proper lighting levels throughout the building but also in the context of historic lighting fixtures. Unlike modern buildings, replacing an incandescent bulb with a compact fluorescent light bulb is not easy. Often historic lighting fixtures left bulbs exposed as electricity and the light bulb were introduced to the building after it was built and therefore may be a character defining feature. A lighting design expert should be able to facilitate acceptable solutions in this area.

Installing a More Energy Efficient Boiler or Furnace that Requires the Addition of Ducts:

While almost any new boiler or furnace will be more energy efficient than an older one, a new unit replacing a unit that is practically historic itself can result in the need for new duct work. A carefully balanced system for the building type is essential to avoid moisture problems. Occasionally a new system will involve new duct work or pipes. Every effort should be made to retain existing walls, ceilings and floors.

If improperly installed, ducts and pipes can introduce moisture and negatively impact the aesthetics of a room. Insulation of existing or new ducts and pipe should be done carefully to avoid moisture introduction. For example the vapor barrier should face out, away from the duct.

Installing a Solar Panel Array on the Roof to Provide a Portion of the Electricity in the Building

The roof line of a historic building, particularly one located in a historic district, must remain unchanged. Roofs are often a significant architectural detail that provides much historic character to the building. Roofs on older buildings also may not be able to handle the weight of a solar array or could suffer greatly from punctures in the roofing material fabric when anchors for a solar array are introduced. Array placement should be considered on outbuildings and mounted on the ground before the roof.

Installing a Geothermal Heating and Cooling System (Which May Require Duct Work)

Drilling near a historic structure could cause problems if the structure's foundation is compromised. Historic landscaping torn up during drilling should be saved and replanted. Duct work associated with the geothermal system could cause problems if not properly placed and installed (see above).

Build an Expansion to the Library Using
Locally Sourced Building Materials

While expanding a historic building is the largest and most costly project, it also holds some of the largest potential for greening the structure. Care should be given to retain as much of the original building as possible. The introduction of green technology and practices will require expert advice from both historic preservationists and green building consultants.

Assembling a contact list of people who are experts on your building is critical to annual maintenance as well as small and large green projects. While there are architects and consultants that specialize in historic preservation, also keep in mind your local experts. Carpenters, plumbers and electricians who may know your building well from having worked on it for years can be an invaluable resource when you undertake a greening project.

Large projects can greatly benefit from Integrated Building Design (IBD). The idea behind IBD is that your team of stakeholders and professionals come together as early as possible in your project to get on the same page about your green goals. This way your historic preservationist, library trustees, architect, engineers, carpenters, plumbers, electricians, library consultant, green consultant or any combination of the above that you plan to work with, all know each other, understand the project goals and intent of the organization to balance the preservation, green and cost aspects of the project.

The earlier your team comes together the better chance you have to keep costs down, finish the project on time and have the most energy efficient and green building you can. Members of your team might include:

- Architect
- Leadership in Energy & Environmental Design Accredited Professional (LEED AP) or Sustainable Building Advisor (NaSBA)
- Structural Engineer
- Mechanical Engineer
- Electrical Engineer
- Contractors
- Lighting Expert
- Commissioning Agent
- Library Staff
- Landscape Architect
- State Energy Authority (Funding Program Connection)
- Interior Designer
- Community Officials

- Other Stakeholders
- Additional Specialists

By creating a team that includes these individuals early in the project the library director and Board, as the owners, can clearly state their combination of greening goals with those related to historic preservation. The earlier this group is formed as a team the earlier team unity will evolve which will hopefully lead to a shared vision that is closely aligned with the owners of the building. Working as a team will allow the group to set shared building performance, construction waste management, site and design goals and to identify potential complications and problem areas earlier than they would if they were working independently. This will save time and money and help guarantee success.

Using LEED as a Framework for Large Projects

The Leadership in Energy and Environmental Design (LEED) Green Rating System from the U.S. Green Building Council has become the standard for defining what qualifies a building as green. There are three potential relevant LEED products for historic buildings—Existing Buildings (EB), Neighborhood Development (ND), and New Construction and Major Renovations/Additions (NC). Libraries in historic buildings may consider pursing LEED certification to help guide rehabilitation, renovation or expansion projects for two reasons. First, LEED criteria can help guide the professionals working on your project (architects, engineers, historic preservationists, designers, construction firms and trades) to move forward more cohesively as a team with clearly defined green goals that have performance measurements tied to them so they know what qualifies as greening a building in a meaningful way. Second, striving for LEED certification helps to elevate the profile of a project which aids in publicity, fundraising and generating community support for a project.

While LEED may add complexity to a project, and add cost in some cases, it provides a framework that can organize a project and provides measurement outcomes that helps to insure that the building will be as green as possible.

Even if a library decides against registering their project for LEED certification with the U.S. Green Building Council the LEED framework can be a tool applied within your project. Using the lens of the LEED-NC checklist to approach greening your library can help you green your library more comprehensively than you otherwise might have.

LEED-NC Categories are divided into six areas: Sustainable Sites, Water Efficiency, Energy & Atmosphere, Materials & Resources, Indoor Environmental Quality, and Innovation & Design.

Sustainable Sites

Historic Buildings automatically earn credits in this area because they are existing structures. This category also addresses connections to public transportation, making room for bicycles and alternative fuel vehicles, restoring natural habitats surrounding your building, and stormwater management on the site.

Water Efficiency

This category covers aspects such as water efficient landscaping and innovative wastewater technologies—replacing the use of potable water for flushing toilets and landscape irrigation.

Energy & Atmosphere

This is the category that everyone expects from LEED as it addresses the energy efficiency of a building. It addresses reducing demand, harvesting free energy, increasing efficiency and the recovery of waste energy. Commissioning, a prerequisite in LEED, is a term that you may not be familiar with but may want to invest in if you are doing a large scale expansion project. A Commissioning Agent can help ensure that the equipment installed to heat and cool your building is actually performing as promised by the manufacturer and has been installed correctly. Investing in commissioning can save your library a lot of money over time.

Materials & Resources

This category addresses aspects both large and small. From having a recycling program for plastic, paper and cardboard to maintaining existing walls, floors and roof in a project. Other features of this category include construction waste management (diverting waste from landfills), reusing building materials, locally sourcing new building materials and using materials made of recycled content, rapidly renewable materials (like bamboo) and certified wood.

Indoor Environmental Quality

Indoor Environmental Qualities of your library include air quality, air temperature, visual comfort (lighting and view to the outdoors), physical comfort (ergonomics) and noise volumes. A healthy, green building is attuned to all of these aspects of the patron and staff experience in the building. Good air quality includes controlling moisture in the building, testing for and controlling Radon and other soil gas levels, proper ventilation and paying attention to the materials used and brought into the building. Look for "Green Label Plus" carpeting, low or no-VOC paints, and avoid purchasing particleboard and medium-density fiberboard (MDF) furniture. While outside of the scope of LEED—consider greening the library's maintenance plan: help educate maintenance staff about the effectiveness of green cleaning products—they really do work! Look for products with the "Green Seal" (Learn more at GreenSeal.org) and consider investing in a high-efficiency (HEPA) vacuum or outside-venting central vacuum.

Innovation & Design

Under LEED the Innovation category is kind of like a bonus round for earning credits towards LEED certification. This category can bring a library full circle in its mission as a library—educating users. Projects going for LEED certification can receive points for signage in and around the building that educate visitors about the green features incorporated into the design. Libraries that have gone green using LEED have earned points through interior and exterior signage, flat panel monitors with animated graphics to demonstrate how day-lighting or solar panels in the building work and interactive components to their web presence that alert library users to the green aspects of the library building.

Educating patrons about the history of their community in the context of an historic building is something many libraries already do. Continuing the idea of the library building as a teaching tool once a facility has been greened is a natural extension of a library's mission to educate.

Libraries are long-standing institutions in the United States and it is common sense that they will remain in existence for many generations to come. Libraries in historic buildings can extend the life of their building, and their operating budgets, by greening their buildings. By investing in the greening of libraries, library stakeholders demonstrate a commitment to taxpayers to keep operating costs down through energy efficiency, to staff and patrons by providing a healthy indoor environment and to the community by taking pride in a shared legacy.

References

Grimmer, Anne E. J.E. Hensley, L. Petrella, A.T. Tepper, "The Secretary of the Interior's Standards for Rehabilitation: Illustrated Guidelines on Sustainability for Rehabilitating Historic Buildings," U.S. Department of the Interior National Park Service, Technical Preservation Services, 2011.

Keeler, Marian and Bill Burke, "Fundamentals of Integrated Design for Sustainable Building," John Wiley & Sons, Inc., 2009.

Myers, John H., "The Repair of Historic Wooden Windows," Preservation Briefs, Technical Preservation Services, National Park Service, U.S. Department of the Interior, accessed 2009.

National Institute of Building Sciences, "Sustainable Historic Preservation," Whole Building Design Guide, accessed January 2010, http://www.wbdg.org/resources/sustainable_hp.php.

National Trust for Historic Preservation, "Repair or Replace Old Windows: A Visual Look at the Impacts," accessed January 2010, http://www.preservationnation.org/weatherization.

Roberts, Tristan, "Historic Preservation and Green Building: A Lasting Relationship," Environmental Building News, January 2007.

Smith, Baird M., "Conserving Energy in Historic Buildings," Preservation Briefs, Technical Preservation Services, National Park Service, U.S. Department of the Interior, accessed 2009.

U.S. Green Building Council, "An Introduction to LEED," accessed August, 2011, http://www.usgbc.org/DisplayPage.aspx?CategoryID=19.

Young, Robert A., "Historic Preservation Technology," Wiley & Sons, Inc., 2008.

Section Two

Green Committees, Services & Programs

From Grass Roots to Vital Player: Michigan State University's Library Environmental Committee

Michael E. Unsworth, Susan K. Kendall & Kriss Ostrom

In the spring of 2008, Michigan State University's Office of Campus Sustainability (OCS) launched an ambitious effort to make the East Lansing campus more sustainable by introducing an Environmental Steward Program.[1] The impetus behind this program was altruism (the University is one of only seven active university members of the Chicago Climate Exchange),[2] tempered with cold fiscal realities (recycling and energy conservation have potential for reducing operating costs).[3] The Office of Campus Sustainability crafted a stewardship initiative that enlisted the occupants and custodial staff of each campus building.[4] However, they did not extend this initiative to the Michigan State University (MSU) Libraries, because its Library Environmental Committee (LEC) already had an active structure in place that addressed sustainability goals, especially in recycling. This essay will describe the MSU Libraries LEC's current organization and operations and how this Committee became a campus leader on environmental matters.

Michigan State University and Its Library System

MSU is the designated land-grant institution for the state of Michigan. For the past three decades, its enrollment has ranged between 40,000 and 47,000 students with over 11,000 faculty and staff.[5] The Michigan State University

Libraries (MSUL) have approximately 4.5 million volumes housed in a Main Library and several smaller branch libraries on the East Lansing campus, with one branch at a small biological station an hour away. The Libraries employ approximately 175 permanent staff members as well as more than 270 students. The Main Library is composed of two wings (one built in 1955; the other in 1967) and has undergone numerous upgrades over its life.[6] It sits at the southern boundary of an area designated MSU's "sacred space," a campus park area among older buildings landscaped with mature trees, other plantings, and pathways, where no further buildings may be constructed.[7] It is also adjacent to an historical botanical garden.[8] The 5,200-acre[9] campus is considered an "arboretum to support the university's teaching, research, and outreach mission."[10] Finally, a strong interdisciplinary Environmental Studies and Policy Program (ESPP) is flourishing on campus, pulling researchers together from multiple MSU colleges.[11]

LEC's Official Status within MSUL

The Library Environmental Committee is part of the MSUL formal organization. Its charge is to:

. . . focus on the Libraries' use of natural resources with an eye toward sustainability, while maintaining and improving our overall working and learning environment.

Areas of concern for the LEC include:

- Paper printing and copier use;
- Energy use—lighting and computers;
- Heating and cooling;
- Cleaning supplies and chemicals;
- Office supplies;
- Recycling and waste reduction;
- Parking and transportation;
- General design issues that have an ecological impact.[12]

The LEC reports to the MSUL Director, without being part of any department or other hierarchy in the Libraries. The Director, the MSUL Executive Council, and individual library units, departments and committees consult with the LEC about its areas of responsibility. The LEC's tasks include:

1) Advising library administration and staff;

2) Providing information for staff;

3) Maintaining a list of resources related to these issues;

4) Acting as liaison with MSU's Office of Recycling and Waste Reduction and contacting other units as required and approved.[13]

Individual staff members are free to interact with the LEC; they do not have to ask a supervisor's permission. The Committee's monthly meetings are open to the staff at large. Its agendas and minutes are shared with the entire staff and posted on the MSUL intranet site.

Structure of the LEC

The LEC has about ten members, all library employee volunteers, both librarians and other staff, who have a personal interest in environmental issues. This personal dedication is key to the success of the committee, as enthusiasm and conviction about environmental causes sustains the members' willingness to work on such matters for the MSUL. There are no requirements that the committee should have representation from all MSUL units, *ex officio* members, or a specified library staff/librarian ratio. Moreover, LEC has no permanent chair or recorder. Those duties are rotated among the members at each month's meeting. There is also no fixed term of membership; members may decide to leave or take a break from the committee at any time. If a member leaves, the committee will recruit a replacement in order to keep the number of members roughly the same. Members find replacements by sending out requests to all library staff for expressions of interest or by personally recruiting library employees who seem to be sympathetic to environmental issues.

This framework, developed over several decades, gives the LEC broad flexibility in carrying out its charges. Its activities are determined by the individual members' concerns, through referrals from official MSUL and University channels, and by direct contact from interested staff members.

While this structure is unconventional, its advantages usually outweigh any disadvantages. First, its members know that they have to share leadership, and no one person feels overburdened. Secondly, these volunteers are enthusiastic because of their interest in environmental matters. Thirdly, each member brings personal interests and expertise which gives the committee a broad knowledge base and many contacts for networking within the libraries, on campus and in the community. Long-time members provide institutional memory.

Without a designated chair/spokesperson, the committee relies on members' self-directed initiative to take the lead for different activities. This has worked because the committee tends to attract dedicated members. Some members naturally are more comfortable with leadership than others so there is informal leadership within the committee, but it does not rest with only one person. One disadvantage of this structure is that administrators are occasionally unsure of a proper contact person in time-critical situations.

Ability to work on projects also depends on different members' workloads, which means that different people will be able to help out more or less at any given time. E-mail enables rapid routing of administrators' concerns amongst the committee members and online discussion of issues that need quick resolution. In most cases, someone from the committee is designated by the group as the person to follow up on a particular concern.

Discussions in LEC meetings are wide-ranging and enrich the members' knowledge bases. The development and maintenance of a website for the LEC has enabled information to be archived and easily retrieved. Participation on the LEC is considered library committee service work by supervisors during annual evaluations, but personal dedication and interest of the members are the primary reasons they are willing to volunteer for a variety of tasks.

Activities Communication/Education

One of the LEC's most visible activities is the monthly email *Ecogram* to all library staff. The subject of each post is chosen at the monthly meeting and is composed by the recorder. Topics are usually of a practical nature and focus on ways to be more environmentally conscious either at work or at home. Past subjects have included:

- Light bulb replacement;
- University-wide recycling goals;
- Library participation in campus-wide "dim-down;"
- Local community recycling programs;
- Energy-saving features on personal computers;
- Tips to make the holidays more green announcements of Earth Day and Smart Commute activities (see below).

Another regular communication with MSUL staff is the email distribution of the minutes of the monthly meeting. In addition to providing the official record of LEC deliberations, the minutes remind the library staff that there is a dedicated, active body devoted to environmental matters in their workplace. Archival copies of the *Ecograms* and minutes appear on the LEC website, and in public folders of the MSUL e-mail server.

The LEC is also involved in educating new library employees on the specifics and importance of recycling and conservation at the MSU Libraries. The LEC has worked with the Libraries' human resources department to be included on the "new employee checklist" of mandated orientations to be completed within the new employee's first weeks on the job. The form gives new hires a contact person within the LEC who will meet with them.

In-person continuing education of current library staff about recycling and conservation also takes place at different occasions, and the LEC looks for these opportunities when possible. The LEC has been invited to present information at all staff meetings and library departmental meetings. The committee has also created a poster about recycling to be displayed at staff social events involving food. Other special events organized by the LEC, such as speaker programs and Earth Day activities (described below), offer opportunities for education.

Reduce, Reuse, and Recycle

Recycling has been and continues to be a primary LEC activity. In fact, an early version of the committee was first formed in the late 1980s as a result of staff volunteer recycling efforts that had been active since the 1970s. Although the LEC does not have any authority to compel the library staff to recycle, its members encourage recycling in various ways.

When the Main Library first began recycling, there was a need to provide education and instruction for staff. This became increasingly important as more types of paper and other solid waste were added to the list of recyclable materials, and education continues to be necessary to this day. The Committee has posted informational signs, offered training to units, encouraged the Library Director to email staff about the importance of recycling, and led recycling efforts by personal example. LEC members also look out for obstacles to recycling efforts and encourage staff behavioral change on a variety of fronts.

In the early days, committee members transported materials to local recycling centers on their own time. Later, when on-campus recycling became available, members went through recycling bins and sorted mixed paper and other materials into appropriate groupings. Fortunately, recent enhancements to the campus-wide recycling program make this no longer necessary as a variety of materials may now be placed in a single container, simplifying the process for those who want to recycle.[14] The Committee now negotiates with MSU Recycling staff for more recycling containers within the libraries. It checks various areas of the libraries to make sure that recycling containers are visible and convenient and that trash cans do not predominate.

LEC volunteers also recycle material from the staff lounge in the Main Library. Thanks to Michigan's "bottle bill" which puts a ten cent deposit on soft drink containers,[15] the committee has accumulated a modest deposit refund which is held in a Library Staff Association account. The LEC uses this fund to buy books and video materials on environmental topics for the Libraries collection. Selections are made at the monthly LEC meetings.

Dedication to recycling as many materials as possible led committee members to look beyond local recycling efforts to find ways to recycle outdated cassettes, CDs, jewel boxes, VHS tapes, and DVDs before the university enabled recycling of these items. Some members took these materials home or on travels to appropriate recycling facilities. Although the Libraries were required by contract to use Canon toner cartridges instead of easier to recycle models, one member found a place to recycle the Canon cartridges.

The LEC's leadership in MSUL's recycling efforts over the years has earned it respect from library administration and other library unit leaders. These units have learned to consult the LEC on policies that may have an environmental impact. For example, the Main Library Copy Center received a proposal from an MSU student regarding a company that would place paid advertising on the back of students' printouts so that their printing would be free. The LEC cautioned that this proposal would likely encourage waste, based on experience from the 1990s when the Libraries provided free printing. The Library administration agreed with LEC's caution, and free printing was not adopted. This policy stance illustrates the LEC's involvement in advocating "reducing and reusing" as well as recycling.

The other side to recycling is encouraging the use of products made from recycled materials. All of the printing and copying in the MSU Libraries provided a good opportunity to use paper made from recycled content. The LEC worked with the Main Library's Copy Center to find 100% post-consumer recycled, non-chlorine bleached paper for copiers and printers. The University General Stores staff was initially reluctant to carry this more expensive product. The LEC convinced the Library administration to purchase the paper directly from the manufacturer instead. The paper was used exclusively throughout the library system. Eventually, General Stores purchased this paper in small quantities and found that other campus units also wanted an environmentally-friendly type of paper. As demand continued to grow, General Stores purchased larger quantities, bringing the price down so that 100% recycled paper became economical as well as sustainable.

The LEC continues to encourage library units to minimize or replace paper publications with electronic ones when possible. Individual members have contacted MSU departments to reconsider their paper publishing practices. The response has been positive since many units now produce e-versions of their publications.

The LEC is concerned not only with recycling but also with energy usage within the MSU Libraries. Energy usage is a more complex issue, however, with less opportunity for the committee to take a hands-on approach. Some years ago the MSU Libraries replaced lights in one wing of the building to much more energy-efficient products to considerably reduce costs. This was a major project that the LEC applauded but was not directly involved in. Some things the committee has been able to do are to meet with members of the MSU Libraries computer systems and information technology staff to discuss ways that staff and public computers can be set up for energy efficiency. Systems staff has implemented some of these ideas, and much energy-saving occurs simply through routine upgrades of equipment. Members of the LEC would prefer to see the MSU Libraries administration require library employees to follow energy-saving recommendations, such as removing screen savers from their computers (which unnecessarily waste energy), but the official policy of the administration has been to make suggestions and encouragements to employees without strict requirements.

Involvement in Campus-wide Initiatives

Two changes at the university, the development of a campus-wide Environmental Steward Program and opening of a new recycling center have evolved the campus recycling program into a disciplined, coordinated effort in all campus buildings. The opening in fall 2009 of a new Surplus Store and Recycling Center has greatly expanded the variety of materials that can be recycled at MSU, enhancing the University's revenue stream and simplifying waste collection.

The Environmental Steward Program is a major initiative that flowed from MSU President Lou Anna K. Simon's 2005 announcement of a "Boldness By Design" vision for the university's future. Its "Strategic Imperative 5" aims to "strengthen stewardship by appreciating and nurturing the university's financial assets, campus environment and infrastructure and people for outstanding performance today and tomorrow."[16] (emphasis added)

As a key element of the stewardship program, the Office of Campus Sustainability assigned each building's custodial staff to become Environmental Stewards and take over emptying all building recycling along with the trash. One member of the LEC had been acting as the MSUL liaison with campus recyclers. This new framework gave that LEC member new opportunity to work directly with MSU Libraries facilities staff, since they oversee the work of custodians and could make sure that problems with recycling are resolved.

Earth Day and Other Outreach Activities

Earth Day provides an occasion for focus and education on environmental topics both on the campus and in the MSU Libraries. Organizing Earth Day programs for the public and staff in the MSU Libraries is another high-visibility LEC activity. Each year, the committee plans activities for the upcoming Earth Day, with individual members taking the lead in implementing them. Earth Day activities have included: Main Library displays relevant to environmental and conservation themes; a staff pizza party that screened environmental videos; continuously running videos on appropriate Earth Day topics in a high traffic public area; a table of pamphlets, library books, and handouts listing websites related to environmental issues, and a "recycling game" developed and run by LEC members in the Main Library lobby aimed at teaching library staff and patrons what kinds of materials can be recycled in appropriate containers.

Besides Earth Day activities, the LEC also arranges outreach and educational programs throughout the year. Since 2008, the committee has hosted a regular series of guided tours of the historical Beal Botanical Garden[17] (located just outside the Main Library building) by the garden's resident naturalist. The LEC has also hosted local speakers on topics such as green LEED-certified building, wind energy, raising backyard chickens, urban farming, and other topics. Initially these presentations were very occasional and informal. In 2010 these events became an official library series, and publicity was more formally coordinated by the Library's PR committee. So far these talks have been primarily attended by MSU Libraries staff, but a goal is to increase visibility for these events to the rest of campus and the public. Publicity consists of news releases, features on the library website, posters, and on flat-screen monitors in the Main Library lobby. One of the first programs, in March 2010, was *What Are the Links Between Hunger and the Environment?* The discussion about food, poverty, and the environment was led by Terry Link, a former MSU reference librarian and the first Director of MSU Office of Campus Sustainability, who is currently Executive Director of the Greater Lansing Food Bank.

The LEC has involved the MSU Libraries not only in campus-wide, but also in Greater Lansing environmental programs. One of these activities, called "Smart Commute", is an initiative that promotes environmentally-friendly transportation options in the Greater Lansing area as an alternative to driving alone. The Smart Commute Challenge takes place over a couple weeks in the spring of each year with different local organizations competing to log the most number of alternative transportation trips by their employees. The alternative trips can include carpooling, telecommuting, biking, walking, or taking public transportation.

Different members of the LEC have taken turns organizing the MSU Libraries' participation as one of the organizations competing in the challenge. One committee member taught Smart Commute cycling classes in the library and in the community during the same period. He taught people how to safely ride their bicycles on city streets during their commutes to and from work. Participation by library employees in the challenge has been excellent. The MSU Libraries consistently placed second in the Large Company category from 2007–2009, and, in 2010, it won that same category with 1,077 trips completed by 40 staff members. The LEC also has contributed some of its own funds as a sponsor of the Smart Commute Challenge.

Current Activities

The current challenge for the LEC is to better coordinate the MSU Libraries' sustainability efforts with the fledgling MSU Environmental Steward Program. All members currently receive monthly reports from MSU's Office of Campus Sustainability with Main Library building information on waste, recycling, and energy use. LEC members have suspected inaccuracies in some of the statistics and are working with OCS for clarification.

One point of information these reports reveals to the committee is that staff recycling and especially energy conservation efforts in a high-traffic public building like the Main Library can only go so far. Its Cyber Café, for instance, is a heavy user of electricity, but neither the LEC nor the MSUL administration has direct control over its usage. Moreover, the Main Library is open 24 hours during weekdays, and patron use of the Main Library's 550 computers and electrical outlets for their personal laptops continues to increase, with resulting increases of our building's electrical use. LEC continues to wrestle with this dilemma.

Recycling and conservation efforts at branch libraries around the campus are also an LEC concern. These branches are located in buildings operated by various MSU Colleges and departments. The MSU Libraries' administration and, therefore, the LEC must work with the Campus Stewards and the policies in these buildings. Even though the Campus Steward Program is MSU-wide, and conservation is a campus-wide goal, different units may be more or less interested or able to enforce policies. Furthermore, branch libraries within these buildings usually must follow decisions of building operators regarding such matters as whether lights will be on all night. On the other hand, the branch libraries provide an opportunity for the LEC and the MSU Libraries to try pilot projects on a small-scale. The MSU business library staff, for instance, is currently piloting a program that puts numerous large containers for plastics and paper recycling in visible places, while removing the usual ubiquitous trash cans. Only very small boxes marked "for landfill" are made available for waste that cannot be recycled. If this program is successful in encouraging even more recycling at the business branch library, it could eventually be expanded to more branch libraries and to the Main Library.

In 2010 the Main Library Building was recognized by the Office of Campus Sustainability's Green Certification Program which "is designed to recognize, assist, and promote units that are taking steps toward reducing their environmental footprint."[18] For this certification, the LEC submitted self-assessment forms about the Main Library in two campus categories: "Information Technology Spaces" and "Offices." The "Info Tech" application measures the effective communication and education of environmental goals and policies, energy efficiency & conservation, recycling & waste reduction, water conservation, and purchasing [of recycled/reused products].[19] The "Offices" application evaluates the use of employees' personal computers, office equipment, printing, copying, and recycling & waste reduction.[20] Green Certification promotes the MSU Libraries' efforts with campus-wide recognition use of a Green Certification Logo, prominent display of a Green Certification Plaque in the Main Library, and a special designation on Environmental Stewardship Reports.[21] Thanks to activities that the committee had already been promoting, the LEC found that the building was compliant with recommendations in almost all of each forms' categories.

Adaptability of the MSUL LEC Model

The MSU Library Environmental Committee demonstrates the value of having an active group devoted to environmental issues within a library. The LEC has been able to establish credibility with the staff and the library administration to the point where it has recently been invited to draft the Libraries' official response to campus administration requests for information on environmental matters.

Many of the activities and programs that MSU's LEC crafts and promotes are the types of activities that could be planned or mandated by a library's administration instead. What the MSU Libraries LEC model uniquely provides is a grass-roots leadership effort that results in longer-lasting staff commitment to sustainable environmental programs. This kind of committee doesn't fit neatly into a very hierarchical structure that some libraries may use for their organization. However, this model does have the potential to work well, since environmental issues do not belong solely to any one unit or department of a library.

Having a committee composed of people from multiple departments who are passionate about environmental issues is a major strength of the model. Concerns particular to different units, such as library facilities or copying/printing departments, are more likely to be discussed knowledgeably. Library employees have their choice of several LEC members with whom they can share concerns or ask questions rather than only one person or one administrator who may be less approachable. Finally, library or campus administration-mandated efforts at recycling or energy conservation are usually framed as ways to save the college or university money. This goal may not necessarily be motivating to employees at all levels. The MSU Libraries has found that when a library administration allows people whose motivations come from personal convictions to take leadership, the efforts become more personally engaging, educational, and are more likely to meet with success.

Endnotes

1. Office of Campus Sustainability. Environmental Steward Program http://www.bespartangreen.msu.edu/envirosteward/ (accessed Apr. 27, 2011).

2. *Chicago Climate Exchange* http://www.chicagoclimatex.com/content.jsf?id=64 (accessed Apr. 23, 2011).

3. Campus Planning and Administration. *Michigan State University Campus Master Plan Update 2007 Executive Summary* [East Lansing: Campus Planning and Administration , 2007] http://prod.gis.msu.edu/construction/pdf/final_executive_summary.pdf (accessed Apr. 27, 2011).

4. Office of Campus Sustainability. *Environmental Steward Program.*

5. *MSU Facts* http://www.msu.edu/thisismsu/facts.html (accessed Apr. 23, 2011).

6. *History of the MSU Libraries* http://www.lib.msu.edu/about/history.jsp (accessed Apr. 23, 2011).

7. Ted Moore, "Creating an Idyllic Space: Nature, Technology, and Campus Planning at the Michigan Agricultural College, 1850–1975," *Michigan Historical Review* 35:2 (Fall 2009): 11, 23–24.

8. *W.J. Beal Botanical Garden* http://www.cpa.msu.edu/beal/ (accessed Apr. 23, 2011).

9. *MSU Facts* http://www.msu.edu/thisismsu/facts.html (accessed Apr. 23, 2011).

10. Michigan State University. Campus Planning and Administration. *Campus Master Plan Update*: Master Plan Update Planning Principles: Planning Principles Related to Land Use and Facilities http://prod.gis.msu.edu/construction/U_planning_principles.jsp (accessed Apr. 23, 2011).

11. *About ESPP* http://www.espp.msu.edu/about/index.html (accessed Apr. 27, 2011).

12. *MSU Library Environmental Committeee* (hereafter cited as *LEC Home*) (accessed Apr. 27, 2011).

13. *LEC Home.*

14. *MSU Recycling* http://www.recycle.msu.edu/index.htm (accessed Apr. 27, 2011).

15. Dave Dempsey. *Ruin & Recovery: Michigan's Rise as a Conservation Leader* (Ann Arbor: University of Michigan Press, 2001), 182–183.

16. "Key Strategies and Focus Areas," Boldness by Design: Strategic Positioning of Michigan State University http://boldnessbydesign.msu.edu/imperatives.asp (accessed Apr. 27, 2011).

17. *Beal Botanical Garden.*

18. Office of Campus Sustainability. *Green Certification* http://www.bespartangreen.msu.edu/greencert/ (accessed Apr. 27, 2011).

19. Office of Campus Sustainability *Application for Green Certification: Information Tech Spaces* http://www.bespartangreen.msu.edu/greencert/applications/it_distributed.pdf (accessed Apr. 27, 2011).

20. Office of Campus Sustainability *Application for Green Certification: Offices* http://www.bespartangreen.msu.edu/greencert/applications/offices_distributed.pdf (accessed Apr. 27, 2011).

21. Office of Campus Sustainability. *Green Certification.*

Tending the Garden: Growing Your Own Green Library Committee

Christine Andresen, Amy Gustavson, David Hisle & Matthew Reynolds

The University of North Carolina is a multi-campus university composed of all 16 of North Carolina's public institutions that grant baccalaureate degrees, as well as the NC School of Science and Mathematics.[1] Within the UNC System, East Carolina University is the third largest research-level university with over 27,000 full-time students and over 5,000 distance education students.[2] J.Y. Joyner Library services the east campus of East Carolina University and holds more than 1.2 million books and 6,000 periodical subscriptions.[3] In January 2008, the UNC Board of Governors adopted a document entitled the *UNC Tomorrow Report* to guide the future of the system.[4] This report identified sustainability as a core value and urged all institutions in the UNC System to increase awareness and research on the topic.

1. (2009). *About the University*. Retrieved from University of North Carolina. Website: http://www.northcarolina.edu/about/index.htm.

2. (2010). *Fact Book 2009–2010*. Retrieved from East Carolina University, Greenville, NC. Website: http://www.ecu.edu/cs-acad/ipar/research/upload/FactBook2009-10.pdf.

3. (2010). *Joyner Library 2010 Annual Report*. Retrieved from East Carolina University, Greenville, NC. Website: http://media.lib.ecu.edu/administration/annualReport/2010/index.cfm.

4. (2009). *UNC Tomorrow Report*. Retrieved from University of North Carolina. Website: http://www.northcarolina.edu/nctomorrow/index.htm.

In response to the *UNC Tomorrow Report*, East Carolina University's Joyner Library formed the Green Task Force, focusing in particular on two of the report's recommendations: recognizing environmental sustainability as a core value for the UNC system, and increasing community awareness of environmental issues. This article is meant to serve as a narrative of the charter year of the Green Task Force. It outlines the Task Force's initial organization and development, as well as its activities. Also included are lessons learned during this first year and advice for starting a similar group. It is intended not only to inform others of our experience, but hopefully to inspire readers to take action in their own institutions and communities.

Sowing the Seeds: Organizing People and Suggestions

The Dean of Academic Library Services at East Carolina University called the first Green Task Force meeting in July 2008 to discuss the scope, focus and future of the committee. With over 20 librarians and library assistants in attendance at this initial meeting, the Dean shared the sustainability section of the *UNC Tomorrow Report* and empowered the attendees to organize the Task Force. The committee spent the remainder of the first meeting tentatively organizing the group, developing a nascent plan, and brainstorming projects for the year.

Throughout the fall semester of 2008, the Task Force structured the committee, compiled suggestions, and organized a great deal of feedback in order to develop a mission. One early challenge was organizing such a large group to include everyone in the decision-making process. The Task Force initially divided members into two subcommittees: an internal group and external group. The internal subcommittee was to focus on planning and implementing events within Joyner Library while the external group would market the internal group's projects and connect with the campus and local community. This model proved too cumbersome and ultimately ineffective, as the split only compounded the communication challenges. The two groups eventually merged into a single large committee with project subcommittees in late fall 2008. The main group met every two months, while the subcommittees met as needed to complete specific projects. This organizational model proved effective because members could self-select short-term or long-term projects that interested them.

Once the Task Force was successfully organized, the next challenge was to improve the management of the group. The chair of the Green Task Force developed a four-step strategy to deal with the large committee. This strategy included asking committee members for input, organizing the feedback, prioritizing the suggestions, and implementing the goals. Reasonable deadlines helped facilitate timely responses from members and allowed the committee to stay on schedule.

First, committee members were asked for input on projects and goals. The next step was for the chair to organize the group's suggestions into a more manageable format. Suggestions were organized under headings in a shared Google document for easy access and decision making. This method was particularly effective during the creation of the annual goals when the Task Force generated a ten-page list of suggestions. The third step required the chair to prioritize these suggestions by ranking projects and goals. This helped the group stay focused on committee objectives throughout the year. Brainstorming ideas were recorded in the minutes and placed on a suggested projects list for later review. Prioritizing goals early in the year helped the committee stay focused on agreed-upon projects. The final step in this strategy was to implement the goals and projects. The chair facilitated project implementation by setting deadlines and offering assistance to subcommittees if needed. Setting firm due dates was critical. The successful completion of these steps resulted in the finalized mission statement of Joyner Library's Green Task Force: *to research, propose, implement, and promote green education and sustainable environmental practices in the university library environment, while raising awareness of green initiatives in Joyner Library, other libraries in the ECU system, and the local community.*[5] Overall, the four-step process allowed the group to create this mission statement and develop both annual and long-term goals, while incorporating many group ideas.

Putting Green Thumbs to Use: Project Management and Green Activities

For its charter year in 2008, the Task Force developed annual goals in keeping with its mission to research, propose, implement, and promote green education and sustainable environmental practices in the university library environment. The Green Task Force initially focused on developing more sustainable practices via department-level goals and library strategic planning recommendations. The committee brainstormed and compiled ideas, and then prioritized a list focused on recycling, printing, power saving initiatives, and office supplies. The first priority was to encourage departmental recycling plans as the library lacked a comprehensive recycling program. Most departments elected to have student workers haul recycled items to the pick-up bins once a week.

5.   (2008) Retrieved from East Carolina University–Joyner Library Website. Website: http://libguides.ecu.edu/gtf.

In an attempt to save paper and reduce ink, an emphasis was put on the reduction of printing. Suggestions were made to print in duplex, multiple pages to a sheet, or in gray scale. Power-saving initiatives included setting computers to shut down at the end of the workday, unplugging computers on Fridays and holiday breaks, and turning off unnecessary lights around the library. Finally it was recommended that departments re-use mailing supplies and purchase earth-friendly office and cleaning supplies, such as garbage bags made from recycled consumer products. Most of the departments in Joyner Library added at least one of these sustainable suggestions to their 2009–10 annual goals.

The second initiative was to develop sustainable goals for future strategic planning cycles, including short-term, long-term and idealistic goals. Short-term goals focused on the next one to two years and included a request for additional recycling bins in public spaces around the library, moving from print to electronic time sheets, asking building security to turn off unnecessary lights at night, adding USB flash drives to the library vending machines for purchase to reduce printing, and placing signs in elevators to encourage use of the stairs. Long-term suggestions focused on replacing a library-owned van with a sedan during the next vehicle rotation and replacing or repairing leaky water faucets over the next three to five years. Idealistic goals included placing solar panels on the roof, the construction of a green roof, and adding hand dryers to library bathrooms to reduce paper towel waste. All three lists of goals were shared with the Dean.

Promoting green education and implementing sustainable practices is an important goal of the Task Force's mission. To this end, the Green Task Force coordinated a series of educational and entertaining projects and events during its first year. Recycling and electricity usage were two areas identified for easy improvement in the first year plan; Earth Day provided us with an education opportunity.

The Task Force took on the responsibility of investigating the optimal placement for the current recycling bins in the building and devised a schedule for emptying them. The Task Force worked with the University recycling program to obtain six new bins exclusively for plastic bottles, making it easier for university employees and students to comply with a new North Carolina law banning hard plastics in landfills. However, purchasing and installing bins is only half the battle. Recycling bins do not empty themselves, so it is important to create a schedule to keep the bins from overflowing. Because of the group's efforts, departmental paper and plastic bottle bins are now emptied on a weekly basis by student employees.

A long-range option for the Green Task Force is the installation of motion sensor lighting in the building. A marked decrease in the number of empty rooms with lights on was accomplished by simply attaching 'Turn off the light' stickers throughout the library building. In North Carolina these stickers are available at no cost from the State Energy Office. Another option is to design your own energy conservation stickers. In less than an hour, three Task Force members were able to canvass the library building and attach the stickers to light switch plates in public areas such as bathrooms and study rooms. This simple action was easily implemented and provided a major impact on the library's efforts to conserve electricity.

In addition to the projects designed to promote sustainable practices, implementing a library-wide celebration of Earth Day was an important focus. Task Force Events and activities for Earth Day celebrations were the responsibility of a Task Force subcommittee. The spring equinox is designated by the United Nations as the date to celebrate Earth Day, and in 1970, the US government decreed April 22 as a nationwide day to celebrate the earth. The Task Force planned activities for both observance dates in 2009.

To coincide with the spring equinox two events were created, a poster contest hosted as a competition between several library departments and a photo shoot arranged for university students to share their green efforts. Five library departments participated in the poster contest including Digital Collections, Interlibrary Loan, Government Documents, Reference and Acquisitions. Each department created posters with recycled materials depicting their interpretations of Earth Day. Voting was open to all library employees to choose their favorite poster. The Task Force provided a pizza party for the participants and displayed the winning poster during the April Earth Day festivities.

The university student photo shoot was the second Task Force spring equinox event. Students positioned themselves under a banner that read "How I'm Green . . ." and held a small white board stating how they helped the environment. The photos documented that several students rode their bikes or skateboards to work and school, while others indicated efforts to turn off lights and electronics when leaving a room. Many photos showed a commitment to using reusable water bottles, while others favored duplex printing. The photo shoot offered an opportunity to highlight participation of the student body.

To celebrate Earth Day, Task Force members designed a bulletin board, made bookmarks using recycled materials, assembled an Earth Day book display, hosted a green speaker, and organized a tree planting ceremony. The pictures from a March photo shoot became part of a bulletin board displayed throughout the month of April. Discarded book jackets were used for the display's background, a recycled brown paper bag was used for a tree trunk, green two-liter bottles for tree leaves, and red aluminum cans for apples. The students' photos were scattered throughout the tree to highlight tips for "going green".

Another Task Force subcommittee used discarded book jackets to create handmade bookmarks to distribute during the week of Earth Day and at various university outreach events throughout the year. Scissors and glue were the only supplies needed to create the bookmarks. They were then laminated for a longer lasting finish. The bookmarks have become one of the Task Force's most popular projects based on favorable responses from staff at the public service desks where they were distributed and from positive feedback received from participants at university events.

To create an Earth Day book display used throughout the month of April, Task Force members gathered topical library materials and arranged them on a table near the library entrance. <u>An Inconvenient Truth</u> by Al Gore and the <u>Planet Earth</u> DVD series were among the items showcased. The Task Force sponsored guest speaker David Emmerling to talk at a second event during the April Earth Day festivities. For the main Earth Day event, the Green Task Force held a tree planting ceremony to highlight the United States' Earth Day celebration. The tree planting ceremony was a successful promotional activity as two local news stations, two campus-produced news segments, and the local newspaper covered the event. A live oak tree was donated and delivered by a local landscaping company for the climactic celebration. The dedication ceremony included an opening address by two Task Force members, a ribbon cutting ceremony by the Dean and Associate Director of the library, and the ceremonial planting of the tree. Live oaks are indigenous to the area, and have a normal life span of several centuries. The tree will be enjoyed by university students and staff for many years to come.

Propagating Ideas: Green Education & Outreach

Creating an electronic newsletter was another effective approach the Task Force used to embrace its mission to promote green education and sustainable practices. Producing a newsletter allowed dissemination of practical "green tips" and a venue to engage others in the mission, while sharing accomplishments with the rest of the library. For the first newsletter, the Task Force had little in the way of accomplishments to talk about, but the group's research into green issues had produced plenty of content, including green living tips and green gadgets. In keeping with the group's mission (and its budget), the newsletter was produced as a PDF, emailed to the wider library, and posted on the library website. The initial response to the newsletter was quite positive. As awareness of the Task Force grew, the group received ideas for article topics. Staff outside the Task Force even volunteered to write articles for future newsletters.

Early in the committee's work it was clear that education regarding green issues would be a large part of the group's focus. Raising awareness of green initiatives both within the library and throughout the larger community became a priority. To accomplish its educational objectives, the Task Force opted to produce an electronic newsletter with a fall, spring, and special Earth Day issue. To bring attention to area green initiatives, the Task Force decided to also sponsor a speaker series.

The first speaker, Jill Twark, was a faculty member in the Foreign Languages and Literatures department and executive director and founder of the Friends of Greenville Greenways (FROGGs). FROGGs is a non-profit, all-volunteer organization that fosters awareness of the importance of greenways, advocates for their use, and solicits funding for their development and construction. Dr. Twark graciously accepted an invitation to speak, and she addressed a full house of more than 30 attendees. She gave an inspiring presentation about the successful implementation of the FROGGS Five Year Greenway Master Plan, which was from the fundraising and grant writing stage, to the eventual construction of over five miles of trails and walkways, an impressive community accomplishment for positive change.

The second speaker event for the spring was part of the Earth Day schedule of events, and featured the executive director of the Pamlico-Tar River Foundation, David Emmerling. The Pamlico-Tar River Foundation is a private, nonprofit group with over 2,500 members dedicated to protecting, preserving and promoting the environmental quality of the Pamlico-Tar River and its watershed. Besides monitoring the health of the river, this group advocates for enforcement of existing laws, for new legislation, and educates others on the importance of protecting local watersheds. Dr. Emmerling's presentation featured an overview of the foundation's struggles and successes in protecting the Pamlico-Tar River. He explained how important it is to educate the community and mobilize the local population in support of an environmental group's endeavors.

Scheduling speakers for green topics has been rewarding as well as remarkably easy. It has been our experience that representatives from nonprofits and advocacy groups appreciate the opportunity to share their project updates with an audience. Best of all, both the Task Force and the audience had the opportunity to learn about green efforts and organizations already operating in the community.

Reaping the Harvest: Lessons Learned and Planning for the Future

The organization of any new group within a library can be an arduous and sometimes daunting process. However, success can be achieved through creative, deliberate work. The first step is to identify a core group that has an interest in creating a green organization. This group should then meet and develop a document that outlines the basics of how they would like to see their committee constructed.

Once the permission to organize a green group is secured from the library administration, work can begin on building a solid foundation for success. Set up an initial meeting inviting everyone in the library to participate. Do not be surprised if you have more people who are interested in joining than you anticipated. Once the groundwork organization is accomplished, it is possible that those who were reluctant to join before will see the momentum the group founders created and be more inclined to participate. At this initial meeting, discuss everyone's expectations of what they would like to see the group achieve. Be sure to have group's members take extensive minutes as this time can be one of great creativity, with ideas for potential projects being voiced from around the room. Do not let these ideas get lost in the shuffle. A wiki can be an excellent way to store and arrange the large number of links and local information your group is likely to generate. Discuss what should be the scope of your activities, especially for the first year. Seek to find a balance between easily achievable projects that will build momentum and *esprit de corps,* and larger projects that will require more in-depth planning.

Once the group has articulated its expectations and an initial plan has been discussed, you can begin the work of developing a strong mission statement for the group. If your group is large, you may want to appoint a subcommittee to craft the statement and then distribute it to the committee for approval. No matter how the work is done, be sure to develop a mission statement that is strong, clear and concise. A solid mission will serve as a reference point for the Task Force during the chaotic first few months of its development and will also serve as a reminder of what to keep in mind when planning projects. In addition, it also serves as a simple statement of purpose for people outside the group who are interested in the group's operating principles. Through discussion of expectations and the development of a solid mission, the group can begin to plan its first projects.

Careful planning can help an idea develop into palpable action. Always keep in mind that while it is okay to think big, it is also okay to start small. Especially in the first year of a group's existence, smaller projects are not only more easily achieved, but can help to build momentum for larger projects. Once a project has been identified, the group as a whole needs to decide how the rest of the planning process should unfold. Larger groups might want to appoint a smaller group of members to organize a series of small scale projects or to break a larger project down into several smaller components. Once the initial planning has been set, inform the rest of the library staff about your plans and invite them to participate. This offers a great opportunity to recruit new members, as the initially reluctant may be more willing to participate after the groundwork has been done.

Look for opportunities to get the word out, not only on campus but to the surrounding community. Assign a representative from the group to be responsible for talking to media representatives and marketing offices in the university and in your community. Your representative can:

- Contact the editor from your campus newspaper about a story;
- Inform the campus marketing office of your plans to see if they are interested in featuring your project in a campus publication or on your university's cable channel;
- Call local news and television outlets.

This representative can also be in charge of contacting the leadership of other green oriented organizations in your area and asking them to inform their membership of your library's activities.

Newsletters are another way reach a broader audience. Opportunities to gather green educational material and generate newsletter content abound. Early meetings can be chaotic as the group gets a sense of its mission, the individual talents and interests of group members, a successful scale for projects and workable goals. When brainstorming for project ideas, keep track of the best research examples. Make sure your green group has someone taking good notes, and mine those meeting minutes. Brainstorming can also produce meaningful newsletter content. While it might not be possible, for example, to add voltage monitors in your library, someone may be intrigued enough by the concept to purchase one for their home. Check your new books shelves for materials on sustainability or environmentalism; write up book reviews, or simply put together a list of recent acquisitions that relate to green living.

Campus and local programs are another great resource for newsletters. Writing about your city's recycling program or university campus's green initiatives can be useful information for two reasons: One, you do not want your green group to duplicate work already being done on campus, And two, people appreciate reminders for questions such as: "Where can batteries be recycled?" or "Which plastics are recyclable?" Links can be saved to a wiki, or maintained on a shared Google document for group members. However you choose to manage links and information, do not let content go to waste. When you need to write a short blurb, you can always refer back to your documentation for links to blogs and organizations for inspiration.

Finally, take advantage of your library's in-house expertise. Joyner Library's reference department employees included a master gardener who committed to a series of articles on organic gardening. Maybe someone in your group, or in your library, is active with a green neighborhood or community group. Perhaps your library has someone with an interest in conservation, or someone who recycles old materials for home crafts.

Once any project or event has been completed, be sure to set up a debriefing meeting with the group. In addition to discussing what worked well, take time to identify problems and get feedback on what can be done differently in the future. Debriefing is important because it serves not only as a time for reflection, but also as a chance to acknowledge the efforts of those who spent time and energy making the project happen. This last part is important to do as the planning and execution process can be draining. Celebrating successes together serves to energize everyone and build momentum toward the next project.

Greening Your Library in Tough Economic Times: Planning Now to Spend Later

Tough budget times on your campus should not prevent your group from planning projects that have a significant funding component. Larger and more expensive projects can be achieved through the use of creative thinking and scouting for funding opportunities. Having a project already planned and waiting for funding can be the key to success in these situations. That way if money becomes available, especially at the end of the budget year when a total expenditure of funds in a timely manner can be key, your group can make its request known in short order. Approaching the administration with a plan in hand rather than a proposal can make a real difference in securing sponsorship for a project. In addition, have your group regularly monitor potential sources for grant funding. If your library has a grant writer be sure to try and recruit them to help in your efforts, even if only to review applications filled out by others. You may even want to the petition university administration to allocate funds for internal grants as is currently being done at universities such as University of California, Berkeley[6] and William & Mary[7] in Williamsburg, Virginia.

---

6. http://asuc.berkeley.edu/asinside.aspx?uid=543.

7. http://www.wm.edu/sites/sustainability/getinvolved/submitproposal/index.php.

Getting Outside the Building and Beyond

Once your group is organized and has a project or two under its belt, it's time to go outside of the library. Look for opportunities to share your experiences with other groups or invite them to share theirs with your group. In a time of scarce resources strength can be found in numbers, so be aware of opportunities for collaboration with other organizations. Sharing the work and financial load can allow for the completion of more ambitious projects. When dealing with community wide issues, such as revamping a city's recycling program, the ability to show a united front across several green organizations can go a long way toward effecting positive change. The beauty of green-focused groups is that they have a vested interest in seeing each other succeed. A victory for one group is a victory for the community as a whole.

The role of libraries in the movement toward more sustainable living is an important one. Libraries are seen by most as repositories of information that promote education and lifelong learning. They serve as spaces for informed discussion and debate of topics that affect the whole community. As librarians, it is our responsibility to promote green practices both on our campuses and in our communities. We should be setting an example by embracing sustainable activities, both at home and at work, and passing the lessons that we learn on to others. This can be accomplished through the organization of a green-focused committee in your own institution. Through careful organization, enthusiastic planning, and encouraging informed discussion, librarians and their institutions can make a positive and lasting impact on their communities.

West Vancouver Memorial Library: Green by Nature

Julie Backer

Modern libraries have always been green, being the epitome of the second of the "Three Rs" of the environmental movement, reuse. In addition to lending and re-lending library materials, libraries or their Friends of the Library groups have further encouraged reuse through their books sales of donated material and library discards. At West Vancouver Memorial Library, we wanted to do more.

West Vancouver Memorial Library (WVML) is a one-branch suburban library in West Vancouver, British Columbia, Canada (population: 42,000) that has almost 37,000 active cardholders and an annual total circulation of over 1,042,000 items. It has a staff complement of 44.4 FTE. Set along the shore of the Pacific Ocean and at the base of the Coast Mountain Range amid the lush green West Coast temperate rainforest of towering trees, we wanted to work in both a literal and metaphorical green environment.

Green Team Beginnings

In 2007 a few staff members came together to do some planning for Earth Day. Out of that planning meeting emerged a grassroots Green Team of committed staff volunteers that has continued to meet to plan and initiate environmentally sustainable practices for WVML. The group was particularly inspired by a then newly-arrived Building Services Supervisor, Chad Arsenault, who had lots of ideas about energy efficiency for our building. The oldest part of our building dates back to 1950, with at least four other extensions added on over the next 50 years.

Green Team Action—Looking In

One of the main reasons for the Green Team's success is that members volunteer to serve on the team. Management, supervisors, and colleagues, however, have been exceedingly supportive and encouraging. Meetings occur every three to four months—more often for Earth Day preparations—and usually before the library opens to lessen the impact on desk scheduling. Team members can follow their own passions or interests after bouncing their ideas off fellow Green Team members.

For instance, one of Chad Arsenault's first initiatives was to implement a variety of energy-saving measures. Following guidelines suggested by our utility company, the electric hot water tank thermostat was lowered by 25°F and the HVAC system was set to come on at 8:45 a.m. rather than 7:00 a.m. (the library opens at 10:00 a.m., and most staff arrive after 8:30 a.m.) He also spearheaded a reminder campaign for staff to turn off lights and computers in staff areas during the day when no one was in the room. Along with phasing out incandescent light bulbs, these actions alone reduced our electricity bill by nearly 20% over the previous year.

Arsenault also championed green housekeeping, purchasing environmentally friendly cleaning supplies and using re-usable rather than disposable cleaning cloths. During the 2007–2009 period, WVML underwent a massive renovation. Arsenault took this opportunity to install low-flow fixtures, use eco-friendly paint, reuse shelving and furniture, and generally implement green options where possible in all remodelling.

While Arsenault's position as Building Services Supervisor allowed him to have the most dramatic impact on greening WVML, his work inspired his coworkers on the Green Team to contribute in other ways. One member, tired of the waste of paper plates and disposable napkins at events in the staff room, arranged for the purchase of a set of china and flatware. To make it even greener—and cheaper!—she purchased mismatched pieces at a local thrift shop. Staff now wash, dry, and put away their own plates and forks after eating cake.

In the past, staff dried their dishes with disposable paper towels in the staff room. Now we have a supply of tea towels. Initially, a staff member took the dirty towels home to launder. However, the library has since purchased a small, stackable high-efficiency washer/dryer unit, used mainly for the Maintenance

Department's cleaning rags, and now for a load of dish towels every few weeks, too.

Others were concerned with the amount of compostable food waste going into the staff room garbage. Coffee grounds, banana peels, apple cores, tea bags, orange rinds and other fruit and vegetable scraps were being thrown out. After experimenting at home, one staff member started a small worm composting pilot project at the Library. While two worm bins, kept in an outdoor alcove, were soon overwhelmed by the volume of compostable scraps produced by staff, the project set an example of what was possible. (Our worm composting bins have also been a source of worms for staff members and, in a couple of instances, members of the public who wanted to start vermicomposting on their own.)

In response to this challenge of too much compostable food waste, another Green Team member stepped forward with an idea. Now, we simply place a lidded empty ice cream bucket beside the garbage can in the staff room. Staff members can put their fruit and vegetable waste in it, and the Green Team member takes the full pail home to her own larger backyard composter. In addition to diverting about five pails' worth of waste a week from the garbage, we also have sources of compost leachate (aka "worm tea") and worm castings to keep our indoor and outdoor plants looking terrific.

Another staff member, who does purchasing for the library, decided to source stationery products from a green vendor. Our paper is now made from 100% recycled post-consumer waste and our refillable pens are made from cardboard and compostable cornstarch.

This same employee noticed the great amount of packing material as she received various shipments addressed to the library. Although the library is able to participate in a curbside recycling program, she was distressed at the amount of packaging waste destined for the landfill. She found a local company that was set up to receive these usually non-recyclable products. Fortunately, the library's output met the minimum requirement for a monthly pickup by the company so we were saved the effort of delivering the recyclables ourselves. Items such as discarded CDs and DVDs as well as their plastic containers and wrapping also go to this same recycling company rather than into the garbage.

In September 2009, one Green Team member organized a "Swap, Don't Shop" event in which staff were invited to bring gently used clothing, accessories, and jewellery for a staff clothing exchange. She set the swap up in a meeting room and staff could pop in on coffee or lunch breaks to peruse the wares. At the end of the day, unclaimed clothing was donated to a local charity thrift store. Although this event did not particularly improve the library's greenness, it did highlight Green Team members' dedication to the environment both at work and at home. Some staff members got a morale boost seeing their once-favorite clothing item find a happy home in someone else's closet!

All of these measures to keep recyclable materials out of the garbage are having an impact on our waste stream output. Although WVML is in the midst of a garbage audit to analyze exact figures, anecdotal reports indicate that our garbage bins are far less full. With the exception of pickup of old drywall, even during our recent renovation, we did not need to arrange for extra garbage pickup.

Green Team Action—Reaching Out to Library Users

In addition to greening internal library practices, Green Team members educated the public on environmental issues. We used traditional methods such as displays on environmental topics and made booklists titled "Global Warming" and "Save Our Planet" available in print and via our website.

Each April in particular, we highlight environmental programs. Our regular children's storytimes during Earth Week, for instance, might feature stories about nature and the environment, and our monthly Philosophers' Café discussion group might discuss water consumption or electric cars. During April our monthly film series would show a documentary relating to an ecological theme.

During Earth Week we also highlight the library's green practices with a display of our green-certified cleaning products, biodegradable garbage bags, and sustainable stationery. Even our worm composting bin goes on display in our public courtyard. In the past, information desk staff received so many questions about the display that we put a list of sources of green maintenance and office supplies on our website as well as information about recycling options. Our graphics technician even supplied templates for recycling signage for other organizations to use.

WVML has also initiated an energy meter lending program. Developed by the library in co-operation with the Power Smart program of BC Hydro, the library's utility company, the program offers a simple and expense-free way for residents to discover the amount of electricity used by plug-in appliances throughout their homes. Six energy meters are available for three-week loan, allowing users to measure the energy consumption of home electrical appliances (and hopefully be inspired to cut down on energy use and costs).

To manage our own power consumption at the library, we have teamed up with a local company, Pulse Energy, and purchased their web-based energy management software which allows us to track our consumption by the month, day and even by the minute. By monitoring our consumption (we have three HVAC systems), we can quickly fix energy-wasting problems, thereby reducing our environmental footprint and our costs. Both staff and the public are able to monitor our energy usage via our website. This software also serves as a "filing system" for our utility bills, allowing us to generate reports about our energy consumption. For example, we calculated that our kilowatt-hour usage declined by 26% between 2006 and 2009.

Along with the expected Info by Topic pages on our website such as "Genealogy" or "Health and Medicine," we also have an "Environment and Sustainability" page, linking users to suggested databases and recommended websites on environmental topics.

In order to highlight all of WVML's green initiatives, we have also added a Sustainability page to the About Us section of our website that outlines our environmental practices.

Green Team Action—Reaching Out to the Profession

WVML's Green Team also promotes its environmental efforts to the library profession. For example, in April 2009 four Green Team members led a roundtable on environmentalism in the library workplace at the annual British Columbia Library Conference. This session generated a network of green librarians and exposed ideas from other libraries in the province.

Later in 2009, a Green Team member was on the planning committee for a one-day staff conference among three public libraries. She encouraged the conference organizers to "think local" in all aspects of planning. For instance, the small thank you gifts for speakers were local products: jars of honey from a neighborhood beekeeper.

Green Team Action—Reaching Out Beyond the Library

The Green Team does more than promote environmental action in the library. In the last year members have staffed a booth at community events such as the West Vancouver Earth Day celebration and the West Vancouver Clean Energy Fair and Forum. At our booth we set up a small display of environment-themed books and DVDs as well as our energy meters. If booth visitors had their library cards with them, they could sign out the items right from the booth. We even took a few reference questions and answered them later in the day!

One idea that came from this outreach was to have a regular display at the local summer Farmers' Market. Displays could follow the growing season, offering items about gardening in the spring and books on canning and preserving in the late summer and early fall. We have yet to follow through on this idea, but we think it is a terrific one.

Our Board Complement

In May 2008 the WVML Board created its own Green Committee. With leadership from Ann Goodhart, then our Director of Library Services, this Committee's chief goal is to achieve LEED® Canada for Existing Buildings certification. We are proud to be the first project to be accepted into this approval process in Canada.

Given the age and history of our building the Board also authorized an Energy Efficiency Building Assessment. The Board is taking a long-term view of infrastructure replacement and maintenance with the intention of retrofitting the building so it is more energy efficient.

A Green Building Operations Policy (www.westvanlibrary.ca/pdf/GreenBuildingPolicy.pdf) has also been developed by the Board. The actions that the Green Team initiated voluntarily in effect have become board policy. Green Team practices continue to assist in reaching the goals stated in this policy.

The Board and management of WVML have been extremely supportive of the Green Team, successfully nominating Chad Arsenault for a local environmental award. Board members take an active interest in the Green Team's activities, even inquiring about the health of the composting worms during a cold weather snap!

Morale

The freedom to implement green practices has allowed library staff to think globally and act locally. One Green Team member commented that demonstrating environmental practices at WVML allows us to build a wealth of knowledge related to sustainability that we can then pass along to interested library users who are trying to implement green practices of their own.

Another member pointed out how much she enjoys being part of a workplace team. Being green is a team effort everyone in the library can be part of. The entire staff is now conscientious about turning off lights, recycling and composting. Yet another Green Team participant appreciates how working on green initiatives makes her values come to life at work. It also makes our library feel modern, part of the current environmental zeitgeist.

Green Dreams

The Green Team is moving toward bigger projects. The latest area of interest is transportation. A team member is working on a project to acquire a workplace bicycle that staff members can use as an alternative to driving.

The Team is also looking to support the 50% of library employees who walk, cycle or take public transit to work, perhaps by providing improved changing facilities and indoor bike storage or providing some sort of incentive to transit users.

What is clear to the Green Team and all staff at West Vancouver Memorial Library is that the process of greening the library is a never-ending one. Currently, the community of West Vancouver is undergoing a process to produce a new strategic plan which includes a mission to "protect, restore, and defend our natural environment." The West Vancouver Memorial Library is proud to be taking a leadership role in our community's environmental stewardship, keeping West Vancouver green, by nature.

Greening a Library, Greening a Community: The Calgary Public Library's Eco-Action Plan

Rosemary Griebel

Introduction

Founded on the principle of reuse, libraries have a long tradition of being environmentally friendly and have been named "one of the seven sustainable wonders of the world".[1] Yet, communities are more likely to think of Wal-Mart as a green champion than the local library. It is no accident that the public has this perception. The greening of Wal-Mart started with the public unveiling in 2005 of a strategic, environmental plan. As libraries strive to be green leaders and position themselves as environmental stewards, one of the key questions is "what is the plan?" Without a comprehensive, strategic framework for the greening of the library, actions can easily become haphazard and out of step with the overall objectives and resources of the organization.

The following article focuses on the Calgary Public Library's experience of developing and implementing an Eco-Action Plan, and demonstrates that if organizations are serious about addressing the environment in a holistic, results-driven manner, a strategic action plan is essential. It cannot be an add-on or afterthought when developing services, programming, staffing and space.

---

1. Ryan, John. *Seven Wonders: Everyday Things for a Healthier Planet.* San Francisco: Sierra Club Books, 1999.

Developing the Eco-Action Plan

In 2007, the Calgary Public Library's CEO, Gerry Meek, announced the formation of a team to develop and write an ambitious environmental action plan. At this time the organization had already established a considerable legacy of environmental leadership. The Library Board had adopted the core values of environment and sustainable resource management in 1995. The Library had constructed two new branches that were among Canada's first certified Leadership in Energy and Environmental Design (LEED) buildings. Energy use had been reduced by 18%, and recycling efforts were well under way.

However, a formalized approach was needed to provide a framework that was congruent with the organizational culture, aligned with the Library's business plan and articulated the Library's commitment to sustainability.

The Eco-Action Team

A cross-sectional team of Library staff was brought together to develop and write the plan. The team represented key sectors of the Library including executive leadership, facilities, purchasing, customer services, human resources and information technology. The challenge was to look at all facets of the organization through an environmental lens.

The plan was to be developed over a six month period. The first three months focused on information gathering and conducting internal and external community scans. This included doing a SWOT analysis of the organization which identified environmental strengths and opportunities which could be built on, and weaknesses and threats which needed to be addressed. For example, the Facilities department had instituted green cleaning practices as early as 2002 which included the use of eco-friendly cleaning products, but the majority of staff was not aware of this practice.

In fact, communication with the Library Board, staff, key stakeholders and community members regarding the Library's greenness became a predominant theme. Closely linked to this was the theme of community engagement and education regarding the environment.

The community scan looked at best practices of leading organizations, emerging funding opportunities and identified a need for enhanced linkages to the community through environmental partnerships and programming. It became evident that environmental issues are at the top of political and community agendas, yet most individuals do not feel they have the knowledge and tools to make the best choices for a healthy future. Environmental issues are often complex and libraries are well positioned to support eco education and awareness.

Guiding Principles for the Eco-Action Plan

As the team began to develop the plan, certain key principles emerged that helped to define the role of the team and the shape of the final document:

- Measurable outcomes—Initiatives would have clear measurable outcomes that reflect social, economic and environmental perspectives;
- Aligned and consistent—Initiatives would be consistent with the core values of the organization and aligned with other strategic plans, particularly the three year business plan;
- Lifelong learning—Acknowledgement that environmental literacy, supported through library collections and programming, is one of the strongest tools to advance stewardship;
- Inclusive and transparent—Collaboration with internal and external networks and partners would guide decisions and interactions;
- Celebrate success—Green initiatives and organizational progress would be recognized, celebrated and communicated.

The Eco-Action Document

It was important that the plan be concise, easily communicated and actionable. To this end, the plan is organized into four broad action areas:

- Increased Commitment to Green Facilities, Energy and Water Efficiency and Recycling;
- Environmentally Responsible Purchasing;
- Engaged Staff Working Together for Environmental Change;
- Enhanced Public Services, Information Resources and Programs that Promote Environmental Awareness.

Under each action area outcomes are arranged by year, and updated annually.

The original Eco-Action plan also included sidebars that communicated environmental practices that had already been implemented. And, since environmental action is about optimism and belief in change, "blue sky goals" were also included. These were goals that were outside the scope of the Library budget, such as using 100% renewable energy at all library locations, but achievements we would continue to strive towards.

Building Understanding and Ownership

To ensure continued commitment and success of the Eco-Action Plan, communication with staff and key stakeholders is paramount.

The Library's "Start Smart! New Employee Bootcamp", includes an environmental component so all new employees are aware of the Library's green practices and initiatives. In addition, all library branches have an eco-champ on staff that provides green leadership. The eco-champs encourage recycling and reduction in the use of energy and other natural resources at their location, monitor and implement green initiatives, solicit ideas and contribute to virtual brainstorming as to how the Library can continually improve sustainability.

An environmentally themed staff newsletter, *GREENprint*, promotes new and ongoing initiatives and encourages employee engagement. A community blog, *Eco-Action* (http://calgarypubliclibrary.com/blogs/eco-action) is on the front-page of the Library's website and is updated weekly by staff bloggers.

Environmental best practices are incorporated into staff and volunteer events to demonstrate tangible change. For example, the Library has moved away from disposable dishes, and ensures that door prizes and awards are environmentally sensitive.

Staff are recognized and rewarded for eco ideas and action with a Green Award. Nominations can come from anywhere in the organization. The Green Award has been given for community work as well as initiatives within the organization.

Ongoing Planning Process

The Calgary Public Library's Eco-Action plan is a living document, and is updated as initiatives and policies develop and evolve. Annual updates and performance metrics are provided to the Library Board and staff highlighting statistical results and documenting achievements in the four key areas. Additionally, the plan itself serves to track and provide an inventory of actions that contribute to a reduced environmental footprint and a more sustainable community.

Planning Results

Has the Eco-Action Plan been successful? Definitely. Within one year of launching the Plan (late 2009) significant achievements include:

- An eco-themed children's summer reading program, Eco-Heroes, that provided a fun approach to waste reduction and environmental education. The program reached over 50,000 school children;
- Elimination of plastic bags at the checkout, and introduction of a stylish, reusable library bag made of recycled material;
- A "Green Before Green Was Cool" media event during environment week to position the Library as a green organization. For example eco-costumed characters distributed mock library cards. The paper of the mock cards contained flower seeds and could be planted;
- Over 50 environmental programs in locations across the city each year
- Collaboration with green organizations to promote environmental awareness. Initiatives like public compost pathways, "eco nooks," and eco business week were some of the results; and
- Introduction of plastic and compost recycling.

Conclusion

Ecological stewardship is one of the most pressing public priorities for communities today. As a valued center of information and community engagement, it is essential that libraries be part of the solution. A systems-oriented approach founded on sound strategic planning is the first step. After that, only our imaginations limit the possibilities.

Library-Sponsored Sustainable Living Outreach in Denver

Kate Lawrence

in collaboration with Simone Groene-Sackett,
Leigh Ann Kennison, and Evi Klett

The Denver Public Library (DPL) takes a keen interest in educating the public about sustainable living. This outreach education has been sponsored primarily by the Transition Libraries Committee and by Fresh City Life, DPL's cultural programming department. Going beyond merely providing resources for patrons to check out, we have sponsored displays and programs to inform and inspire, and have partnered with other community organizations to broaden our outreach. Our projects have led to greener fundraising events, distribution of infomarks, displays, and increased networking with local organizations and city government. The projects have also heightened interest in the energy usage meters, an unconference in conjunction with the 2009 American Library Association Midwinter Meeting, a community conversation with Dr. David Korten on strengthening local businesses, bicycle commuting and maintenance workshops, and even a Living Library event with experts available for patrons to check out.

A "Green Tie" Event

In 2007 a DPL staff member approached the DPL executive team about emphasizing to the public the sustainable nature of public libraries, in particular how libraries promote resource sharing and community building. The administrators decided to use an environmental theme for the 2007 Booklover's Ball, one of the DPL Friends Foundation's major annual fundraising events. An administrator wrote, "We think it will be the first major fundraiser that will be 'green'." The Ball, attended by hundreds of donors, was officially themed a "green tie" event, with attention being paid to using recyclable table service and to sourcing locally produced foods as much as possible for the banquet. Event publicity on DPL's website included a listing of the library's many environmentally beneficial aspects. Since 2007, awareness of sustainable values in organizing the Ball and other events has continued, although the theme changes each year.

Transition Libraries Committee

The DPL Transition Libraries Committee (TLC) formed in the fall of 2008, about the same time as the citywide Transition Denver Initiative. The Transition Towns movement, which began in the U.K. in 2005, seeks to build resilient, locally focused communities better prepared to weather the profound changes coming in the years ahead. These changes, arising from peak oil, climate instability, industrial agriculture, and increasing population, will mean higher prices for food, energy and everyday commodities, but especially for fossil fuel-based transportation. Because of these changes we will need to localize and simplify dramatically, but if we prepare by learning necessary skills and strengthening our local communities, these changes can bring enrichment instead of deprivation. Public libraries, long established as community centers in urban neighborhoods, can play a pivotal role in easing this transition.

TLC's mission is to foster and support community sustainability efforts and awareness through the library. Our goals include:

- Securing official committee status, and identifying a staff member in each branch cluster who can serve as a liaison for our projects;
- Improving DPL's collection of sustainability resources, both print and online; and
- Developing partnerships:
  - Internal—pooling resources, raising staff awareness, forging interdepartmental and intercluster relationships and maintaining clear communication within the committee.
  - External—creating a database of green-friendly organizations and establishing relationships with them, offering chances to work together, and consulting with and to other organizations.

Infomarks, Exhibits, and Special Projects

One of TLC's first projects was to begin creating infomarks on topics related to sustainability. We refer to them as infomarks, instead of bookmarks, because they list websites, magazines, and DVDs in addition to books. Our infomark themes included Global Warming & Peak Oil; Local & Sustainable Food; Gardening & Growing; Sustainable Transportation; and Energy Conservation. An artistic staff member created an engaging graphic design concept that lent a unified theme to the five infomarks, pulling them together as a series. A small trifold Farmer's Market infomark, not formally a part of the series, was also created. It included subcategories of: The Growing Experience; In the Kitchen; Eating Real Food Locally and Sustainably; Growing Your Own—A Sampler of Gardening Books; GMOs; DVDs; and Websites. This infomark was featured at one of our larger branches along with a display highlighting farmers' markets in town.

In the future our committee will collaboratively edit and update these infomarks as new books and other information resources are published. We also plan to pass the infomarks on to our web team so they can be available online.

We've been able to pair the infomarks with exhibits displayed in Schlessman Hall, the main lobby at DPL's Central Library. Exhibit themes have included Going Local, which focused on local food, energy, economy, and community cultivation; and Transition to Sustainability, which explained the Transition Towns movement and encouraged people to grow food locally as part of a "Grow Local Colorado" campaign. We were able to highlight our collection, as well as local organizations such as Denver Urban Gardens, Denver Metro farmers' markets, the Mile High Business Alliance, our local Redirect Guide (a green pages for the Denver/Boulder/Ft. Collins area), and our local Transition Denver group. We also assisted with placing an advertisement describing library services in the Redirect Guide.

Another exhibit evolved through DPL's partnership with Xcel Energy, the main energy company operating in Colorado. The partnership promoted energy conservation by making "Watts Up?" meters donated by Xcel available for library checkout. The amount of energy used by an appliance can be measured by plugging the appliance into the meter. This gives people the ability to audit their energy use in order to help them assess where they may want to change their habits. For TLC's exhibit, a table was set up in Schlessman Hall with two lamps, one with a compact fluorescent light bulb and one with a conventional incandescent bulb. Both lamps were hooked up to a Watts Up? meter to illustrate that the one using a CFL bulb used 1/10th the amount of energy as the conventional bulb. Books and DVDs on green remodeling, alternative energy, and global warming were also displayed and available for checkout. DPL's web team did such a great job of highlighting these meters that we had 300 patron holds placed on them. It was a very successful collaborative effort.

Networking with Local Organizations and the City

A few of us on the Transition Libraries Committee are active in community organizations. We attend presentations, film showings, conferences, and workshops dealing with aspects of sustainability in the community. We find this to be an excellent way to network with knowledgeable community members. As a result we have been able to collaborate with these organizations in terms of putting together exhibits, finding individuals to participate in panel discussions, providing the Denver community with free information resources, hosting library co-sponsored meetings and events, and potentially finding individuals to offer workshops through our adult and youth programming efforts.

The library has also partnered with the city's Greenprint Denver Initiative. Sustainability has been identified as a core value of the Denver city government, and Greenprint Denver has been tasked with educating the public and providing services related to sustainability measures. Former Denver Mayor John Hickenlooper, whose administration developed the Greenprint Denver Initiative, was known for occasionally wearing a green leaf jacket designed by a DPL staff member. We highlight the Greenprint Denver agenda in our exhibits and through DPL's website. Our website provides information about our own greening efforts at the library and resource lists for adults, teens and children. The website also features GreenFILE, a database that covers all aspects of human impact on the environment including global warming, green building, pollution, sustainable agriculture, renewable energy, recycling and more.

In the future we hope to improve our communication and information resource sharing with our web team and to interact with the public about sustainability through DPL's various blogs.

Unconference and Community Conversation

In January of 2009, on the pre-conference day of ALA's midwinter meeting in Denver, we organized an unconference on Transition Libraries. Approximately 30 people attended from DPL, the Denver/Boulder community, and library systems both within and outside of Colorado. Debra Slone, an MLIS professor at the University of South Florida in Tampa, who wrote a pivotal article in the March 15, 2008 issue of *Library Journal* on the role of public libraries in a post peak oil society, set the stage for the day. Leslie Glustrom, of Clean Energy Action, passionately informed us of the status of fossil fuels and the possibilities of a renewable energy future. Kenzie Davison, a local permaculturist, explained the Transition Towns movement, which has mushroomed all over the U.S. After lunch we had a panel discussion on the "Elements of Transition." Ellen Rosenthal spoke on permaculture and growing food locally. Annelle Norman, a homeopathic healthcare professional, discussed sustainable medicine. Mickki Langston of the Mile High Business Alliance spoke on growing the local economy. Marilyn Megenity, owner of Denver's Mercury Cafe, discussed sustainable business and the importance of nourishing community. Finally, Peter Roper spoke about CU-Boulder's sustainable transportation program. The final segment of the unconference focused on where we go from here. We brainstormed ideas on educating, supporting, and networking on behalf of our communities.

In May of 2009 we were lucky enough to present David Korten, author of *The Great Turning: From Empire to Earth Community* (2006) and *Agenda for a New Economy: From Phantom Wealth to Real Wealth* (2009), as part of a community conversation we hosted at the Central Library. The theme of the conversation was "What Does a Healthy Economy Look Like and How Do We Get There from Here?" Dr. Korten was in Denver to attend the BALLE (Business Alliance for Local Living Economies) conference and was available and willing to join our program at the library. The format for our two-hour event consisted of a 15-minute presentation by Dr. Korten, a 50-minute panel discussion moderated by a news director of our local community radio station, and a 45-minute Q & A with audience members. The panelists included Dr. Korten, Mickki Langston from the Mile High Business Alliance, Kendra Sandoval from Blue and Yellow Logic, Ashara Ekundayo from the Eastside Growers Collective, Carolyn Bninski from the Rocky Mountain Peace and Justice Center, and Doug Linkhart from Denver's City Council. What was particularly interesting about the panel discussion and the Q & A session was the wide range of ideas considered. Participants established a respectful democratic space in which to discuss many issues and perspectives related to the economy. Despite the last minute organizing of the weekday morning event we were able to get 40 people to attend, with a later broadcast on KGNU community radio and on the nationally broadcast Free Speech TV. DPL's events room coordinator, public relations manager, and web team were instrumental in providing the venue and getting the word out to our community.

In the future we would like to continue the "Sustainable Living—Community Conversation" series. Upcoming topics may include "How do we create a thriving local economy?" and "Could industrial hemp boost Colorado's economy?" These conversations give us an opportunity to engage the local community and to collaborate with local groups working on sustainability issues.

Bicycle Commuting Workshops

TLC offers ongoing workshops at the Central library for staff and the general public on how to get started commuting to work by bicycle. Scheduled at the start of each season—winter, spring, summer and fall—the classes offer tips, tricks and techniques and answer participants' questions. Local area bike dealers, as well as volunteers from Bike Denver, a local bicycling advocacy group, offer their insights on the various types of bicycles, safety, clothing, and equipment.

Fresh City Life Environmental Programming

Fresh City Life (FCL) has been the adult cultural programming department of the Denver Public Library since 2004. Its mission is two-fold: to offer free diverse monthly programming; and to serve as a spokesperson for DPL, representing the library to the community.

The varied programs that FCL offers are all intended to bring a slice of joy to the people of Denver, allowing them to pursue life-long learning goals and find fellowship and new friends. FCL promotes the library through its own web page on the library's website and a colorful and widely-distributed brochure. FCL reaches many more people on Facebook and Twitter. Several times a year a program or event generates news media coverage.

Increasingly, Fresh City Life is committed to fostering green and sustainable programming. Cooking demos have featured such titles as "It Came From Planet Organic: what to do with strange vegetables in your CSA box." Several FCL craft projects have incorporated recycling old things to make new things, for instance making fashionable belts out of old ties, and magnets out of beer bottle caps. Almost all of the Fresh City Life programs are presented by local artists, teachers and business people, and the library often pursues official partnerships with these entities in order to increase their perceived value to the community by this association.

Nuts & Bolts Bike Maintenance Class

In the summer of 2009, the Denver Public Library's Fresh City Life department hosted a three part series on basic bike maintenance, one each month of the summer. Taught by a local bike shop owner and sponsored by Izze, a local beverage company, Nuts and Bolts Basic Bike Maintenance classes focused on the types of maintenance and repair tasks that can be completed with minimal tools and time: fixing a flat tire, adjusting brakes and evaluating gear problems.

These free programs were held on the main library's patio, attracting the attention of curious passersby. The class began with modest attendance but quickly increased in popularity, in large part because of local media coverage. Participants from all walks of life attended these classes: children and seniors, men and women, people for whom bikes are their only mode of transportation, and people who are hobby bicyclists. Several DPL employees also attended the event.

The first part of the class entailed our teacher demonstrating a technique in front of the group. Then he and his assistants would answer any and all questions the students generated, often specific to their own bikes, which they often brought with them. The teacher would frequently use students' bikes as examples, helping students fix their own bikes with coaching on the side.

The Fresh City Life department received several inquiries from other libraries on how the program was organized and implemented, so it seems we inspired our colleagues.

Living Library

In the summer of 2010, Fresh City Life presented a Living Library on green sustainable living for the people of Denver. "Books" (who are really community leaders and local business owners, all experts on green topics) were available for a 25-minute checkout, during which time the patron conversed with the book on such topics as composting, urban gardening, eating healthier, buying local products and getting around without a car. The Living Library also functioned as a local information fair and community incubator. The "books" brought pamphlets and flyers about their organization or business, as well as providing referrals to shops and other organizations around town.

The Living Library sprang out of a partnership with more than twelve Denver organizations including businesses, city agencies, civic renewal groups and co-ops. Those who participated were enthusiastic, and eager to see the Living Library offered again.

Fresh City Life also encompasses the social element of sustainability, creating opportunities for friendship and community—qualities often lacking in our modern world. The latest endeavor of this department is a Hungry to Help database that puts Denver's citizens in direct contact with Denver organizations that need time, money and helping hands to achieve their missions, whether that be feeding the homeless, supporting new refugees or volunteering at the library.

Through all of the activities described above, and many more to come, the Denver Public Library encourages residents from all walks of life to learn and practice sustainable living.

Going Green @ Your Library: One Librarian's Lessons in Programming

Robbie Sittel

The Environmental Protection Agency's website states "America is shifting to a 'green culture' where over 300 million citizens are embracing the fact that environmental responsibility is everyone's responsibility."[1] Americans do seem to be embracing environmental responsibility and in a variety of ways that range from urban homesteading to purchasing energy efficient appliances. As Americans begin to explore options for greener living, libraries can be available to offer collections and programming that assist their patrons in discovering green alternatives. In 2008 the Tulsa City-County Library decided to embrace a greener side through programs and collections to help educate and connect customers to cleaner, greener, more sustainable living.

A Little About Tulsa and the Tulsa City-County Library System

The Tulsa City-County Library System (TCCL) is a system of 25 locations serving a county-wide population of a little more than 600,000.[2] The system has branches serving smaller communities around the county, but the greatest number of library branches is within the city of Tulsa. In addition to branches TCCL also offers four regional libraries. The regional libraries are intended to

---

1. EPA Go Green Monthly Newsletter. http://www.epa.gov/newsroom/gogreen/.
2. U.S. Census Bureau, 2009 Population Estimates, Census 2000, 1990 Census.

serve as hub libraries, available to provide larger collections, additional meeting spaces, computer labs, and additional services to smaller branches within each of the four county regions—north, south, east and west.

Tulsa County consists of rural areas but is most heavily populated in the urban and suburban areas. Tulsa County, overall, has embraced sustainable living in varying ways and with varying fervor. The City of Tulsa and some of the smaller surrounding communities offer curbside recycling programs. Despite the seeming accessibility to curbside recycling, an April 2010 news article in the Tulsa World reported that only 22% of Tulsa residents recycle.[3] In contrast to the communities' recycling efforts, Tulsa has an active gardening community and residents show great support of local farmers and local foods. This is evidenced by a number of farmers markets, food cooperatives, public gardens, and plant-related festivals. Though it still has a way to go, Tulsa is looking at more viable mass transit. Tulsa has an active cycling community with a network of bike trails and green spaces for off-road riding. These are just a few ways the residents of Tulsa City and County support and explore sustainable or green living choices.

In 2008, to further personal and community involvement in sustainability, a group of 20 TCCL employees formed a committee to design and implement a variety of programs that would offer library customers and the larger community access to information about community organizations and ways people, on an individual basis, can live cleaner and greener. The committee, which included public and non-public service staff, associates, clerks and librarians, came to be known as the Green Team. In addition to programming, the committee purchased books and videos that would engage customers in the Library's collections and, once the program ended, provide additional support. Three years later the Green Team continues as a standing library committee, offering programs and building collections.

If You Build It They Will Come . . . Sometimes.
The Green Team's First Year.

For many library workers, programming is a cornerstone of their job responsibility. For others, it's the furthest thing from their minds. And for any library worker who has toiled and phoned and set-up and photocopied for a program that was attended only by one or two people, the afterthought can be

---

3. HYLTON World Staff Writer, S. (2010, April 22). Reconsidering recycling. *Tulsa World (OK)* (Final ed.), A11. Retrieved April 15, 2011, from NewsBank on-line database (America's Newspapers).

"was it really worth all of the effort," sometimes yes and sometimes no. The first year of Green Team programming suffered defeat with some program ideas and met great success with others, but overall it was well worth the effort

The inaugural year of green programming at TCCL consisted of a series of eight programs offered over a nine week period. The series was dubbed Going Green @ Your Library. The programs, offered primarily on Saturdays, were intended to appeal to a wide audience and traveled around the system; programs were at three of the four regional libraries, the Central Library, one library branch and the local art house theater. By offering the programs as a series the committee intended for each program to segue into the next, continuing to build the public's interest from one Saturday to the next. This did not turn out to be the case. Instead, each program drew a new crowd with little carry over in attendance from week to week.

Here is a sampling of the eight programs offered that first year: *Going Green @ Your Library Kick-Off*, a resource fair intended to connect local residents with community resources from bee keepers to recyclers; *Green Up Your Diet*, a second resource fair focused on connecting attendees to local growers, groceries, and healthier food options complete with a local nutritionist presenting on stretching a family's food dollar through healthier shopping; *Green Cleaning*, this program offered a lecture about the health hazards of many cleaning products followed by the opportunity to make and take a cleaning products from ordinary house hold items (vinegar, baking soda, etc); *Composting & Rainwater Harvesting*, a lesson in composting and rainwater harvesting taught by a local master gardener.

What makes a successful program? Is there really an answer to that question? Sometimes programs suffer the fate of weather, good and bad. Tulsa experienced a late season blizzard the morning of the food program, conditions deteriorated quickly and TCCL closed all library locations early thus ending the program early. The *Kick-Off* event saw rain and cold; the cleaning program ushered in sunny skies and cool breezes more apt for working in the garden than experiments in cleaning science. Of the programs outlined above the *Composting & Rainwater Harvesting* program was the most successful. The program was held on a rainy morning in April, but drew an all-ages crowd of over 20 from throughout the Tulsa metro area with many of the most pertinent questions coming from the younger attendees.

Weather aside, the inaugural year offered some ideas about what the public was interested in learning. In planning the first year of programs the committee brainstormed trying to consider what might be relevant to the general public. Often though, the committee focused on member's interests for program ideas and drew on personal and community connections to find organizations to present or participate in the programs. Developing programming this way was not always the best approach, as it did not fully consider our audience. Truly considering whom the program is targeting and what it's intending to impart might be better than making an easy scapegoat of the weather.

A Few Lessons Learned

Community partnerships can be a key in developing successful programs. Tulsa County has a number of groups that offer community education opportunities. The most successful programs the first year and in the subsequent years have been programs that feature speakers on topics that interest the public from organizations that carry community trust and respect. One example is urban farming and homesteading. The Green Team has worked to develop a relationship with the County Extension Office, a rural organization that sits in the heart of the city that offers training and assistance with gardening, farming and the raising of livestock. Programs with the County Extension have repeated the composting class and also offered canning, urban gardening, and poultry workshops, all of which draw a substantial crowd regardless of the number of times it's offered. These are topics that community members could visit the extension office or website for guidance and information, but the venue of a library hosted workshops brings in an expert with the opportunity for questions, answers, a bit of bragging and hearing some of the successes and failures of other would-be urban farmers.

To keep theses community partnerships strong, it is important to have a healthy turnout at a program, something that is not always guaranteed. One way to draw attendance is to offer programs with public interest or a topic in which the public has a stake. This might seem straightforward, but it's not always. The first year the Green Team offered programs members thought would be of interest to the public, some were and some weren't. The lesson here is that it's important to know the library's community. Read the local papers; know what local government is doing; talk to organizations about popular offerings. Conduct an environmental scan to gather information for programs that will reflect the pulse of the community and current or prospective development projects. Keeping community development in mind, subsequent Green Team offerings have included programs that look at residential garbage and recycling services (Tulsa is about to revamp its trash collection) and plans for development of better mass transit (a county-wide initiative soliciting community response). This is an example of how libraries can serve as community partners by both informing of local government initiatives and offering programs that fit a theme.

Branding is something else that can help the cause of successful programs. Not all library staff want to join a committee, but many put together amazing programs. One way the Green Team has furthered its reach is by staying on top of what's happening throughout the Library system and putting its brand on it. TCCL has the fortune of a public relations office and a graphic designer who developed a Green Team logo. The logo can easily be added to fliers, entries in the library event guide or the library's website. Recent Green Team committee chairs have contacted staff system-wide, who happen to be offering programs that fit the green model and have asked that the logo be added to any publicity material. The Green Team thus adds its name to another program, builds a relationship with staff not on the committee, and continues to further its reach throughout the library system and county.

Finally, it is important to get staff buy-in. The Library can offer programming, but if the System and its staff aren't doing their part in many ways the efforts seem in vain. The first year of the Green Team, the committee hosted a contest to recognize the greenest employee. The contest asked participating staff to keep track of their green habits for a month. At the end of the month, the employee with the highest green ranking won a prize. This was far too much to ask of staff. The most recent Green Team has adopted the Greenbacks program, where staff can recognize staff with a $5 Whole Foods gift card for simple acts of green. These acts might include taking the branch's recyclables to a drop-off location or stocking a staff break room with non-disposable plates and cutlery. Simple tasks that no one needs to keep track of, just recognize.

Library programming is a kin to the 500 pound gorilla in the room, sometimes it's painful to recognize but it is often necessary *and* rewarding. Programs can connect library patrons to organizations and expose them to new ideas or perspectives and ultimately draw them into the library, its collections and its greater service offerings. Sometimes green seems trendy but little changes can make a difference. Libraries can find themselves as relevant connectors between community organizations, local government and library patrons helping to facilitate the little changes. Making these connections can be successful, frustrating and sometimes painful; but ultimately it serves a greater good of helping the community become more conscious of their environment, their choices and their community.

Bookmobiles are Going Green

Kathryn Totten

Anythink in Motion, as our bookmobile is called, is a green machine. The bookmobile is a branch of Rangeview Library District and Adams County, Colorado. This district is committed to sustainability. The Rangeview Library District Board of Trustees decided to make the 2008–2010 capital construction projects as sustainable as possible. The district now has two silver and one gold LEED certified library buildings that use natural light and ground-source heating and cooling to reduce the carbon footprint. As the manager of Outreach Services for Rangeview Library District (branded as Anythink libraries), I was involved in the design and purchase of the new bookmobile. We looked for a vehicle with many green features. Our new vehicle, Anythink in Motion, was delivered in October of 2008. The bookmobile has energy efficient and clean features that make it a complement to the sustainable branches of Anythink Libraries.

The Anythink in Motion bookmobile, built by Moroney in Worcestershire, MA, has a fuel efficient diesel engine which runs on very low sulfur diesel fuel. It is possible to run it on biodiesel. Carbon monoxide exhaust is minimal and the engine does not have the bad smell of earlier diesel engines. Not only is the emission clean, the vehicle is green because it will last longer. The life of diesel engines is generally twice as long as that of gasoline engines. Diesel engines are more fuel-efficient than gasoline engines because of a higher temperature of combustion. This brings down the cost of operation. Diesel engines also require less maintenance than gasoline engines.

Lighting on this bookmobile is bright and natural. Moroney builds bookmobiles with a bank of skylights running the full length of the truck body. The exclusive Monolite roof brings in the daylight but blocks out the harmful direct rays of the sun. With this natural light the stacks are much easier to read, and we only need to run electric lights on the cloudiest days.

Heating the vehicle with a Wabasto sub-floor hot water radiant heat system keeps the bookmobile warm and the carpet dry in winter months. The diesel powered Wabasto heats a mixture of water and antifreeze that is pumped through pipes under the bookmobile floor. Heat radiating from the floor keeps the vehicle warm enough on most days. On very cold days we use zone controlled auxiliary electric heaters at the foot of both desks.

The bookmobile has a bank of batteries and a power inverter that provides electrical power for the lights and computers. The system recharges while we drive to the next stop, and each evening when we plug it into AC power in the garage. With this system we have less need to run the generator. Using the inverter provides clean and quiet energy.

On hot summer days when we need air conditioning we run our Onan Quiet diesel generator. The generator has much cleaner emissions than older generators and creates less smell. This generator is very quiet, making conversation in the bookmobile much more comfortable. It is also quieter outside the vehicle, causing less of a disturbance to our neighbors at our bookmobile stops.

We keep efficiency in mind as we plan our bookmobile routes, vehicle maintenance appointments and fuel stops. Economic route planning saves fuel as well as travel time. Our county is large, so we schedule bookmobile stops in circular routes that are grouped by location, for example, on Mondays we go north, on Tuesday we go east, and so forth. Grouping our stops together allows us to have shorter routes, which require less fuel.

Fueling the vehicle is planned into our schedule to occur on days when the bookmobile stops are near a large truck stop fueling station. This station is the most convenient one for fueling our large vehicle. We also keep the tank at least half full, which is a good practice for both safety and efficiency.

Regular service on the vehicle keeps it running at maximum efficiency. Tire pressure, brakes, and fluid levels are maintained. The generator requires oil and filter changes regularly, after 100 hours of usage. Our bookmobile drivers perform daily vehicle checks, which sometimes catch potential problems before they become a real hazard.

Driver training has been a factor in our fuel savings as well. Although our vehicle is below the weight that requires Commercial Drivers License drivers, when we received our new vehicle all bookmobile drivers attended truck driver training. This training included fuel efficiency practices such as maintaining even speed and timing arrival at intersections to minimize braking for traffic lights. We received basic Smith System training. The System teaches drivers to stay aware of what is happening ahead of them and around them, to leave a way out, to communicate with other drivers on the road, and get the big picture. Smith System driver training can be the most effective method of reducing your fuel costs.[1] The trainer coached our drivers to check mirrors constantly and use fuel-efficient driving habits.

Taking our bookmobile into rural and suburban communities that are miles from a library branch means fewer patrons driving personal vehicles to the library. Bookmobile service results in less air pollution from vehicle emissions. In the summer of 2008, when gas prices were over $4 per gallon, many parents thanked me and the outreach staff for bringing library services into their community. Their family budget did not allow for many trips into town. According to federal data and a USA Today poll, record high gas prices "prompted Americans to drive less for the first time in nearly three decades, squeezing family budgets and causing major shifts in driving habits."[2] Taking the library to these outlying communities is a much needed service that is also eco-friendly.

Anythink in Motion is a green machine, but we do not claim to be unique in environmental awareness. Each year the American Library Association (ALA) Annual Conference includes a full day program for outreach called Bookmobile Sunday. This event is organized by the Office of Literacy and Outreach Services subcommittee on bookmobiles. The event brings outreach library professionals together for a full day of workshops, and also gives bookmobile vendors an opportunity to show their vehicles at the bookmobile parade.

At the ALA Annual Conference in Washington DC, in 2010, I toured two notable new bookmobiles with green features. The Meridian bookmobile is built on a Dodge Sprinter high roof van. The shelves are made from strong and light aluminum built by Acore Shelving. There are four removable Acore carts so the collection can be rotated. A lift in the rear of the vehicle provides the means of changing out these carts. LED lighting is efficient and comfortable for the eyes. Solar panels on the roof charge the batteries, and an inverter converts the power to run the computers and lights. This vehicle does not have a generator. When air conditioning or heat is required the vehicle's Mercedes-Benz diesel engine provides the power. The fuel efficient engine gets about 22 miles per gallon. This small bookmobile can carry a collection of about 2,000 items.

American Specialty Vehicles (ASV) showed a low floor bookmobile that runs on clean natural gas. This vehicle has a range of 150 miles and can be refueled at the end of the day on the library property from an on-site natural gas tank. ASV also builds bookmobiles with gasoline, diesel or propane power. The type of fuel is matched to the kind of service planned for the bookmobile. The battery and inverter will power the lights and computers for 4 ½ hours. A short 30-minute drive will recharge the battery and provide an additional 4 ½ hours of power. The vehicle is plugged in to AC power each night to fully recharge for the next day of service.

Bookmobile and outreach services library professionals gather at the Association of Bookmobiles and Outreach Services (ABOS) conference each October. This is another opportunity to see and compare bookmobiles. Each year libraries showcase their bookmobiles and vendors bring their latest models and show off their innovative designs. Dates and locations for future ABOS conferences can be found at the ABOS website (http://www.abos-outreach.org/). OBS recently displayed a new low floor vehicle that has many well-designed green features. This vehicle has automatic doors which keep the inside temperature steady, and it uses solar technologies together with a hybrid generator with variable speed and variable output. Roof-mounted solar panels are angled to maximize exposure to the sun. The constant, low amperage electrical output charges the bank of batteries. The inverter powers computers, lighting and even air conditioning and heating with quiet comfort. The generator comes into the system only when the battery bank is depleted to a pre-set level. This system results in a 20% reduction in fuel consumption and a 50% reduction in noise and vibration.[3]

Each year the ABOS conference also features bookmobiles built by Matthews Specialty Vehicles and Farber Specialty Vehicles. Matthews Specialty Vehicles offers nine vehicle bookmobile styles. "We build vehicles with solar panels, power inverters, and energy efficient lighting. Each vehicle is designed with the features the library needs," says Tami Kane of Matthews Specialty Vehicles. Farber Specialty Vehicles builds bookmobiles in various styles from walk-in low floor vehicles to the Book Hauler which is made to carry many book carts for lobby services. The Matthews and Farber bookmobiles have similar green features and may use either gasoline or diesel fuel. They are built in various lengths and styles to accommodate the type of service the library wants to provide.

The ABOS conference is a great place to see and compare the features of bookmobiles and see them fully stocked with books and media. Touring the vehicles makes it easier to decide what kind of vehicle will best meet the library service needs. The ALA Office of Literacy and Outreach Services hosts a bookmobile wiki on their website. This is a good resource for any library considering adding bookmobile services. The wiki includes a list of bookmobile vendors and their contact information.[4]

Bookmobiles vary in size and are typically built on a truck, van or bus frame. They are hybrid or powered by natural gas. It can be a daunting experience to purchase a bookmobile. "There are so many options for green features and all of them have a direct impact on cost," says Michael Swendrowski of Specialty Vehicle Services. "You can retrofit solar panels and inverters into older vehicles. Cutting down on generator use is the easiest way to be eco-friendly. And those retrofits are relatively easy."[5] Whether you are designing a new bookmobile or updating an older one with green features, it can be cost effective to get advice from a specialty vehicle consultant. The resulting vehicle will be something you will be pleased to have in service for years to come.

Longevity is another eco-friendly feature of bookmobiles. Bookmobiles are built to last. They are often in service for a long time; many are on the road for 15 years or more. By keeping the bookmobile well-maintained, we are saving the environment by not discarding and replacing our vehicles as often. Older bookmobiles have been remodeled into mobile computer labs, giving them a second life. As service models change, a bookmobile can be transformed into a van for preschool literacy classes or a lobby stop vehicle for delivering senior services. Recycling a bookmobile is a very eco-friendly option. So even if they are well loved and used bookmobiles can keep *going green.*

Endnotes

1. "Right Foot Fuel Economy," Accessed December 5, 2011, http://www.smith-system.com/downloads/RFFEbooklet.pdf.
2. Judy Keen and Paul Overberg, "Gas Prices Rattle Americans," USA Today, May 9, 2008.
3. Paula Trenta, "OBS Inc.'s Green Report," September 17, 2009, Accessed December 5, 2011, http://www.obsinc.net/ green_report_volume_1_issue_1.pdf.
4. "Bookmobile Vendors/Manufactures," http://olos.ala.org/bookmobiles/ index.php?title=Bookmobile_Vendors/Manufacturers.
5. "Farber Specialty Vehicles: Bookmobiles," Accessed December 5, 2011. http://www.fsvcc.com/bookmobiles/.

Section Three

Green Resources & Reflections

Toward Sustainable Conferences: Going Green at the 2009 ACRL 14th National Conference in Seattle

Charles Forrest, Karen Munro & Kate Zoellner

Introduction

Technological innovation is transforming scholarly communication. New modes of interaction and dissemination are emerging to support research, publication and conversation between and among colleagues and a larger professional audience. Face-to-face opportunities can now be augmented, or perhaps replaced, by a variety of individual and social networking opportunities, prompting professional associations and other institutions to re-imagine the experience, and thus reaffirm the value, of professional meetings, institutes and conferences. The business model for the professional meeting must actively account for the cost to individuals, the association, the profession—and the environment. Is the professional association conference as we know it sustainable as we end the era of cheap energy and enter the social networking age? Sustainability is defined as meeting the needs of the current generation without compromising the ability of future generations to meet their needs. Recognizing the fundamental importance of face-to-face communication in our professional lives, can we invent a new model for the conference experience that we can pass on to future generations of librarians and scholars?

The 14th National Conference of the Association of College & Research Libraries (ACRL) in Seattle in 2009 was the first to incorporate a sustainability planning and educational initiative, realized through the cooperative efforts of the Green Component Planning Committee and the Association. The initiative was born during the ACRL 13th National Conference in Baltimore in 2007. ACRL's Green Component Committee was charged by Betsy Wilson, Dean of the University of Washington Libraries and Chair of the ACRL 14th National Conference, to recommend to the Conference Chair, ACRL Staff, and the other conference planning subcommittees environmentally friendly practices to enhance the national conference and reduce its impact on the environment. The Committee's work aligned with the ACRL Strategic Plan 2020's goal of sustainability, specifically with the first strategic objective, to "[e]xpand commitment to adopting green and sustainable business practices for ACRL offices, conferences, continuing education and operations with business partners."[1]

The Committee was composed of ACRL members drawn from college and university libraries across the country, led by co-chairs Charles Forrest, Director, Library Facilities, Emory University Libraries and Karen Munro, Head, University of Oregon-Portland Library & Learning Commons.[2] ACRL staff member Tory Ondrla served as staff liaison for the Committee, and was closely involved in all activities.

The Committee's work resulted in:

- Widespread participation in sustainable conference behaviors;
- Reduced paper and materials waste;
- Increased composting, recycling, and charitable donations; and
- The development of best practices to inform future ACRL and ALA conferences and meetings.

This chapter draws heavily from the Committee's final report on its activities.[3]

1. ACRL Executive Committee, "Charting Our Future: ACRL Strategic Plan 2020," Association of College & Research Libraries, May 13, 2009, http://www.ala.org/ala/mgrps/divs/acrl/about/whatisacrl/strategicplan/index.cfm.

2. In addition to co-chairs Charles Forrest and Karen Munro the Committee included: Nancy Huling, Head, Reference & Research Services Division, University of Washington Libraries; Juliet Kerico, Electronic Resource Coordinator, Indiana State University; Kerri A. Odess-Harnish, Reference/Instruction Librarian, Gettysburg College; Sarah Sheehan, Education & Nursing Reference/Liaison Librarian, George Mason University; Paula Walker Director, Libraries Space Planning, and Special Assistant to the Dean, University of Washington Libraries; and Kate Zoellner, Education, Human Sciences and Psychology Librarian, The University of Montana.

3. Kate Zoellner and Charles Forrest, "ACRL 2009 Green Component Planning Committee Conference Planning Report," Online report, July 27, 2009, From ACRL 14th National Conference Website, http://www.ala.org/ala/mgrps/divs/acrl/events/seattle/GreenCommReport07270.pdf.

Methods

The Green Component Committee organized its work into three areas: 1) communication with attendees; 2) concrete on-site actions; and 3) encouragement for members to commit to sustainable behaviors at the conference and beyond it. To accomplish these goals, the Committee focused its efforts on the following:

- Informing other conference planning committees and attendees about the environmental footprint of the conference, and influencing behavior through collaboration, communication, and marketing;
- Reducing, reusing, and recycling materials used in the planning and implementation of the conference, by changing association practices, contractual arrangements, and attendee behavior; and
- Committing to sustainability in the association by building best practices into the planning of future conferences of the association, and documenting the work of the Committee to provide a model of environmental responsibility for ALA and its divisions.

Communication with Attendees

To build awareness and understand membership concerns about sustainability, the Committee developed, delivered, and analyzed the "ACRL 14th National Conference Member Opinion Survey on Greening ACRL National Conference 2009." Conducted in February 2008, the online survey provided 663 responses that documented members' primary concerns about sustainability and helped lay the foundation for the Committee's work.

The Committee also worked to establish a sustainability-oriented conference by crafting a call for program proposals on topics related to greening libraries. This call was part of the general ACRL call for proposals, which included five themes:

- Cast a Net (networking, telecommunication, inclusivity, marketing);
- Feel the Buzz (trends, new roles, blurring boundaries, public engagement);
- Get It to Go (mobile technologies, training for emerging technologies, usability, collaboration);
- Scale the Heights (career paths and development, work-life balance, organization development); and
- Harvest and Sustain (sustainability and related topics)

The sustainability-oriented "Harvest and Sustain" theme called for proposals related to archiving and preservation, library fundraising, collection development, and ecological sustainability. For the full wording of the call, see Appendix A.

Throughout its work, the Committee used various means to keep members informed of its activities. The conference website featured information about the Committee and its charge, and a special "green leaf" logo was designed to draw attention to new green initiatives. The Committee also updated members through the ACRL podcast "Greening Seattle" and through several *C&RL News* articles published during the lead-up to the conference date.[4] The podcast and articles highlighted sustainable changes to the conference, and suggested ways attendees could practice sustainably both during the conference and afterwards.

During the registration period, the Committee gathered information from the conference hotels about their sustainable business practices and posted this information on a web page linked to the registration site.[5] The Committee also profiled local businesses and vegetarian restaurants on the interactive conference map and wiki to keep members thinking sustainably about their dining and purchasing habits in Seattle.

At the conference, the Committee staffed a booth in the high-traffic registration area, to answer questions about the sustainability of the conference. We also presented a panel session on greening library meetings and conferences, offering an overview of our work and suggesting best practices for future events. In addition, we arranged for a special featured "green" speaker. Robin Chase, founder of the Zipcar car-sharing program, lectured on the similarities between lending libraries and other resource-sharing programs. Jackie Belanger, reflecting on Chase's talk, noted: "She encouraged all the attendees to think about

---

4. "Go Green @ ACRL," *C&RL News* 70 (January 2009): C-2.; "The Greening of Seattle," *C&RL News* 70 (September 2008): 483.; Juliet Kerico and Karen Munro, "Six Steps to Greening your ACRL 14th National Conference Experience," *C&RL News* 70 (February 2009): 100–101, http://www.ala.org/ala/mgrps/divs/acrl/publications/crlnews/2009/feb/sixstepstogreen.cfm; Karen Munro, "Going Green," *C&RL News* 70 (June 2009): 331, http://www.ala.org/ala/mgrps/divs/acrl/publications/crlnews/2009/jun/confwrapup.cfm; Kristen Shuyler and Dalia Corkrum, "Green Dining in the Emerald City," *C&RL News* 70 (February 2009): 99–103, http://www.ala.org/ala/mgrps/divs/acrl/publications/crlnews/2009/feb/greendining.cfm; and Scott Walter, Juliet Kerico, and Karen Munro, *Greening Seattle*, ACRL Podcast, September 23, 2008, http://www.acrl.ala.org/acrlinsider/2008/09/23/acrl-podcast-greening-seattle/.

5. Association of College & Research Libraries, "Eco-friendly Hotel Practices," From ACRL 14th National Conference Website, http://www.acrl.org/ala/mgrps/divs/acrl/events/seattle/housing/Greenhotelpractices.cfm (accessed February 1, 2010).

where there was 'excess capacity' in our lives that was not being used, and how that could be shared to reduce our consumption of scarce resources . . . her talk inspired me to think about other ways I can use the 'excess capacity' in my life so that someone else doesn't have to buy what they don't really need."[6]

The Committee also worked to inform conference vendors about our sustainability goals, and to encourage them to promote their sustainable business practices. The Exhibitor Service Kit sent by ACRL to all conference vendors included a form allowing vendors to self-report their green activities. As another paper savings, for the first time the Exhibitor Service Kit was disseminated electronically rather than in print. Seven exhibitors self-identified as having sustainable business practices and were featured in the printed conference program as ACRL Green Exhibitors (Absolute Backorder Service, Archival Products, Better World Books, Brodart Co., Palmieri Furniture, Paratext, and ProQuest). These exhibitors presented products containing high percentages of post-consumer recycled waste, reuse of books, journals and other printed materials, LEED (Leadership in Energy and Environmental Design) certifiable manufacturing processes and materials, paperless business offices and processes, and in one case even a lightweight, energy-efficient conference exhibit booth.

Overall, the Committee's efforts to communicate its mission and strategies to membership were highly successful, with over 98% of respondents to a post-conference evaluation indicating that they were aware of the efforts made to green the conference.[7]

Concrete On-Site Action

The Green Component Committee's opinion survey yielded many suggestions from members about how to improve paper recycling, waste reduction, and other aspects of the on-site conference. These responses led the Committee to partner with ACRL staff and the Washington State Convention and Trade Center on several concrete sustainability projects. Some of these were improvements to already-standard conference features, while others were entirely new to ACRL's previous planning work. ACRL and the Convention Center agreed to:

- Provide visible recycling and composting stations;

---

6. Belanger, Jackie. *Saturday & Final Thoughts*. Blog post, March 15, 2009. From ACRL 2009 Virtual Conference Blog. http://www.learningtimes.net/acrlconference/category/conferenceblog/.

7. Kate Zoellner and Charles Forrest, "ACRL 2009 Green Component Planning Committee Conference Planning Report," 49.

- Set lights and HVAC systems at low levels for conference set-up and take-down;
- Reduce catering food waste through donations to charities (covered, un-served food) and composting of both food and bamboo utensils;
- Design exhibit hall materials (such as pipe and drape) to be reused at future ACRL conferences;
- Use exhibit hall carpeting made of recycled material;
- Donate over 1,100 books from the exhibit hall to Better World Books, resulting in roughly $1,000 in donations for the National Center for Family Literacy;
- Donate two large conference signs with the 2007 thunderbird motif to a local theater group for re-use in stage sets;
- Use live potted plants in lieu of cut flowers;
- Print the conference program book on recycled paper using soy-based ink;
- Make conference mailings electronic, saving approximately 240,000 pages of paper;
- Make badge holders of recycled materials, and provide a badge holder recycling bin on site; and
- Make conference give-aways more sustainable. The sponsored conference bag was made of recycled materials; the coffee mug was made of non-BPA corn-based plastic; and a special four-minute shower timer was included. If members declined give-aways, these were donated to charity.

Key to the success of these efforts was the fact that the Washington State Convention and Trade Center was well-prepared to host a more sustainable conference, and had already implemented some of these features.[8] ACRL staff were also well-informed of sustainability opportunities and willing to change established practices.

Committing to Sustainability

The Committee worked to encourage members to act sustainably at the conference and afterwards. Fundamental to this effort was the Green Pledge, a

---

8. The Washington State Convention and Trade Center has in place energy and water conservation practices such as lowering lighting, heating and cooling during move-in and move-out times. "Special Services—Room Sets & Custodial," Washington State Convention and Trade Center, http://www.wsctc.com/our_services/special_services.aspx (accessed February 1, 2010).

document designed by the Committee asking conference attendees to commit to sustainable behaviors such as recycling, reducing their energy use, and avoiding disposable items while at the conference (see appendix B). The Pledge was made available for members to sign when they registered online for the conference, as well as at a booth in the conference registration area. Vendors were also invited to sign the Green Pledge. Attendees who signed the pledge were given a special conference name badge with a watermark of the "green leaf" logo behind their name, to further promote awareness and participation.

In the lead-up to the conference, the Green Pledge generated comments from some ACRL members. Virtual Conference blogger Sarah Ward wrote: "I've been mulling over the Green Pledge since registering for the conference, and I decided to challenge myself to get through the entire thing without using a single plastic bag or water bottle. I came armed with my Sigg water bottle, and I hear tell that the conference swag includes a reusable coffee mug—swell! This also means that every time I stop at the drug store, or buy a cheesy Space Needle snow globe I will have to remember to refuse the plastic bag and put whatever treasures I collect into my handy conference tote bag. Isn't that why we get them in the first place? Is anyone else challenging themselves to uphold the pledge?"[9]

Responses to the membership survey showed that virtual conference attendance—the ability to view conference presentations and materials remotely—ranked as a high sustainability priority. ACRL 2009 offered a more robust virtual conference experience than at previous conferences, using a dynamic screen capture system to record lectures and present recordings simultaneously with presentation materials. Presenters were strongly encouraged to upload handouts to their virtual conference presentation space, rather than providing hard copies at the event. The virtual conference website continues to offer members access to conference materials in the form of podcasts, webcasts and dynamic screen captures.

After the conference, the Committee's co-chairs and ACRL staff liaison hosted an ACRL OnPoint chat sesion titled, "Lessons Learned from the Seattle Green Conference." This session was intended to continue the conversation after the conference in April 2009.[10] Thirteen individuals joined the discussion.

---

9. Ward, Sarah. *Sunny Seattle?* Blog post, March 12, 2009. From ACRL 2009 Virtual Conference Blog. http://www.learningtimes.net/acrlconference/category/conferenceblog/page/8/.

10. Karen Munro, Charles Forrest, and Tory Ondrla, *Lessons Learned from the Seattle Green Conference,* ACRL OnPoint Chat Archive Transcript, April 29, 2009, From ACRL, http://www.ala.org/ala/mgrps/divs/acrl/events/onpoint/archives/2009-04-29.cfm.

Challenges

The scope of the Green Component Committee's work was broad, and we faced some challenges to accomplishing all of our goals. While we foresaw some challenges, others were a surprise.

Logistically, our work was daunting because of its broad scope, the complexity of communication required, and the degree of forethought and planning necessary to make changes to such a large-scale event. After generating lists of good ideas for implementing the Committee's charge, our task was to define a realistic set of action items that could be achieved in a reasonable amount of time with the resources available. Although the Committee was appointed and began its work well in advance of the conference, we were surprised to learn how early schedules were set, and bookings and other conference arrangements were made. Our work was made substantially easier by the hard work and experience of Tory Ondrla, our ACRL liaison, as well as by the preparations and policies already instituted by the Washington State Convention and Trade Center. Throughout our term, we were challenged to conceive of our work in ways that made it both feasible to accomplish and amenable to clear communication to members and other planning committees. We used several communication tools, including a wiki, regular conference calls, and email, to keep all Committee members on task and ensure that no project was left behind.

We anticipated mixed feedback from our initial membership survey, and were not surprised when we received it. While the majority of responses were positive and supportive, some critiqued aspects of the conference we did not control, or challenged our assumptions about membership priorities and beliefs. In some cases, this changed our approach to our charge: we chose not to pursue a carbon-offset program for conference travel, due to the controversial nature of carbon-offsets and feedback we received from membership. In other cases, we attempted to inform and influence membership opinion: rather than move to reduce on-site attendance, we helped promote the virtual conference as an option for those who chose not to travel.

Several hotels were slow to respond to our requests for information about their sustainable business practices, making it difficult to post clear and complete information for conference attendees. Similarly, most vendors did not take full advantage of the opportunity to promote their sustainable business practices via the Exhibitor Service Kit. This was a surprise, as we had expected vendors and hotels to see this as a means to promote their services and distinguish themselves. We occasionally encountered resistance to our ideas from conference partners, and often found that we could use these situations as opportunities for professional education. For example, Tory Ondrla, our ACRL liaison, was able to overcome the Convention Center Catering Manager's initial resistance to donating unused food to a local charity by explaining the *Good Samaritan Food Donation Act* and working out a compromise by which food would only be unwrapped as it was needed.[11]

Evaluation and Results

The Green Component Committee worked with ACRL staff to include several questions about the greening of the conference in the final conference evaluation. (For the full text of these questions, see appendix C.) Members' responses to these questions reveal that 98.2% of respondents were aware of the Committee's green conference initiatives. Most attendees learned about the initiatives from the conference website and the registration confirmation they received. When asked to rate the importance of the conference's sustainability features, more than three-quarters of respondents rated as "very important" the following features: providing ways to recycle handouts; using recycled or reusable materials for set-up and signage; substituting digital for paper handouts; and donating or composting food waste.

Of the 1,339 members who responded to the final conference evaluation, 514 answered the following open-response question: "Describe any changes you made at the conference to reduce your environmental footprint." Select responses to this question include:

- I simply recycled as much as I could. You guys made it easy for me, and I appreciate that.
- Took notes on my blackberry rather than on a notepad.
- Attended virtually rather than flying from the east coast.
- Curtailed use of electricity in hotel room; walked or used public transportation to and from most destinations; used reusable drink container; recycled paper.
- Ate local foods at restaurants suggested on wiki. Did not take paper handouts from vendors. Drank from cans and recycled them.
- I did not bring any paper handouts to my presentation. It was good to know that I wasn't wasting any paper.
- I have tried to be more environmentally aware for many years, but even I was more careful about the amount of disposables I collected (even purchasing a reusable bag at one Seattle shop). I also made sure to recycle

---

11. *Model Good Samaritan Food Donation Act,* Public Law 104-210, *U.S. Statutes at Large* 110 (1996): 3011–3012.

my conference badge holder, which I normally do not think about until after I've returned home.

Some responses urged the Committee, ACRL, and ALA to go farther in making conferences more sustainable:

- Don't print *Footnotes*—it's not very "green"!
- . . . if I had known a program would be given out at the conference, I wouldn't have printed out what I got from the session builder. It seemed a waste of paper, particularly for a green conference.
- If this were truly a green conf. we wouldn't need the program or pocket program books. I would LOVE to see us move away from the big badge holders and all of the printed materials.

While others argued for moderation:

- I need the program book in print. Please do not become too green and take it away.
- I was looking forward to the ACRL calendar paper pad to take notes on. I don't think we had to go SO green that we didn't receive a notepad. I didn't bring anything with me to write on, so that was not very nice.

Some comments reflect misunderstandings of the options and programs available to members, and speak to the difficulty of communicating a complex project to a large and decentralized group. Many members, for instance, did not realize that declined conference bags and other give-aways would be donated to charity. Others were confused about how to access materials available on the Virtual Conference website. In addition, membership opinions often clashed on which conference features were important to retain, and which should be changed. Feedback from the final evaluations is valuable in pointing out areas where future committees could improve communication and understanding across ACRL membership.

In addition to responses on the final conference evaluation, the Committee's success in meeting its charge may also be measured in terms of conserved resources and changes to member behavior.

- Over 80% of conference attendees signed the Green Pledge;
- More than 240,000 pages of paper were saved by switching from print to electronic mailings;
- The program book was printed on recycled paper;

- Approximately 500 coffee mugs were donated to the local food bank Northwest Harvest and community-building organization Solid Ground, and 500 conference bags were donated to the foster care support organization Treehouse; and
- Over 1,100 books were donated to Better World Books, resulting in roughly $1,000 in donations for the National Center for Family Literacy.

A key goal for the Committee was to produce documentation to support greening future conferences. The Committee's recommendations and strategies, as well as a fuller analysis of membership feedback, are documented in the *ACRL 2009 Green Component Planning Committee Conference Planning Report.*[12]

Next Steps

Lessons Learned

Through sixteen months of work, we learned a number of lessons and generated many ideas for consideration in the planning of future ACRL, ALA, and other professional conferences and events. These lessons can be broken into three areas: membership initiative, communication, and partnerships.

It was critical for the Green Component Committee to engage the membership from the start of the association's efforts to green the conference. This engagement kept us grounded and guided by members' ideas, which provided support and member buy-in on green initiatives. Communication among multiple parties was critical between Committee members and our ACRL liaison, among other ACRL component planning committees, and between the Committee and ACRL members. We communicated with ACRL membership via the member opinion survey, the conference website, and other media including a podcast and several *C&RL News* articles. Partnering with the Convention Center, caterers, suppliers, hotels, and the local community was also important to planning for sustainable conference practices. It was critical for us to understand the practices of the businesses with which we worked, both to promote those that were sustainable and also to draw attention to those that were not.

Association Changes

The ACRL Strategic Plan 2020 lists sustainability as a goal, with a strategic objective to "[e]xpand commitment to adopting green and sustainable business

---

12. The report is available online at http://www.ala.org/ala/mgrps/divs/acrl/events/seattle/ GreenCommReport07270.pdf.

practices for ACRL offices, conferences, continuing education and operations with business partners."[13] ACRL's efforts toward these ends began prior to the 2009 Green Component Committee initiative and will continue beyond it. In 2005, an ACRL Online National Conference was offered as a separate yet parallel professional development experience from the ACRL 12th National Conference, the start of online conference offerings. In 2010, at the ALA Midwinter Meeting, many ACRL section committees met virtually instead of in person.[14]

ALA and ACRL are making other changes to their policies, in response to recommendations from members and the reports of specific groups such as the ALA Task Force on Electronic Member Participation (TFOEMP). The draft document *Architecting Participation: New Ways of Convening @ ALA,* outlines ways in which members can participate and convene within the association without traveling. While the recommendations of TFOEMP specifically address the participation of board, committee, and task force members, the *Architecting* document approaches participation in a broader sense, addressing participation in conferences and other professional development and educational programs.[15] In this way, the association is concurrently addressing the sustainability of the association, concerns and needs of members, opportunities for professional development, and impact on the environment; changes being made impact sustainability in many senses of the word.

Future Considerations

Attendees suggested a number of future initiatives, via both the member opinion and conference evaluation surveys. Recurring suggestions include: eliminating the face-to-face conference; not printing a program book; requiring presenters to post supporting conference materials (e.g., handouts) online prior to the conference; purchasing carbon offsets for travel; providing attendees with the option to decline a conference bag and mug on the registration form; and encouraging vendors to offer fewer give-aways. Even more creative suggestions included offering a scholarship for people who use alternative transportation (e.g., bicycles) to get to the conference, and featuring green library stories.

---

13. ACRL Executive Committee, "ACRL Strategic Plan 2020."

14. Clara Fowler, "From the Desk of the Instruction Section Chair," *Instruction Section Newsletter* 26 (Fall 2009): 2.

15. "Re: E-Participation Update, Architecting Pariticipation: New Ways of Convening @ ALA," ALA Executive Board Document #2.13, January 4, 2010, http://connect.ala.org/files/4161/e_participation_doc_17311.doc (accessed February 1, 2010).

The large number of attendees who took time to comment on the member opinion survey and conference evaluation indicates strong interest and opinions regarding greening and sustainable initiatives. The three areas of the Committee's work are instructive for organizing further efforts: communicating with conference attendees to inform and influence behaviors; acting on-site by reducing, reusing and recycling materials as well as developing more sustainable contractual agreements; and committing to sustainability throughout the association.

There is great potential for involving conference attendees in sustainability efforts prior to an event, through surveys, online chat, discussion lists, and blog discussions. These communications may also serve as a means to recruit volunteers. In terms of reduction of resource consumption, many attendees indicated on the final conference evaluation that they would have preferred not to have received the conference bag, coffee mug, program, and *Footnotes*; others indicated they did not want to give up these items. Providing an "opt-out" option upon registration would allow ACRL to reduce initial purchasing of items. Most attendees indicated that they felt paper could be further reduced at the conference and that they could do without handouts if supplementary session documents were posted to the virtual conference site prior to the session. In order for this to effectively reduce paper use, an association-wide policy would need to require presenters to post materials online prior to their sessions. Committing to sustainability means that ACRL will need to take an active role in educating partner vendors and hotels about sustainable practices and members' opinions. For example, members indicated that they did not want paper mailings and that vendors should be encouraged to email information, and that they want recycling bins to be visible in hotel guest rooms.

Conclusion

While face-to-face communication is of fundamental importance in our professional lives, technological innovations in scholarly communication combined with the need to conserve diminishing environmental resources are driving professional associations and learned societies to invent a new model for the conference experience that is cost-effective in the near-term, and sustainable in the long-term. The work of the ACRL 14th National Conference Green Component Committee was a significant first step for ACRL toward designing sustainable conference practices, and toward working with conference partners in new ways. Asking ourselves, our professional colleagues, and our commercial partners questions about sustainable behaviors and practices led us to think further about the environmental impact of our actions and changes we can make to reduce that impact. These issues are very important to ACRL members, and critical for the larger society. We must build upon our success as we work to better manage our association's environmental impact, share best practices, and develop a new business model for sustainable conferences.

References

Association of College & Research Libraries. "Eco-friendly Hotel Practices." From ACRL 14th National Conference Website. http://www.acrl.org/ala/mgrps/divs/acrl/events/seattle/housing/Greenhotelpractices.cfm (accessed February 1, 2010).

Association of College & Research Libraries Executive Committee. "Charting Our Future: ACRL Strategic Plan 2020." Association of College & Research Libraries, May 13, 2009. http://www.ala.org/ala/mgrps/divs/acrl/about/whatisacrl/strategicplan/index.cfm.

Belanger, Jackie. *Saturday & Final Thoughts*. Blog post, March 15, 2009. From ACRL 2009 Virtual Conference Blog. http://www.learningtimes.net/acrlconference/category/conferenceblog/.

Fowler, Clara. "From the Desk of the Instruction Section Chair." *Instruction Section Newsletter* 26 (Fall 2009): 2. http://www.ala.org/ala/mgrps/divs/acrl/about/sections/is/projpubs/newsletter/2009fall.pdf.

"Go Green @ ACRL." *C&RL News* 70 (January 2009): C-2.

"The Greening of Seattle" *C&RL News* 69 (September 2008): 483.

Kerico, Juliet, and Karen Munro. "Six Steps to Greening your ACRL 14th National Conference Experience." *C&RL News* 70 (February 2009): 100–101. http://www.ala.org/ala/mgrps/divs/acrl/publications/crlnews/2009/feb/sixstepstogreen.cfm.

Munro, Karen. "Going Green." *C&RL News* 70 (June 2009): 331. http://www.ala.org/ala/mgrps/divs/acrl/publications/crlnews/2009/jun/confwrapup.cfm.

Munro, Karen, Charles Forrest, and Tory Ondrla. *Lessons Learned from the Seattle Green Conference*. ACRL OnPoint Chat Archive Transcript, April 29, 2009. From ACRL. http://www.ala.org/ala/mgrps/divs/acrl/events/onpoint/archives/2009-04-29.cfm.

"Re: E-Participation Update, Architecting Pariticipation: New Ways of Convening @ ALA." ALA Executive Board Document #2.13, January 4, 2010. http://connect.ala.org/files/4161/e_participation_doc_17311.doc (accessed February 1, 2010).

Shuyler, Kristen, and Dalia Corkrum. "Green Dining in the Emerald City." *C&RL News* 70 (February 2009): 99–103. http://www.ala.org/ala/mgrps/divs/acrl/publications/crlnews/2009/feb/greendining.cfm.

"Special Services—Room Sets & Custodial." Washington State Convention and Trade Center. http://www.wsctc.com/our_services/special_services.aspx (accessed February 1, 2010).

Walter, Scott, Juliet Kerico, and Karen Munro. *Greening Seattle*. ACRL Podcast, September 23, 2008; 5 min., 36 sec. From ACRL. MPEG, http://www.acrl.ala.org/acrlinsider/2008/09/23/acrl-podcast-greening-seattle/.

Ward, Sarah. *Sunny Seattle?* Blog post, March 12, 2009. From ACRL 2009 Virtual Conference Blog. http://www.learningtimes.net/acrlconference/category/conferenceblog/page/8/.

U.S. Congress. *Model Good Samaritan Food Donation Act*, Public Law 104-210, U.S. Statutes at Large 110 (1996): 3011–3012. http://frwebgate.access.gpo.gov/cgibin/getdoc.cgi?dbname=104_cong_public_laws&docid=f:publ210.104.

Zoellner, Kate, and Charles Forrest. "ACRL 2009 Green Component Planning Committee Conference Planning Report." Online report, July 27, 2009. From ACRL 14th National Conference Website. http://www.ala.org/ala/mgrps/divs/acrl/events/seattle/GreenCommReport07270.pdf.

Appendix A

"Harvest and Sustain" Call for Conference Proposals

Careful stewardship and cultivation of our cultural and financial resources are familiar territory for academic and research libraries. As the world around us changes at an ever-increasing pace, we are becoming more aware of the need to conserve our environmental resources as well. Sustainability—of our collections as well as of our buildings and work process—has become more important than ever. How do we ensure that future generations will have access to increasingly digitized and licensed collections? How do we make our collections accessible to the widest possible user group? How do we pursue these goals, and all the other work we do in our libraries, with an eye to lightening our environmental footprint, and preserving resources for the future? As we tend to our growing array of library services and resources, how can we use our experience and knowledge to plan for green and fruitful libraries well into the next century? Possible topics for this theme include, but are not limited to, the following:

- Projects addressing the environmental footprint of libraries
- LEED and libraries
- Sustainable library programs
- Greening the resource base: innovative fundraising and new partnerships
- Persistent metadata and sustainable access
- Preservation of materials and collections
- Electronic resource management: Will you still be there tomorrow?
- Acquiring and preserving out of print works
- Developing print on demand projects
- The effects of mass digitization projects
- Digital preservation in libraries
- Traditional preservation and conservation (physical)
- Ejournals and Eresources (including LOCKSS)

Appendix B

The Green Pledge

During the ACRL 14th National Conference in Seattle, I will endeavor to . . .

Learn: Educate myself about the environmental impact of conferences.

Inform: Share information about available green services and programs with colleagues.

Think: Make a sustainable mindset second nature.

Act: Put sustainable ideas into practice. Suggested activities: Take public or shared transportation to and from the airport. Walk or use public transportation in Seattle. Consult the ACRL interactive conference map for local and green restaurants and businesses to patronize. Consult the ACRL conference program to learn which vendors provide sustainable services and practices, and visit them in the exhibit hall.

Reduce: Use digital copies of handouts and presentation materials whenever possible. Turn off lights and unplug personal electronics when I'm not using them in my hotel room. Take shorter showers.

Reuse: Use my ACRL or other reusable mug for coffee, water and other beverages. Participate in my hotel's towel and linen reuse program if available.

Recycle: All paper materials that I don't take home from the conference, as well as food and other containers whenever possible.

Appendix C

Conference Evaluation Questions Related to the Committee's Efforts

- "Rate the value of each featured presentation that you attended" listed "Invited Green Speaker—Robin Chase"
- "Rate the following aspects of the conference experience" listed "Green Conference initiatives"
- "The 14th National Conference sought to implement sustainable 'green' practices, raise conference attendees' awareness, and suggest ways in which individuals could reduce their personal footprint. Were you aware of this initiative?" "If so, how did you hear about it?" Options: American Libraries, C&RL News, Colleagues, Conference program book, Conference registration confirmation, Conference website, Conference wiki, Discussion list, Footnotes, Green booth, Signage, Other (please specify)
- "Please rate the importance of the following activities in reducing the environmental impact of the conference." Items included: Donating or composting food waste from catered events. Encouraging attendees to eat locally and support sustainable businesses in Seattle. Encouraging attendees to reduce their energy consumption in conference hotels by limiting the frequency of laundering linens and the length of their showers. Encouraging vendors to highlight their sustainable business practices. Providing a reusable coffee mug. Providing ways for attendees to recycle paper handouts. Reducing the number of paper handouts by substituting digital copies. Using recycled or reusable materials in conference setup and signage.
- "Describe any changes you made at the conference to reduce your environmental footprint."
- Comments about the sustainability of the conference were also found in response to the following open-response evaluation questions:
  - "Do you have any suggestions to improve the ACRL National Conference? If so, list below."
  - "If you would like to provide a positive quote about your ACRL conference experience that may appear in promotional materials for the next conference, please use space below."
  - "Please share any additional comments you have about the ACRL 14th National Conference."

Green Librarians Blogging

Beth Filar Williams

Today there is an abundant number of web-enabled applications built from user-generated or user-manipulated content called Web 2.0 tools.[1] This Web 2.0 era has created an online, engaged community of users who are globally sharing, connecting, collaborating, and communicating. Information can be pushed out to the online community and pulled in by individuals through any number of tools—immediately. These systems for disseminating and receiving information are evolving into quick but key methods for global conversations.

Many librarians have been using Web 2.0 tools such as blogging, wikis, Facebook, or Twitter, for several years to connect with their users and colleagues.[2] More and more green library blogs are popping up (see an ongoing list on my own blog).[3] Why wouldn't patrons find a green-related library blog exciting to read if it includes local and global news items, reviews green resources in the library collection, spotlights a "green patron of the week," highlights ways the library is going green (and possibly saving its taxpayers money!), promotes local green events and resources, and offers tips and ideas on going green?

Blogging allows anyone, anywhere, the opportunity to post their opinions, share ideas, and converse with others on a specific topic.[4] Blog posts can be short bursts of information, news or resources, opinions and commentary, or long research-intensive articles. Users can subscribe to the blog's RSS feeds and get various blog syndications through a tool of their choice such as Google Reader. Bloggers can also use free tools to push their blog content into Twitter, Facebook, websites, nings or other tools. Blogs are easy to use and free to set up. Often small libraries use blogs for their websites, departments or committees create blogs to share group info, and any librarian can start a blog on any topic—especially useful in large organizations where individuals have limited access to edit their websites. For a committee, a blog can help disseminate information on what you have accomplished or projects in process and to gather ideas or comments from your readers and allow everyone on the committee to participate by creating their own posts. Blog RSS feeds can be pushed into such places as a sidebar on your library website or a portal of subject-specific resources. Video, audio, or other presentation files (such as ones from a green library event) can easily be embedded in the blog post to allow better dissemination of information in a multimedia format. Greg Schwartz offers some simply stated comments in his WebJunction article on what blogs are and why librarians should consider reading and blogging.[5] He mentions some key points: a blog keeps you writing, can really be an advocacy tool which builds a community, and gives voice to individuals to express their uniqueness.

In light of expressing uniqueness in librarianship, I started a blog a few years ago: *Going Green @ your library* (http://greeningyourlibrary.wordpress.com). At this time, January 2008, there were no published green/sustainable library blogs. I began by suggesting to the American Library Association that they start promoting green library ideas through their website or newsletters, as they are the leading library organization. A year later, they did start their own green blog but they were not ready to jump in at that time.

I have always been an environmental-minded, nature-centered, person. I was happily raised by parents who taught me to respect the natural world and live in balance with the environment, not try to dominate it—that the concepts of an environmentalist should be commonplace in every living person. My educator parents showed me first hand that "saving the earth" is not so much the agenda, but limiting the impact humans have on the earth, trying to be part of the solution than the problem, and educating others through modeling behaviors or disseminating information.

I longed to alleviate ignorance surrounding this topic and promote the amazing happenings and ideas in and outside the library world, yet I hesitated to jump in and start blogging. Why? I am no expert in environmentalism, don't have a degree in that general area, am not a writer, and never aspired to be a blogger.

I contacted a few well-known library bloggers I follow—especially those who might offer "green library" posts every so often—to ask about best practices for blogging. With their encouragement, I took the leap on New Year's Day 2008, and started my blog:

Happy New Year 2008 . . . a year to start Going Green?
January 3, 2008

Filed under: Uncategorized—filarwilliams @ 7:01 pm
Tags: environmental, green, greening, greenpractices, libraries, library

>*Welcome to a new blog—Going Green @ Your Library! My goal for this blog is to create short posts with links to "green" ideas, practices, tools, resources, companies, and techniques to help libraries and librarians become more environmentally friendly. Some ideas can even save or raise money for the library. I'd love to hear any comments and ideas you might have to share.[6]*

One reason I decided to start blogging was personal—to create a place where I could store these intriguing green ideas or events. I wanted something that was easily searchable, so I could find what I needed, when I needed it. I had many links saved in my Delicious bookmarks[7] from the green, sustainable blogs I follow, but often times just a link, even with a description in Delicious, did not allow me to fully annotate or embed other links, images, or videos within that one concept. Blogging allows me to tag posts with numerous keywords and concepts, organize posts into categories, embed a video or images, and include extra pages for lists of resources. By choosing a blog to store and organize these concepts, others can more easily follow it online or through RSS feeds. Hence my beliefs in educating others are also met, and allow people to follow my blog by their choosing, rather than my pushing ideas on them directly. Through blogging, I can take non-library ideas or concepts and bring them to the attention of librarians. I can also share with the greater library audience amazing green happenings and idea in libraries worldwide.

My blog tends to be an aggregator of information more than personal vignettes on green and sustainable libraries. I subscribe to many green-themed blogs or follow these types of folks on Twitter, and find it beneficial for discovering ideas. Outside the library arena there is a plethora of green, sustainable focused blogs. A Google advanced blog search with "green" in the blog title returns almost 4 million hits. These are very useful resources, not only to gain ideas that could be applied to a library setting, but also for education and news on this growing sector in our society. Discovering news about possible grants for green building of public facilities in your community when your library is considering a remodel; reading a news interview of a renewable energy expert in your own community whom your library could bring in for its eco-lecture and discussion series; or learning how to more efficiently manage your energy cost thus saving the library thousands of dollars—all these are worth the time to stay informed outside the library world. Finding out what is happening in the green arena will not only provide important knowledge and insights but disseminating this information to patrons in your community can only be beneficial: knowledge = power and sometimes green saves green.

Soon after I began blogging other green library blogs appeared such as The Green Library blog (http://thegreenlibraryblog.blogspot.com/) and the Alliance Library System's Going Green blog (http://alsgoesgreen.wordpress.com/). Sadly in the past few years many of these have gone defunct. When I inquired of various green librarian bloggers about reasons for lack of blogging, several responses were either "lack of time" or that the institution closed (in the case of Alliance Library System). Someone inspired by an idea, from attending a workshop or participating in a class or school might create a blog with good intentions, but keeping up the blog on a regular basis can be a struggle. Most bloggers who keep at it for two-and-a-half years or more tend to continue blogging.

This typical problem of blogging—finding the time to maintain it with useful information—is one I struggle with myself. I have gone over a month without a blog post at times when work and life got especially busy. My blog—its focus being more an aggregator of information than personal opinion—could lend itself to quick posts highlighting key events, ideas or information tidbits. But adding more useful information to it than simply a cut and paste requires researching the item in more depth, determining the authority, possibly finding a review or press release on the item, summarizing the key points and even contacting a person if necessary to verify or follow up. The extra effort is worth the time, as it gives readers a more in-depth human touch to the post, making it appear more "real."

My posts range from ideas or news from a variety of libraries such as a green teen program at a public library to sustainability issues at academic libraries. I frequently receive emails from commercial entities wanting me to highlight their product or service. Many times the products they suggest aren't really related to a library at all. Even if they are, I hesitate to promote a product I don't use. If I can find a library using it and advocating for the product or service, more likely I will add it to my blog. I also get suggestions from other librarians which I often post, giving them credit when due. My blog topics include posts on upcoming events, opportunities, news items, resources, ideas and highlighting green libraries. Sometimes I can post in 15 minutes; other posts require an hour or research before posting. Finding a chunk of open time, I can create a few posts and then schedule them to publish at another time. Sticking to a schedule is often the best way to stay engaged in blogging whether you set it in your to-do list each week, schedule it in your calendar, or make it a goal. Having an Agraphia Group at my library is a motivator to blog regularly—tenure-track librarians meet every two weeks to revisit our previous writing goals for those weeks pasts, and set new ones, holding each other accountable for what we say we will do. Nonetheless, it's a constant struggle to maintain a blog for many people, but if a blog isn't updated regularly, readers will disappear as well.

Blogs are key tools in the social web scene, promoting themselves as natural discussion boards on a posted topic. The nature of my blog as an aggregator of information does not appear to lend itself to discussion as much I had hoped. Over the past few years, I have received only a few "comments," which is usually the benefit of blogging—readers can comment on your posts and others' comments. I generally only know my readership via blog statistics and through personal communication. Other blogs have a much larger readership and comments and discussions; for example the American Library Association (ALA) offers a Green Your Library blog through the *American Libraries* magazine online.[8] This blog was created in January 2010 with their first-year blogger Laura Bruzas, a PR writer often writing about green and healthy living topics. ALA, with tremendous membership and hence readership, is a perfect venue to promote the ideas of green libraries. Posts often have numerous comments, dialogue and suggestions from its readers. Guest bloggers, such as myself, were included a few times as well to offer other perspectives from libraries in the field. Unfortunately, Laura stepped down as blogger after one year and was not replaced by ALA. Though the organization sporadically will offer useful posts, there have only been five of them in the ten months since.

Another active, useful green library blog started in January 2010 is called *Sustainable Libraries* by Librarian Rebekkah Smith Aldrich—Coordinator for Library Growth & Sustainability at the Mid-Hudson Library System, certified Sustainable Building Advisor (NaSBA), and Leadership in Energy & Environmental Design Accredited Professional (LEED AP). Rebekkah's credentials show her expertise in this area and she has offered a number of useful posts, sometimes highlighting her own articles or presentations but often ideas, suggestions, highlighting of other libraries green practices and lots of useful information. Like my blog, Rebekkah's disseminates lots of information but doesn't often have many comments or discussion from readers. She was active with numerous posts in 2010 but only about one a month in 2011—yet still a blog and a green librarian to keep up with! When I asked Aldrich why the cut back in blogging she said "I get more bang for my buck through my Facebook page http://www.facebook.com/ SustainableLibraries . . . far more interaction with people and can get more info up more quickly. My blog posts automatically feed to my Facebook page so that the audience just sees it as supplemental to the other posts." So some green librarians find better avenues to reach their audience and can integrate various Web 2.0 tools to be more efficient.[9]

Library blogging grew tremendously from about 2004 to 2009, with about 237–265 blogs created between these years, according to Walt Crawford's *Cites & Insights* publication. Thus it appears that once blogging was well established in library world in the mid-2000s, non-typical bloggers such as green-minded librarians, ventured down this avenue. From Crawford's analysis of library blogs' longevity by months from 2007–2010: "The average and median are surprisingly close in this case: 39.2 months on average, 36 months as the median." Crawford almost evenly grouped the blogs according to longevity showing that blogs which have been around the longest (5 years to 11 years), tend to stay fairly active with only 7% moribund, with the second longest blogs in existence (4–5 years) are about half or 11% moribund; the third group (2.5–3.5 years) with about one-six moving to extinction, or 16%; group four (1+ to 2.5 years) are 28% moribund; and the lowest blog group (1 month to 1+ year) where more than half or 48% are moribund. As Crawford summarizes, "Blogs tend to die young."[10] This data can be a similar trend for green and sustainable library blogs—motivated at first, but blogging dwindles over time.

Blogging has also become an adult pastime rather than one for youth and teens who probably prefer using a mobile device for sending and receiving quick, short bits of information than reading or writing long blog posts. Two recent Pew Internet Project surveys indicate a decline in teens blogging—with a rise in adults over 30 years of age blogging—as teens are more apt to visit social networking sites (73% in 2009) over adults (40% only in 2009).[11] With wireless connectively rising in youth age group, "We often look to younger generations to see where technology use might be headed in the future," lead author Amanda Lenhart noted. "People under 30 have often been in the vanguard of internet and cell-phone use, and it will be interesting to see how much of their enthusiasm for new gadgets is a time-of-life issue, and how much will ripple through the broader culture in the coming years."[12] Keep this in mind when thinking about your audience for your blog. Are the youth in your community interested in green and sustainable activities? Perhaps a blog is not the best way to reach them on this topic. But adults might be keen on the idea of a green-themed blog.

Though most individual librarians' blogging about green and sustainable practices are low, many more actual libraries are green blogging for their library patrons or community. Burbank Public Library has a very active blog, started in January 2008, with a frequent variety of posts aimed at "everything green in Burbank, CA."[13] The Schaumburg (IL) Public Library's *Come to the Green Side*, matches Burbank's in longevity, frequency of posts, and audience.[14] The Calgary Public Library is another great example of an active, current, useful blog but with a team of eco-bloggers—a fabulous idea to keep a blog effective and active.[15] Unfortunately, though, many library green-themed blogs are becoming defunct but perhaps that's a sign that we citizens don't need a specific blog on green practices anymore because the ideas are so integrated into our lifestyles and communities that being green is not a new concept. Well . . . maybe not, but I can dream!

Endnotes

1. Peltier-Davis, Cheryl, "Web 2.0, Library 2.0, Library User 2.0, Librarian 2.0: Innovative Services for Sustainable Libraries." *Computers in Libraries* 29, no. 10 (2009): 16–21. From Library Lit & Info Full Text, Wilson-Web. (accessed December 9, 2009).

2. Lietzau, Zeth, "U.S. Public Libraries and Web 2.0: What's Really Happening?" *Computers in Libraries* 29, no. 9 (2009): 6–10. From Academic Search Premier, EBSCO (accessed December 8, 2009).

3. Filar Williams, Beth, "Other green Library Pages," Going Green @ your library (blog), October 18, 2011 (1:17pm), (accessed October 15, 2011). http://greeningyourlibrary.wordpress.com/green-library-committees-blogs-and-more/.

4. Draper, Lani, & Turnage, Marthea. "Blogmania: Blog Use in Academic Libraries." *Internet Reference Services Quarterly* 13, no. 1 (2008): 15–55. From Library Lit & Info Full Text, WilsonWeb. (accessed December 9, 2009).

5. Schwartz, Greg, "Blogs for Libraries." WebJunction Idaho OCLC. October 8, 2007. Updated May 2010, (accessed 10/24/11). http://id.webjunction.org/technology/web-tools/-/articles/content/430713.

6. Filar Williams, Beth, "Happy New year 2008 . . . a year to start going green?," Going Green @ your library (blog), October 16, 2011 (8:39 a.m.) (accessed October 15, 2011). http://greeningyourlibrary.wordpress.com/2008/01/03/happy-new-year-2008-a-year-to-start-going-green/.

7. Filar Williams, Beth. Delicious.com. filarwilliams "Greenyourlibray" tag. (accessed 10/15/11). http://www.delicious.com/filarwilliams/greeningyourlibrary.

8. "Green Your Library." *American Libraries* Magazine. http://americanlibrariesmagazine.org/green-your-library (accessed 10/18/11).

9. Aldrich, Rebekkah Smith. "Re: green & sustainable library blogging." Message to Beth Filar Williams. October 17 2011. E-mail.
10. Crawford, Walt. *Cites & Insights: Crawford at Large* 11, no. 1 (2011): 9–18. http://citesandinsights.info/civ11i1.pdf.
11. Lenhart, Amanda, Purcell, Kristen, Smith, Aaron, & Zickuhr, Kathryn. Report Teens, Social Networking, Mobile, Generations, Blogs, Web 2.0: Social Media and Young Adults, Pew Internet & American Life Project, February 3, 2010. (accessed 10/24/2011). http://www.pewinternet.org/Reports/2010/Social-Media-and-Young-Adults.aspx.
12. Ibid.
13. Burbank Public Library. "Green Pages." (accessed 10/18/11). http://burbankgreenpages.blogspot.com/.
14. Schaumburg Public Library. "Come to the GREEN side blog." (accessed 10/18/11). http://schaumburglibrarygreenside.wordpress.com/.
15. Calgary Public Library. "Eco Action." (accessed 10/18/11). http://blog.calgarypubliclibrary.com/blogs/eco_action/default.aspx.

Resources for Greening Libraries

Laura L. Barnes

Green has become an extremely popular color in the past several years. Companies, from multinational corporations like Wal-Mart and Clorox to local businesses like dry cleaners, are clamoring to show consumers how concerned they are about the environment. I knew that environmentalism had moved from the fringes to the mainstream when I saw *Sustainable Living for Dummies* in my local bookstore as part of a huge display of green lifestyle books several years ago. So where do libraries fit into this new green culture? The good news is that the library's core services are already eco-friendly because they encourage people to borrow rather than buy materials. That's an excellent place to start.

Albert Einstein once said, "Setting an example is not the main means of influencing others; it is the only means." Libraries are trusted information sources for their communities and are in an excellent position to lead community sustainability efforts by holding green programs and modeling sustainable behavior. This annotated bibliography is intended as a starting point for librarians who want to bring some green to their library operations. It also includes links to case studies and resources to help libraries develop environmental programming for their communities.

General Sustainability

Bardeline, Jonathan. "The Zero-Waste Office: Is It Possible?" GreenBiz.com, April 10, 2008, http://www.greenbiz.com/ feature/2008/04/10/the-zero-waste-office-is-it-possible (accessed October 24, 2011).

Discusses the concept of zero waste and applies it to office settings.

Carlson, Kim. *Green Your Work: Boost Your Bottom Line While Reducing Your Carbon Footprint.* Avon, MA: Adams Business, 2009.

Targeted at businesses, although most information is applicable to any organization. Particularly helpful is the chapter on pitfalls to avoid when implementing a sustainability program.

City of Portland, Office of Sustainable Development. *Green Office Guide: A Guide to Greening Your Bottom Line through a Resource-Efficient Office Environment.* Portland, OR: City of Portland, Office of Sustainable Development, 2001. http://www.oregon.gov/ENERGY/CONS/BUS/docs/ Green_Office_Guide.pdf (accessed October 24, 2011).

A good beginner's guide to making offices more environmentally friendly, although the resource list is fairly specific to Oregon. Because of the age of the guide, phone numbers, websites, and e-mail addresses may be outdated.

Gale, Sarah Fister. "Taking Green Initiatives to the Next Level." GreenBiz. com, September 2, 2008, http://www.greenbiz.com/feature/2008/09/02/ taking-green-initiatives-next-level (accessed October 24, 2011).

Uses Interface Carpets, Enterprise Car Rental, and PB Copy to show how these companies go beyond implementing a few eco-friendly ideas by changing their corporate culture and transforming into sustainable organizations.

Illinois Green Government Coordinating Council. *Sustainability Planning Guide for Illinois State Agencies.* Springfield, IL: Illinois Green Government Coordinating Council, 2007. http://www.standingupforillinois.org/ uploads/Guide.pdf (accessed October 24, 2011).

Created to help state executive agencies identify and evaluate their environmental impacts in a systematic manner. Also provides a roadmap to assist them in identifying priorities for improving their sustainability efforts and meeting the requirements of the Green Governments Illinois Act. Although written for Illinois government agencies, the information is general enough to be useful for any library.

———. *Sustainability Plan Template for Illinois State Agencies.* Springfield, IL: Illinois Green Government Coordinating Council, 2007. http://www.standingupforillinois.org/uploads/Template.pdf (accessed October 24, 2011).

Companion to the above sustainability planning guide. Designed to give agencies a defined framework for creating a sustainability plan that complies with the Green Governments Illinois Act. As with the planning guide, the template is general enough to be useful for libraries anywhere.

Kansas Green Team, http://www.kansasgreenteams.org/ (accessed October 24, 2011).

Developed to help Kansas government agencies operate more sustainably. Includes information for schools, businesses, organizations, and government agencies. Although the focus is Kansas, there is a wealth of general information here for any organization.

Hitchcock, Darcy; Willard, Marsha. *The Step-by-step Guide to Sustainability Planning: How to Create and Implement Sustainability Plans in any Business or Organization.* London; Sterling, VA: Earthscan, 2008.

Detailed guide to creating a sustainability plan and sustainability report. Each chapter contains background reading, tips, case studies, and worksheets to help with the process. While targeted at businesses, library administrators should also be able to apply the information to their operations.

Natural Resources Defense Council. "NRDC Greening Advisor." Natural Resources Defense Council, http://www.nrdc.org/enterprise/greeningadvisor/ (accessed October 24, 2011).

Includes information on green business principles and policies, energy and water efficiency, waste management, and green purchasing. An excellent overview for businesses and organizations that will also be helpful for libraries.

RePaper Project, The. *Recovering & Rediscovering a Resource: Recovered Office Paper Guide*. Asheville, NC: Environmental Paper Network, [2009?]. http://www.environmentalpaper.org/repaper-docs/finalrecoffpapguide.pdf (accessed October 24, 2011).

This how-to guide not only compiles the basic steps of setting up a successful paper recycling program but also covers other topics that today's office and building managers encounter, while explaining how organizations fit into the overall system of recycled paper manufacturing.

Xerox. "Xerox Sustainability Calculator." Xerox, http://www.consulting.xerox.com/flash/thoughtleaders/suscalc/ xeroxCalc.html (accessed October 24, 2011).

Tool to help organizations determine the energy, greenhouse gas, and solid waste impact of their office printing operations based on current operations and optimized scenarios.

Zero Waste Alliance, http://www.zerowaste.org/ (accessed October 24, 2011).

The Zero Waste Alliance promotes the use of zero waste strategies. Their website includes information on the case for zero waste, an outline of their approach, and links to publications and resources.

Library Sustainability

Antonelli, Monika. 2008. "The Green Library Movement: An Overview and Beyond." *Electronic Green Journal* 1,(27): Article 1, http://repositories.cdlib.org/uclalib/egj/vol1/iss27/art1 (accessed October 24, 2011).

Review article covering history and current state of the art in green library buildings, programming, and associations. Includes an extensive bibliography.

Barnes, Laura L. 2011. Green Libraries LibGuide, Champaign, IL: University of Illinois Library, http://uiuc.libguides.com/green-libraries (accessed October 24, 2011).

An annotated guide to sustainability resources relevant to libraries and librarians. Continuously updated.

Bennett, Connie J. 2007. "Institutionalizing Sustainability: An Emerging Trend," *OLA Quarterly* 13, (4): 2–6.

Describes city-wide efforts to institutionalize sustainability in Eugene, OR through public policy initiatives. Also details the library's contribution to the effort.

Filar Williams, Beth. Going Green @your library blog, http://greeningyourlibrary.wordpress.com (accessed October 24, 2011).

The blog's tagline is "environmentally friendly practices for libraries and beyond." Posts cover everything from solar powered e-book readers to green buildings.

Harger, Elaine. 2008. "Global Warming and Us: Assessing Our Environmental and Professional Responsibility." *American Libraries* 39,(4): 35.

An essay contemplating the author's individual carbon footprint, along with some suggestions for things librarians can do to encourage their patrons to consider their individual impacts.

Indianhead Federated Library System. "Eco-Friendly Libraries." Indianhead Federated Library System, http://www.iflsweb.org/ContinuingEd/EcoFriendlyLibraries/tabid/632/Default.aspx (accessed October 24, 2011).

Links to handouts for a green libraries program sponsored by Indianhead Federated Library System in Eau Claire, WI. Handout topics include environmental programming ideas, resources, mindful practices, and the Natural Step framework.

Meyer, Jennifer. 2008. "Global Warming's Library Challenge," *Library Journal*, 133,(18): 26–9, http://www.libraryjournal.com/article/CA6606477.html (accessed October 24, 2011).

Discusses the impact of climate change on the environment, how it affects libraries, and what librarians can do about it. Includes an extensive resource list and bibliography.

Miller, Katheryn. *Public Libraries Going Green*. Chicago, IL: American Library Association, 2010.

Includes information about greening facilities, routine library operations (collection development, ILL, weeding, etc.), and programming, but does not go into great detail about any of them. An extended bibliographic essay, rather than a reference volume, with good lists of resources.

Mulford, Sam McBane. *How Green is My Library?* Santa Barbara, CA: Libraries Unlimited, 2010.

This book is aimed at "novice to intermediate ecological sophisticates" to help them improve the sustainability of their libraries. Mulford (a planner) and Himmel (a librarian) both have experience with greening library buildings. Includes checklists, lists of definitions and resources, sample project forms, and a model planning and facilitation process. Excellent resource for libraries that are beginning to green their facilities.

Norton, Judith. 2007. "A How-to: Conduct an Environmental Audit in Your Library." *OLA Quarterly* 13,(4): 9–11.

Provides a nice overview of environmental audits and a worksheet for conducting them in libraries.

Oregon Library Association. *Going Green: Libraries and Sustainability*. La Grande, OR: Oregon Library Association, 2007, http://data.memberclicks.com/site/ola/olaq_13no4.pdf (accessed October 24, 2011).

The Winter 2007 issue of *OLA Quarterly* focused on libraries and sustainability. Article topics (many cited elsewhere in this list) included green building, recycling media, and a sustainability reading list.

Reed, Lori. 2008. "Going Green: The Un-Handout and Handout Alternatives." Library Trainer blog, posted 6/3/08, http://lorireed.com/going-green-the-un-handout-and-handout-alternatives/ (accessed October 24, 2011).

Post discusses reasons for not providing printed handouts at presentations and offers alternatives to keep people's minds engaged.

Urbanska, Wanda. 2009. "A Greener Library, A Greener You." *American Libraries* 40,(4): 52–5.

Gives a good overview of things that libraries are doing to go green, from green building to eco-activism.

Case Studies

Christo, Steve. "What's Red on the Outside and Green on the Inside?" Presented at the West Virginia Library Association Conference, White Sulphur Springs, WV, December 2008, http://www.wvla.org/conference/2008/postcon/presentations/green.pdf (accessed October 24, 2011).

Cabell County Public Library built a new branch that incorporated many energy-saving and eco-friendly features. This presentation describes the green features of the new building, which includes a rainwater recycling system.

Dempsey, Mary and Erin Lavin Cabonargi. "The Chicago Experience, Making Green Routine." Presented at the 2007 Library Journal Design Institute, http://www.pbcchicago.com/pdf/green_routine.pdf (accessed October 24, 2011).

Outlines the City of Chicago's efforts to conform to LEED standards when building new city facilities.

Griebel, Rosemary. "Calgary Public Library Eco-Action." ImagineCalgary, http://www.imaginecalgary.ca/library/Libary_collective_action_imagineCALGARY.pdf (accessed October 24, 2011).

Presentation details the Calgary Public Library's green efforts and how they relate to those of imagineCalgary, a community-wide sustainability effort in Calgary, Alberta.

LeBer, Jeanne Mariel; Gregory, Joan M. 2004. "Becoming Green and Sustainable: A Spencer S. Eccles Health Sciences Library Case Study." *Journal of the Medical Library Association* 92(2), 266–268, http://www.ncbi.nlm.nih.gov/pmc/articles/PMC385309/ (accessed October 24, 2011).

Article details the sustainability efforts of the Spencer S. Eccles Health Sciences Library at the University of Utah. Includes a discussion of actions taken and barriers encountered during their ongoing process of going green.

WebJunction Ohio. "Green Libraries." WebJunction Ohio,
http://oh.webjunction.org/grlibs (accessed October 24, 2011).

Links to case studies of sustainability efforts in Ohio libraries.

Long, Sarah. 2006. "Skokie Library Goes Green for Remodeling." Library
Beat, http://www.librarybeat.org/read/show/273 (accessed October 24,
2011).

Column detailing the green features of the remodeled Skokie Public Library, including a green roof.

Collection Development

Clark, George E. 2007. "Bytes of Note—Environment on Film." *Environment*, September 2007, http://www.environmentmagazine.org/Archives/
Back%20Issues/September%202007/Bytes-s07.html (accessed October
24, 2011).

Bibliographic essay on web resources for identifying and locating films with
environmental themes.

Eagan, Robert. 2008. "Sense & Sustainability." *Library Journal*, 133,(2): 40–3,
http://www.libraryjournal.com/article/
CA6523447.html?q=energy+conservation (accessed October 24, 2011).

Annotated bibliography of sustainability titles recommended for public and
academic library collections. Includes suggestions for criteria to use when
weeding older materials in this subject area.

Engberg, Gillian. 2009. "Top 10 Books for Youth on the Environment." *Booklist*, 105,(12): 92, http://www.booklistonline.com/
default.aspx?page=show_product&pid=3298051 (accessed October 24,
2011).

Annotated list of the top ten environmental books for youth reviewed in
Booklist in 2008. Appears in the February 15 issue each year. Includes both
fiction and non-fiction.

Lake County Library System. "Going Green @ My Library." Lake County
Library System, http://www.lakeline.lib.fl.us/going_green.aspx (accessed
October 24, 2011).

Pathfinder for Lake County, FL library patrons about green lifestyle materials available in the library's collection. Good selection of books on various environmental topics, although it lacks some newer titles.

Mother Nature Network. "Top 10 Environmental Books of 2009." Mother Nature Network, http://www.mnn.com/lifestyle/books/photos/top-10-environmental-books-of-2009 (accessed October 24, 2011).

Annotated list of Mother Nature Network's picks for the best environmental books of 2009. MNN's Books News section (http://www.mnn.com/news/lifestyle/books) is an excellent resource for reviews and information about current books with sustainability themes.

Newton Marasco Foundation. "The Green Earth Book Award." Newton Marasco Foundation, http://www.newtonmarascofoundation.org/programs/a_ge.cfm (accessed October 24, 2011).

Annual award given to books that inspire young readers to appreciate and care for the environment. Awards are given in January of each year. Categories include picture book, children's fiction, young adult fiction, and non-fiction. Includes lists of current and past winners.

Seaman, Donna. 2009. "Top 10 Books on the Environment." *Booklist*, 105,(12): 25, http://www.booklistonline.com/default.aspx?page=show_product&pid=3297823 (accessed October 24, 2011).

Annotated list of the top ten environmental books reviewed in *Booklist* in 2008. Appears in the February 15 issue each year.

Society of Environmental Journalists. "Society of Environmental Journalists Books page." Society of Environmental Journalists, http://www.sej.org/library/books/overview (accessed October 24, 2011).

Includes links to books recommended or authored by SEJ members.

Crafts with Old Books and Other Recyclables

Campbell, June. "The Altered Book: A Cyber Home for the Altered Book Artist." Altered-Book.com, http://www.altered-book.com/ (accessed October 24, 2011).

Created by June Campbell, an altered book artist. Includes an FAQ, instructions for making different types of altered book projects, and extensive book and supply lists.

CanadianLiving.com. "Make a Recycled Book Lamp." CanadianLiving.com, http://www.canadianliving.com/crafts/home_and_garden/ make_a_recycled_book_lamp.php (accessed October 24, 2011).

Step-by-step instructions for making a desk lamp from recycled books and a lamp kit or recycled lamp parts.

CreativityPortal.com. "Getting Started with Altered Books and Other Altered Art.", CreativityPortal.com, http://www.creativity-portal.com/howto/ artscrafts/altered.books.html (accessed October 24, 2011).

Links to specific projects and general resources for making crafts out of old books.

Instructables.com. "Green Crafts." Instructables.com, http://www.instructables.com/tag/type-id/category-green/category-craft/ (accessed October 24, 2011).

A treasure trove of environmental craft ideas.

Hatzigeorgiou, Karen J. "Altered Books Gallery." Karenswhimsy.com, http://karenswhimsy.com/altered-books/ (accessed October 24, 2011).

Photos and descriptions of altered book art projects created by artist Karen J. Hatzigeorgiou.

Phillips, Caitlin. "Recycled Hardcover Book Purse", HGTV.com, http://www.hgtv.com/crafting/recycled-hardcover-book-purse/index.html (accessed October 24, 2011).

Detailed instructions for making a purse out of an old hardcover book.

StudentHacks.org. "10 Creative Ways to Recycle Old Books." StudentHacks. org, http://studenthacks.org/2008/06/11/old-book-hacks/ (accessed October 24, 2011).

Links to ten ideas for turning old books into something new and useful.

Electronics

Electronics TakeBack Coalition, http://www.computertakeback.com/ (accessed October 24, 2011).

The Electronics TakeBack Coalition (ETBC) promotes green design and responsible recycling in the electronics industry. Their electronics recycling guide (http://www.electronicstakeback.com/recycling/find_a_responsible_recycler.htm) is an excellent resource for ensuring that your library disposes of its old electronics responsibly.

EPEAT, http://www.epeat.net/ (accessed October 24, 2011).

EPEAT helps purchasers evaluate, compare and select electronic products based on their environmental attributes. Includes resources for specifying greener computers when purchasing new systems.

Federal Electronics Challenge, http://www.federalelectronicschallenge.net (accessed October 24, 2011).

The Federal Electronics Challenge (FEC) is a partnership program that encourages federal facilities and agencies to purchase greener electronics, reduce the impacts of electronic products during use, and manage obsolete electronics responsibly. Managed by the U.S. Environmental Protection Agency and the Office of Federal Environmental Executive. Includes an extensive list of resources for buying, operating, and disposing of electronics while keeping the environment in mind.

Greenpeace. *Guide to Greener Electronics.* N.p. : Greenpeace, last updated October 2010 . http://www.greenpeace.org/international/en/campaigns/toxics/electronics/Guide-to-Greener-Electronics/ (accessed October 24, 2011).

Greenpeace releases this quarterly guide that ranks electronics manufacturers based on specific environmental criteria. Links to previous editions of the guide are provided at http://www.greenpeace.org/international/campaigns/toxics/electronics/how-the-companies-line-up.

Naditz, Alan. 2008. "Green IT 101: Technology Helps Businesses and Colleges Become Enviro-Friendly." *Sustainability: The Journal of Record* 1,(5): 315–18.

Discusses ways that organizations can make their IT departments greener.

TechSoup. "Reduce Your Environmental Impact and Save Money." Tech-Soup, http://www.techsoup.org/greentech/ (accessed October 24, 2011).

Portal for TechSoup's GreenTech initiative, which encourages non-profits to be more environmentally responsible about managing technology. Also includes a link to their Refurbished Computer Initiative (http://www.techsoup.org/greentech/getstuff/), where non-profits and libraries can buy low-cost, refurbished computer equipment.

Energy

American Council for an Energy-Efficient Economy. *Commercial Sector: Buildings and Equipment.* Washington, DC : American Council for an Energy-Efficiency Economy, http://aceee.org/sector/commercial (accessed October 24, 2011).

Portal to energy efficiency information for whole buildings and building equipment. Includes links to standards and related publications.

Dean, Edward M. *Daylighting Design in Libraries.* Cerritos, CA : Libris Design Project, 2004. http://www.librisdesign.org/docs/DaylightDesignLibs.pdf (accessed October 24, 2011).

Provides an overview of designing library buildings to take advantage of daylighting.

Dean, Edward. *Energy Management Strategies in Public Libraries.* Cerritos, CA : Libris Design Project, 2002.

Provides detailed information about energy use in public library buildings and offers suggestions for improving efficiency.

DoItYourself.com. "Buying Guide—Understanding Energy Efficient Ratings." DoItYourself.com, http://www.doityourself.com/stry/energyratings (accessed October 24, 2011).

This easy-to-read guide explains how appliances are rated for efficiency, what the ratings mean, and what to look for while shopping for new appliances. Useful for ready reference and for purchasing new appliances for employee break areas.

Energy Star, http://www.energystar.gov/ (accessed October 24, 2011).

Energy Star, a cooperative effort of the U.S. Department of Energy and the U.S. Environmental Protection Agency, is the federal government's energy efficiency portal. Includes a wealth of information on all aspects of energy efficiency, including statistics. Librarians will find *Bring Your Green to Work with ENERGY STAR* (http://www.energystar.gov/index.cfm?fuseaction=bygtw.showSplash) very helpful when trying to make their workplaces more energy efficient. Extensive list of resources includes printable tip cards and posters, green team basics, fast facts about building energy use and global warming, and an EnergyIQ quiz.

———. "Computer Power Management Savings Calculator." EnergyStar, http://www.energystar.gov/ia/products/power_mgt/LowCarbonITSavingsCalc.xls (accessed October 24, 2011).

Downloadable Excel spreadsheet that calculates energy and money saved by adjusting the power settings on your organization's computers.

N.C. Solar Center. "Database of State Incentives for Renewables and Efficiency (DSIRE)". N.C. Solar Center, N.C. State University, Department of Engineering, http://www.dsireusa.org/ (accessed October 24, 2011).

Comprehensive database of state, local, utility, and federal incentives and policies that promote renewable energy and energy efficiency. Established in 1995 and funded by the U.S. Department of Energy, DSIRE is an ongoing project of the N.C. Solar Center and the Interstate Renewable Energy Council. Excellent resource for locating funding for energy efficiency projects.

U.S. Department of Energy Office of Energy Efficiency & Renewable Energy. "Estimating Appliance and Home Electronic Energy Use." Washington, DC: U.S. Department of Energy, 2009. http://apps1.eere.energy.gov/consumer/your_home/appliances/index.cfm/mytopic=10040 (accessed October 24, 2011).

Provides a general formula for estimating energy consumption of appliances, along with a list of typical wattages for various appliances.

———. "Federal Energy Management Program." U.S. Department of Energy, http://www1.eere.energy.gov/femp/ (accessed October 24, 2011).

This program assists federal agencies with using energy wisely. Includes information on purchasing energy efficient products, deploying renewable energy technologies, identifying funding opportunities, and inventorying and managing greenhouse gases. Although federal agencies are the target audience, these resources will also be useful to library administrators.

Piotrowicz, Lynn and Scott Osgood. 2009. "Building Science 101: Save Money, Energy, and Resources by Getting a Better Understanding of How Your Building Works." *American Libraries* 40,(4): 56–8.

Introduction to how HVAC, thermostats, and ceiling fans work. Includes a checklist to ensure that all systems are properly set, which increases energy efficiency and saves money and resources.

Primary Research Group. *Library Energy Conservation Benchmarks*. New York, NY : Primary Research Group, 2009.

Results of a survey conducted by Primary Research Group about what libraries are doing to conserve energy.

Rusk, Todd. *Power and Energy Basics: Calculating Energy Use & Savings*. Champaign, IL : Illinois Sustainable Technology Center, 2009. http://www.istc.illinois.edu/main_sections/info_services/library_docs/TN/tn10-095.pdf (accessed October 24, 2011).

Provides basic information about power and energy, along with examples of simple electricity and natural gas calculations, which are useful when trying to calculate baseline energy use.

Thumann, Albert. *Handbook of Energy Audits*, 8th ed. Lilburn, GA; New York, NY: Fairmont Press; Marcel Dekker, c2010.

Guide to planning and carrying out an energy audit of any type of facility, including electrical, mechanical and building systems analysis. Includes forms, checklists and working aids.

Wood, Damon. *Lighting Upgrades: A Guide for Facility Managers*, 2nd ed. Lilburn, GA; New York, NY: Fairmont Press; Distributed by Marcel Dekker, c2004.

A step-by-step guide to upgrading lighting systems, either through retrofits or complete redesign. Discusses lighting quality, upgrade strategies, applications, technologies, economics, maintenance, project implementation, and methods for assessing specific opportunities.

Woodruff, Eric A. *Green Facilities Handbook: Simple and Profitable Strategies for Managers*. Lilburn, GA: Fairmont Press, 2009.

Includes information about all aspects of making green facilities decisions, including implementing solar projects. Although it is targeted at business owners, library administrators will also find this valuable.

Green Building

Antonelli, Monika. "Green Libraries: A Website for Information about Green and Sustainable Libraries." GreenLibraries.org, http://www.greenlibraries.org/ (accessed October 24, 2011).

Directory of green library building projects in the United States and Canada. Includes an extensive resource list.

Barack, Lauren. 2009. "Green Libraries Grow in SL." *School Library Journal*, 55,(1) (January): 12–3, http://www.schoollibraryjournal.com/article/CA6624892.html (accessed October 24, 2011).

Profile of the creators of the Sustainable Living Library in Second Life. The virtual library, located on SL's Emerald City, gives real-world librarians ideas for designing green library buildings.

Fialkoff, Francine . 2008. "Green Libraries Are Local," *Library Journal*, 133,(11): 8, http://www.libraryjournal.com/article/CA6566439.html (accessed October 24, 2011).

Discusses several recently built or renovated library buildings in the San Francisco (CA) Public Library System that incorporated green building principles during construction.

GE Lighting. "Frequently Asked Questions—Lamp Disposal, Recycling & Environmental." GE Lighting, http://www.gelighting.com/na/business_lighting/faqs/disposal.htm (accessed October 24, 2011).

A FAQ with information about recycling fluorescent lamps and ballasts. Includes links to information for home and business.

Kilgarlin Center for Preservation of the Cultural Record, School of Information, the University of Texas at Austin. *From Gray Areas to Green Areas: Developing Sustainable Practices in Preservation Environments Symposium Proceedings*. Austin, TX: The Kilgarlin Center for Preservation of the Cultural Record, School of Information, the University of Texas at Austin, 2009. http://www.ischool.utexas.edu/kilgarlin/gaga/proceedings.html (accessed October 24, 2011).

Proceedings of a conference held in 2007 and sponsored by the University of Texas School of Information. Papers examine all aspects of sustainable practices in cultural heritage preservation environments. The main focus is green building practices.

National Electrical Manufacturers Association. "LampRecycle.org.", National Electrical Manufacturers Association, http://www.lamprecycle.org/ (accessed October 24, 2011).

A one-stop information source about recycling lamps (the term used in the lighting industry to refer to all types of light bulbs). Includes a recycling directory, links to energy efficiency resources, and a guide to federal and state laws and regulations.

National Institute of Building Sciences. "Whole Building Design Guide: Libraries." National Institute of Building Sciences, http://www.wbdg.org/design/libraries.php (accessed October 24, 2011).

Excellent information on all aspects of building planning and design for public, academic, school, and special libraries. Includes links to relevant standards and resources. Lots of emphasis on sustainable building design.

Sands, Johanna. *Sustainable Library Design*. Cerritos, CA : Libris Design Project, 2004. http://www.librisdesign.org/docs/SustainableLibDesign.pdf (accessed October 24, 2011).

Discusses how to design library buildings to minimize their environmental impact.

SF Environment. *Energy Efficient, Low-Mercury Lighting for Your Home or Organization: Approved for City & County of San Francisco Departments*. San Francisco, CA: SF Environment, 2008. http://www.sfenvironment.org/downloads/library/sf_approved_lamps._10308_small_file.pdf (accessed October 24, 2011).

Manufacturers are not required to indicate how much toxic mercury is in lighting products. To address this issue, SF Environment created this list, which includes the amount of toxic mercury in over 700 energy efficient, long-lasting lighting products by major manufacturers. Use this list to purchase greener energy efficient lighting.

U.S. Environmental Protection Agency Office of Resource Conservation and Recovery. "Mercury Containing Light Bulb (Lamp) Recycling." U.S. Environmental Protection Agency, http://www.epa.gov/epawaste/hazard/wastetypes/universal/lamps/index.htm (accessed October 24, 2011).

From the website: "This web site is intended to increase awareness, provide resource tools, information to users, and to encourage the recycling of all mercury-containing light bulbs, including compact fluorescent light bulbs (CFLs) after they burn out." Includes links to information about what to do if a CFL breaks and how to dispose of them when they burn out.

Green Cleaning

GreenYour.com. "Janitorial and Cleaning." GreenYour.com, http://www.greenyour.com/office/office-operations/janitorial-and-cleaning/tips?category=9470 (accessed October 24, 2011).

Includes links to facts, tips, and products for making your janitorial service more environmentally friendly.

U.S. Department of the Interior. *Guidance and Training on Greening Your Janitorial Business*. Washington, D.C. : U.S. Department of the Interior, 2008. http://www.doi.gov/greening/links/intro.html (accessed October 24, 2011).

This manual provides basic information about preferred cleaning products and processes that can reduce health, safety, and environmental risks associated with janitorial services. It also outlines a strategy for building managers to transition from traditional cleaning systems to "green" cleaning systems.

U.S. Environmental Protection Agency Environmentally Preferable Purchasing Program. *Greening Your Purchase of Cleaning Products: A Guide for Federal Purchasers*. Washington, DC: U.S. Environmental Protection Agency, 2010. http://www.epa.gov/epp/pubs/cleaning.htm (accessed October 24, 2011).

Guide developed to help federal purchasers make more informed decisions when purchasing cleaning products. Includes an overview of the benefits of green cleaning products, what to look for when purchasing cleaners, and where to look for more detailed information.

Western Sustainability Pollution Prevention Network. "Janitorial Products Pollution Prevention Project." Western Sustainability Pollution Prevention Network, http://wsppn.org/Janitorial/jp4.cfm (accessed October 24, 2011).

Includes basic information about why green cleaning is important, links to fact sheets about cleaning specific building areas, and tools to help evaluate the hazards of cleaning products.

Zudonyi, Corinne. 2007. "Turning Clean into Green." *Housekeeping Solutions* June, http://www.cleanlink.com/hs/article.asp?id=6834 (accessed October 24, 2011).

This article outlines the benefits using green cleaning products and provides tips for starting a green cleaning program.

Paper

Environmental Defense. "Paper Calculator v.2.0." Environmental Defense, http://www.edf.org/papercalculator/ (accessed October 24, 2011).

Shows the environmental impacts of different papers across their full life cycle. Useful for quantifying the benefits of better paper choices.

Environmental Paper Network. http://www.environmentalpaper.org/ (accessed October 24, 2011).

Cooperative effort of several environmental organizations to improve environmental practices in the pulp & paper industry. Website's resource list includes a guide to purchasing environmentally friendly paper. Two of their initiatives include What's In Your Paper (http://www.whatsinyourpaper.com/), which encourages sustainable paper purchasing, and the RePaper Project (http://www.environmentalpaper.org/repaperproject/index.shtml), which educates organizations about paper recycling.

Minnesota Pollution Control Agency. 200?. "Become a Paper-Less Office." Minneapolis, MN: Minnesota Pollution Control Agency,
http://156.98.19.245/paper/. (accessed October 24, 2011).

Discusses the environmental impact of office paper and offers suggestions
for reducing paper use. Includes an office paper reduction toolkit. Although
the target audience is Minnesota companies, the tips offered are widely applicable to organizations everywhere.

World Resources Institute & World Business Council for Sustainable Development. *Sustainable Procurement of Wood and Paper-based Products:
Guide and Resource Kit: Version 2*. Washington, D.C. : The Institute; The
Council, 2011. http://www.wri.org/publication/
sustainable-procurement-wood-and-paper-based-products (accessed October 24, 2011).

A comprehensive guide to purchasing sustainable wood and paper products.
See also the companion website at http://www.sustainableforestprods.org.

Programming

Bordson, Lauren and Laura L. Barnes. *Environmental Novels: An Annotated
Bibliography*. Champaign, IL : Waste Management and Research Center,
2007. http://www.istc.illinois.edu/info/library_docs/other_pubs/
Environmental-Novels.pdf (accessed October 24, 2011).

Annotated bibliography of novels for young adults and adults, subdivided
by genre. Does not include picture books. Useful for book clubs.

Bosben, Pamela. *Environmental Programming for All Ages*. Eau Claire, WI :
Indianhead Federated Library System, 2008. http://www.iflsweb.org/
Portals/0/Environmental%20Programs%20for%20All%20Ages.doc (ac-
cessed October 24, 2011).

Detailed list of environmental programs sponsored by Rosemary Garfoot
Public Library (Cross Plains, WI). Also includes program suggestions from
librarians throughout the U.S.

Calgary Public Library Eco-Action Blog, http://blog.calgarypubliclibrary.com/
blogs/eco_action/ (accessed October 24, 2011).

From the About page: "Building a healthier environment and reducing Calgary's ecological footprint is a challenge we all share. Written by knowledgeable Library staff who are passionate about the environment, this blog focuses on news and information that will assist you in making smarter, greener choices." An excellent example of how libraries can be sustainability leaders in their communities as well as a good source of information on green lifestyle issues.

Cantu, Ann and Beth Andersen. 2003. "It's Not Easy Being Green, But It Sure Is Fun: Sustainability Programming at the Ann Arbor District Library." *Public Libraries* 42,(4): 240–4.

Case study of a month-long series of sustainability programming for children and adults at the Ann Arbor (MI) District Library. Includes details of the planning process, which included community members, as well as potential pitfalls and lessons learned.

Hudson, Randee. "Millburn Central School to Facilitate Solar Energy Activities." North Suburban Library System, http://www.nsls.info/articles/detail.aspx?articleID=153 (accessed October 24, 2011).

Describes a program at Millburn Central School in Wadsworth, IL that integrated energy activities into their school library media center.

Minnesota Pollution Control Agency. "Environmental Books for Students." Minnesota Pollution Control Agency, http://www.pca.state.mn.us/oea/ee/booklist.cfm (accessed October 24, 2011).

Annotated bibliography of children's books with environmental themes, subdivided by grade level. Mostly older titles. Particularly useful as a story time resource.

Princeton Public Library. "Princeton Environmental Film Festival." Princeton Public Library, http://www.princeton.lib.nj.us/peff/ (accessed October 24, 2011).

This annual film festival, sponsored by the Princeton, NJ Public Library, features environmental documentaries and is designed to encourage discussion about the environment. The festival is planned by librarians and community members. The site also includes an extensive list of resources (http://www.princeton.lib.nj.us/peff/resources.htm), including reading lists, blogs, and state and local resources.

Purchasing

Arnold, Dana. *What is Green Purchasing Anyway?* Washington, DC : Office of the Federal Environmental Executive, n.d. http://www.fedcenter.gov/_kd/go.cfm?destination=ShowItem&Item_ID=14261 (accessed October 24, 2011).

Slides from green purchasing training provided to federal agencies by the Office of the Federal Environmental Executive. Presentation covers executive order and statutory requirements, Federal Acquisition Regulation provisions, each of the components of the Federal green purchasing program, examples of cool stuff from Federal agencies, sample contract language, and lots of references. Notes are provided.

Brower, Michael; Leon, Warren. *The Consumer's Guide to Effective Environmental Choices: Practical Advice from the Union of Concerned Scientists.* New York, NY: Three Rivers Press, 1999.

Helps consumers figure out which purchasing decisions have the most environmental impact. Although targeted at individuals, the information also applies to businesses and organizations.

P2RIC. "Green Procurement Topic Hub." P2RIC, http://www.p2ric.org/p2information/topichubs/index.cfm?page=toc&hub_id=13&subsec_id=7 (accessed October 24, 2011).

A guide to basic information about green purchasing with links to additional resources.

U.S. Environmental Protection Agency. "Environmentally Preferable Purchasing (EPP)." U.S. EPA, http://www.epa.gov/epp/index.htm (accessed October 24, 2011).

The federal government's green purchasing portal. Includes links to policies, product guides, tools, and publications related to green purchasing.

Green Product Guides & Certification

Cradle to Cradle Certification, http://www.c2ccertified.com (accessed October 24, 2011).

Certifies a variety of product types. Includes links to their certification criteria.

Demco. "Earth-friendly Products." Demco, http://www.demco.com/ goto?GREEN_EARTH&BKM0000 (accessed October 24, 2011).

Demco's line of green products.

Ecolabel Index, http://www.ecolabelindex.com.

Comprehensive directory of over 300 green product certification programs.

EnergyStar, http://www.energystar.gov/index.cfm?fuseaction=find_a_product (accessed October 24, 2011).

Certifies electronic equipment and appliances. Information about product specification criteria located at http://www.energystar.gov/index.cfm?c=prod_development.prod_development_index.

EPEAT, http://www.epeat.net/Criteria.aspx (accessed October 24, 2011).

EPEAT is the required method of product environmental assessment for desktop computers, laptops and monitors for federal agencies.

Forest Stewardship Council, http://www.fscus.org/ (accessed October 24, 2011).

Products bearing the FSC logo guarantees that the wood from a certified well-managed forest. Includes a retailer database at http://www.fscus.org/productsearch/retailers/.

Gaylord. "Everyday Green." Gaylord, http://www.gaylord.com/everydaygreen.asp (accessed October 24, 2011).

Gaylord's line of green products.

Green Guide, The. "Buying Guides." National Geographic, http://environment.nationalgeographic.com/environment/green-guide/buying-guides/ (accessed October 24, 2011).

Product guides for a wide variety of consumer products.

The Green Office, http://www.thegreenoffice.com (accessed October 24, 2011).

One stop shop for green office products.

Green Seal, http://www.greenseal.org (accessed October 24, 2011).

>   Certifies a wide variety of products and services. Product guide at http://www.greenseal.org/findaproduct/index.cfm.

GreenGuard, http://www.greenguard.org (accessed October 24, 2011).

>   Establishes acceptable indoor air standards for indoor products, environments, and buildings. Product database available at http://www.greenguard.org/en/QuickSearch.aspx.

Greenraising, http://www.greenraising.com (accessed October 24, 2011).

>   Fundraising site for schools and nonprofits that features eco-friendly products.

North American Green Purchasing Initiative. *Buying Environmentally Preferable Office Equipment: A Buyer's Guide*. Montreal, Quebec: The Initiative, 2008. http://www.cec.org/files/PDF/ECONOMY/NAGPI-Office%20Equipment-FS_en.pdf (accessed October 24, 2011).

>   Guide to purchasing green office equipment. Includes a discussion of the environmental impacts of office equipment, how to establish a green purchasing program, and a list of resources.

Office Depot. "Your Greener Office." Office Depot, http://www.officedepot.com/a/browse/your-greener-office/N=5+11332/ (accessed October 24, 2011).

>   Office Depot's portal to green office supplies. Includes a green buying guide and green purchasing FAQ.

Staples. "EcoEasy." Staples, http://www.staples.com/sbd/cre/marketing/ecoeasy/index.html (accessed October 24, 2011).

>   Staples' portal to green office supplies.

WaterSense, http://www.epa.gov/watersense/ (accessed October 24, 2011).

>   EPA-sponsored program to promote water efficiency. Certifies products and services. Search for products at http://www.epa.gov/watersense/product_search.html.

Worldwatch Institute. *Good Stuff? A Behind-the-Scenes Guide to the Things We Buy.* Washington, DC : Worldwatch Institute, 2004. http://www.worldwatch.org/taxonomy/term/44 (accessed October 24, 2011).

Guide to purchasing everything from appliances to chocolate.

Greenwashing

EnviroMedia Social Marketing. "Greenwashing Index." EnviroMedia Social Marketing , http://greenwashingindex.com/ (accessed October 24, 2011).

Website that allows consumers to post ads that might be examples of greenwashing and rate them on a scale of 1 to 5. Also includes an explanation of greenwashing and how to identify it.

Federal Trade Commission. 1999. *Sorting Out 'Green' Advertising Claims.* Washington, D.C.: Federal Trade Commission, Bureau of Consumer Protection, Office of Consumer and Business Education. http://www.ftc.gov/bcp/edu/pubs/consumer/general/gen02.pdf (accessed October 24, 2011).

Factsheet that describes the FTC's efforts to regulate false environmental claims and offers consumers some guidelines for distinguishing between fact and fiction when shopping for green products.

Terrachoice Environmental Marketing. *The Seven Sins of Greenwashing: Environmental Claims in Consumer Markets.* Ottawa, Ontario : Terrachoice Environmental Marketing, 2009. http://sinsofgreenwashing.org/findings/greenwashing-report-2009/ (accessed October 24, 2011).

Detailed report on how companies mislead consumers about the environmental benefits of their products. Companion website at http://sinsofgreenwashing.org provides tools and tips for taking action.

Walsh, Bryan. 2008. "Eco-Buyer Beware: Green Can Be Deceiving." *Time Magazine*, September 11, http://www.time.com/time/magazine/article/0,9171,1840562,00.html (accessed October 24, 2011).

Article that explains greenwashing and how to identify and combat it.

Wood, Deb. 2007. "Guard Against Greenwashing." *Colorado Construction*, November, http://colorado.construction.com/features/archive/ 0711_feature1e.asp (accessed October 24, 2011).

Focuses on greenwashing as it applies to building and maintenance.

Weeding

CD Recycling Center of America, http://cdrecyclingcenter.org (accessed October 24, 2011).

Accepts CDs and DVDs for recycling at no charge. Customer pays shipping. Includes educational materials. Located in NH.

Cole,Maureen. 2007. "From Worthless to Worthy: Turning Media Trash into Recycling Treasure." *OLA Quarterly* 13,(4): 22–24.

Describes the Eugene (OR) Public Library Technical Services Department's efforts to recycle their discarded materials, rather than throwing them away. Includes a good discussion of the barriers encountered during the project and how they were overcome.

Green Weeding Wiki, http://greenweeding.pbworks.com (accessed October 24, 2011).

Links to information about a wide variety of options for donating, selling, trading, and recycling discarded library materials.

Penniman, Sarah & Lisa McColl. 2008. "Green Weeding: Promoting Eco-friendly Options for Library Discards." *Library Journal* 133,(15): 32–3.

Suggests options for reusing or recycling discarded library materials rather than throwing them away.

Water Efficiency

GreenBiz. 2008. "Water Conservation." GreenBiz.com, October 3, http://www.greenbiz.com/resources/resource/water-conservation (accessed October 24, 2011).

Guide to water conservation basics includes links to other resources.

Lindstroth, Tommy. 2008. "Water Savings 101: Top 10 Tips for Commercial Buildings." GreenerBuildings.com, September 10, http://www.greenerbuildings.com/news/2008/09/10/ water-savings-101-top-10-tips-commercial-buildings (accessed October 24, 2011).

Identifies ten things that facilities managers can do to save water, many of which are fairly low cost and easy to implement.

New Mexico Office of the State Engineer. *A Water Conservation Guide for Commercial, Institutional and Industrial Users.* Albuquerque, NM: The Office, 1999, http://www.seo.state.nm.us/water-info/conservation/ pdf-manuals/cii-users-guide.pdf (accessed October 24, 2011).

Detailed guide to implementing a water conservation program. Some of the technical solutions and cost savings figures are outdated, but most of the information is still relevant.

Beyond Swag: Reflections on Libraries, Pencils, and the Limits of "Green" Consumerism[1]

Dave Hudson

Locating "Green" Swag

As evidence of the ecological crisis we face has become harder to ignore, so too have expressions of environmental concern become increasingly prevalent within mainstream public discourse. Given the primacy of our identification as consumers in life under global capitalism, it is not surprising that such concern has asserted itself forcefully through an explosion in market demand for "green"[2] products. Indeed, alongside public expectations of demonstrated corporate environmental responsibility, such demand for genuinely "green" products has continued to grow in spite of the global recession, with consumers indicating ethical motivations as well as a general willingness to pay more for such products (Manget, Roche, and Münnich 2009; Cone 2009; National Geographic and GlobeScan 2009).

Corporate response to such demand has been significant, with report after report indicating a growing recognition among companies of the value of

1. I am grateful to Kim Garwood, as well as to the editors of this anthology, for their critical comments on my writing.

2. I have chosen to enclose "green" in quotation marks throughout this chapter where I feel its credibility as a signifier of environmental responsibility ought to be flagged. While this may interrupt the landscape of this chapter's text, my feeling is that it is more important to maintain a critical distance from such language where its naturalization in the course of conversation masks environmentally questionable practices.

"green" business practices (Bockman 2009). To use one commentator's colorful (albeit disturbing) imagery, "[a]mong countless brands across countless categories, we're in the midst of a kind of arms race to be the greenest" (Erdman 2008, 18). It would indeed seem that one cannot take a step towards a cash register these days without bumping into a shelf of "eco-friendly" products. From biodegradable laundry detergent and the now-commonplace compact fluorescent light bulb, to biodegradable poop n' scoop bags and organic avocados, to high-end recycled gold and conflict-free diamond jewelry, the landscape of "green" alternatives appears endless in both variety and extent.

Such trends towards ecologically-conscious purchasing behavior have not been limited to individual retail consumerism: as part of the broader realm of organizational purchasing, libraries have displayed a seeming affinity for "green" alternatives from ENERGY STAR-qualified office machines (Poudre River Public Library District 2009) to 100% post-consumer waste recycled printer and copy paper (University of Western Australia 2009) to conference badges that include recycled materials (Blumenstein 2008). Indeed, my own workplace recently underwent an extensive lighting retrofit: our new energy efficient bulbs have prevented 617 tons of CO_2 emissions (equivalent to removing 154 cars from the road), while contributing to substantial energy cost savings and aiding the work of our stack maintenance staff (the reduced-wattage bulbs are, ironically, brighter) (University of Guelph 2008; Pitman 2009; University of Guelph Library 2009a).

Among the most visible elements of the library world affected by this trend towards "green" products are those ubiquitous promotional products—or swag, to use the colloquial shorthand—that appear in conference participant packages, on trade show floors, and at reference desks. At a conference expo in 2009, I spent some time at the booth of the company that had supplied the official attendee bags, which were made of recycled plastic bottles. At another conference the preceding fall, the swag within my participant package included a recycled paper notebook and a recycled cardboard and plastic pen. Visitors to promotional product suppliers' websites these days are likely to encounter prominently-displayed collections of items under headings such as "eco products," "environmentally friendly products," and "promotional products for your conscience," alongside invitations to "go green" and "shop eco-friendly" (Fairware 2009; Amsterdam Products, Ltd 2010; 4imprint Inc. 2010). Options include everything from biodegradable corn-based highlighters to bamboo business card holders to organic cotton ball caps to solar-powered pedometers, all available with customized imprints.

There is certainly something to be said for the marriage of environmental consciousness and promotional products, for visibly "green" swag, as it were.

Thoughtfully selected and circulated swag in general has long been understood to be effective as a means of promoting organizations and initiatives, even in non-profit contexts (Self 2001): it would seem that folks are quite simply more likely to feel affinity with promotional messaging if they have access to a physical reminder.[3] It could be argued, in turn, that the circulation of "green" swag sends a twofold message: *we wish to give you this item by which to remember who we are and what we do, but we also share concerns about the ecological impact of our doing so, about the state of the world in which we all live.* Given the increasing public concern over the state of the environment, our choice, of "green" alternatives when purchasing promotional products, has the potential to resonate powerfully with our library users as a sign of our commitment to ecological responsibility.

I used reasoning similar to this in the summer of 2009 when it came time to re-order promotional swag for the University of Guelph Library and Learning Commons to hand out during our fall orientation week for incoming students. I had never ordered promotional products before, but my own interest in reducing ecological footprints wherever possible led me to explore the availability of a "greener" giveaway. Conversations with other colleagues closely connected to student life suggested that other "green" initiatives undertaken by the library had been well received by students: in particular, students had appreciated the library's decision to phase out paper due-date slips for borrowers, a decision announced through modest signs that read, "It just got easy to be green." My subsequent foray into the catalogues of promotional product suppliers demonstrated not only the above-noted variety and widespread availability of "green" alternatives, but also the perhaps counterintuitive reality that such options are not necessarily more expensive. We eventually decided on pencils with casing made of recycled newspaper rather than virgin timber. Pencils had been popular in previous years and the use of recycled materials seemed like a move that would indeed result in a reduced ecological footprint, given that the production of traditional wooden pencils has tended to rely on the clear-cutting of old growth forests and/or use of herbicide-dependent monoculture plantations ("Pencils" 2008). In keeping with the theme initiated at the phase-out of paper due date slips, we produced a small "It's easy to be green" countertop sign to display with the pencils at the reference desk and at external organizational events, presenting the pencils to users as a symbol of our efforts at "green" initiatives in the library. These efforts have been well received.

---

3. While not surprising, it is nonetheless worth noting that the most prominent studies supporting such conclusions come from representatives of the promotional products industry itself, including the Promotional Products Association International and the Advertising Specialty Institute (ASI) (see, for instance, PPAI Research 2009; ASI 2008).

Troubling "Green" Consumption

Questions remain, however. Despite its lack of controversy and relative insignificance as an environmental intervention, my experience introducing the "green" pencils while considering the broader contexts of consumerism outlined above has forced me to re-examine the assertion that it is indeed "easy to be green." I question, specifically, whether environmental responsibility really can be presumed to align so neatly with our current ways of operating in the world. To what degree does the integration of environmental consciousness into our practices as library professionals hinge on our choice of "eco-friendly" products, on "green" consumerism? Is the process of greening libraries simply a matter of, as it were, greening our swag? Or does it require a more fundamental questioning of the prevailing assumptions that inform our lives as professionals and global community members alike?

Such questions are hardly new, of course, balanced as they are on the tension between status quo consumption levels and environmental change, a broader context of criticism that offers important insights for any practice of "greening." In particular, those concerned with ecological sustainability have long pointed to the link between environmental degradation and consumer culture, a culture that pays little attention to the ecological interventions, contexts, and impacts associated with the cradle-to-grave lifecycle of consumer products at each stage—raw material exploration, extraction, and transportation; refinement, marketing, and manufacturing; packaging, storage, and distribution; and use and disposal. And yet, as has also been widely noted, our ecological health has come to be threatened not simply by the *techniques* of our consumption, but also the sheer *extent* of it, particularly in the minority world:[4] ours is a culture

---

4. The phrases "minority world" and "majority world" have come to be used as alternative terminology within those discussions of geopolitical poverty, wealth, and empowerment traditionally marked by dualisms such as "First World" and "Third World," "developed" and "developing" countries, "East" and "West," and the "Global North" and "Global South." In the words of Shahidul Alam (2008), who coined the concepts of majority and minority worlds, traditional expressions such as "'Third World' or 'Developing World' or even LDCs (Least Developed Countries) [. . .] have strong negative connotations that reinforce the stereotypes about poor communities and represent them as icons of poverty. They hide their histories of oppression and continued exploitation [. . .] and hinder the appreciation of the cultural and social wealth of these communities" (89). Alam offered the phrase "majority world" as a way of pointing to "the fact that we are indeed the majority of humankind. It also brings sharp attention to the anomaly that the Group of 8 countries—whose decisions affect the majority of the world's people—represent a tiny fraction of humankind. [. . .] It also defines the community in terms of what it has, rather than what it lacks" (89). For this reason, I have

beset by seemingly insatiable consumerism, a point worth recalling even if it seems obvious on the verge of cliché. Commitments to civilizational progress and community well-being (be it local, national, or global) are measured chiefly in terms of material accumulation and constant growth; and personal happiness, care for others, and a whole host of other relations are centrally negotiated through shopping within a cultural surround that devalues the old, the slow, and the long-term, while romanticizing the new, the fast, and the immediate—a culture of swag, fears of obsolescence, and constant upgrades.[5]

Our rates of resource consumption indeed continue to rise globally. Between 1961 and 2002, for instance, human demands on the biosphere grew from one half to 123% of the biosphere's total carrying capacity (Kitzes et al. 2008). The International Energy Agency (IEA) has projected a startling 40% increase in global energy demand between 2007 and 2030 (IEA 2009). Such increases cannot, moreover, be attributed simply to expanding population, as consumption growth rates have far exceeded population growth rates in recent history (Dauvergne 2008; Princen, Maniates, and Conca 2002b), with the minority world continuing its long-standing trend of grossly disproportionate resource use (Worldwatch Institute 2008). If current *global* consumption growth rates continue, we will require two planets to sustain our "needs" by the early 2030s (WWF International, Global Footprint Network, and Zoological Society of London 2008); if global consumption rates were to unfold solely on *North American* and *Western European* rates, our ecological footprint would increase to a whopping three to five times the earth's carrying capacity (Kitzes et al. 2008, 468).

It is within the context of these particular trends and cultural contours that compelling questions about the limits of "green" consumerism have been raised. Critical discussion of "green" consumerism is expansive and perspectivally varied, and the scope of this essay does not permit an exhaustive review of such writing's critical contours and nuances.[6] However, perhaps the most central among such critiques is the simple observation that the privileging of

---

chosen to use these phrases throughout this essay, though I extend their use here to encompass those systemic inequalities in resource access and consumption *within* countries such as Canada and the United States (Macedo 1999), as well as those dynamics that mark the broader global stage.

5. Portraits of the fervent and deeply entrenched consumerism of our society are widespread. See, for instance, *Not Buying It* (Levine 2006); *Affluenza* (De Graaf, Wann, and Naylor 2005); or *The Age of Missing Information* (McKibben 1992).

6. Though for evidence of such nuanced critical divergences, see, for example, Soper, Ryle, and Thomas (2009); Muldoon (2006); Wapner and Willoughby (2005); Princen, Maniates, and Conca (2002a); Wood (2002); and Salvador and Samosky (1991).

"eco-friendly" product choice as the chief expression of environmental concern (entrenched within both corporate and formal government sustainability strategies [Seyfang 2005]) does little to address the key problem of overconsumption and the logics and behaviors that fuel it. I may decide to buy "eco-friendly" shoes made of post-consumer rubber, bamboo textile, and plant cellulose fiber, but the very conclusion (however implicit) that I need an additional pair of shoes in the first place—for "laid-back meetings" or "après fun" (Backcountry. com 2009)—is not brought into question. Likewise, I might decide to restyle my bathroom using bamboo floors, recycled porcelain tiling and countertops, and low-VOC paint, but the fundamental decision to gut the entire space simply because it is "small, old, [and] just out of style" (Ecoteriors 2008, 1st para.) remains untroubled.[7] "Green" consumerism practices a logic whereby, to use Princen, Maniates, and Conca's (2002b) words:

> Consumption becomes sacrosanct. If water supplies are tight, one must produce more water, not consume less. If toxics accumulate, one must produce with fewer by-products—or, even better, produce a cleanup technology —rather than forgo the production itself. Goods are good and more goods are better. Wastes may be bad—but when they are, more productive efficiencies, including ecoefficiencies and recycling, are the answer. Production reigns supreme because consumption is beyond scrutiny. (5)

The trouble with the explosion of "eco-friendly shopping," in other words, is not only its concrete dependence on status quo consumption growth levels, but also what Kahn (2009) notes as its "ecopedagogy"—that is, its (re)circulation of a particular lesson about how to act on one's environmental concerns: where we are told, to use one initiative's language, that we can "shop for the planet" while "[shopping] as [we] normally do" (Community Environmental Council 2009, para. 5, 6), we are taught, implicitly, to leave broader questions of need unexamined and ignore the environmental costs of even the most "eco-friendly" consumerism—the reality that my recycled rubber shoes and bamboo flooring still contribute to ecological degradation where processes of gathering raw materials, manufacturing, transportation, use, and disposal are concerned. As Kahn (2009) states, "[i]n the form of a feel good catharsis, the take home message of green consumerism is largely to stop worrying about the big problems and to instead do one's little part for sustainability through endless repetitions of spending on behalf of 'the planetary good'" (49). Moreover, "green" consumerism not only promotes illusory "guilt-free" shopping, but, through largely uncritical circula-

---

7. A similar criticism might also be made of Apple's iPad, which, at the time of this writing, has just been released as, in part, Apple's revolutionary "environmentally responsibility" incarnate (Apple 2010).

tions of catch-all modifiers like "green" and "eco," tends to blur the very question of environmental impact with which it is ostensibly concerned: indeed, Cone's 2008 Green Gap Survey found that "almost half (48%) of the population erroneously believes a product marketed as 'green' or 'environmentally friendly' has a positive (i.e., beneficial) impact on the environment. Only 22% understand these terms more accurately describe products with less negative environmental impact than previous versions or competing products" (2008, para. 3).

Critics point to another strategic shortcoming in "green" consumerism: the reduction of environmental action to individual product choice is fundamentally limiting because the problem of environmental degradation is one of collective and systemic (ir)responsibility, connecting not simply to the sum total of all consumer transactions, but to the broader corporate, cultural, and governmental policy frameworks that enable and privilege particular sorts of ecological interactions while severely constraining, if not altogether precluding, others (Kahn 2009; Dauvergne 2008; Seyfang 2005; Wapner and Willoughby 2005; Maniates 2002). Seyfang (2005) offers a compelling example:

> A person might choose one brand of washing-machine over another because of its greater energy-efficiency, but what they cannot easily choose is to purchase collectively and share common laundry facilities among a local group of residents. Consumers are effectively locked in to particular consumption patterns by overarching social structures of market, business, working patterns, urban planning and development. (297)

Our solutions to these problems, such critics observe, must therefore ultimately be similarly collective, extending to the fundamentals of how we operate as communities, whether it be globally or locally. "Confronting the consumption problem," Maniates (2002) writes, "demands [. . .] the sort of institutional thinking that the individualization of responsibility patently undermines. It calls too for individuals to understand themselves as citizens in a participatory democracy first, working together to change broader policy and larger social institutions, and as consumers second" (46–47).

Beyond Swag

This is not to suggest that libraries are prime examples of the sort of hyperspeed, impulse-driven, retail-therapy-and-patriotic-duty individual consumerist excess that is perhaps most easily brought to mind by the critiques outlined above. Indeed, libraries are often cited as quintessential models of resource-sharing. There is also an important difference between individual retail consumerism and the sorts of purchasing typically practiced within organizations like libraries: the latter takes place (at least theoretically) within an environment of collective accountability, in which levels of scrutiny to matters of cost, need, and overall efficiency tend to make for a somewhat slower, more considered process. Inasmuch as such scrutiny is understood to be antithetical to the ("green") "capitalism without friction" (Gates 1999) that fuels demand for (hybrid) SUVs and (ENERGY STAR-rated) 70 inch LCD TVs, critiques of frenetic, rapacious consumerism would not, at first blush, seem well applied to libraries.

And yet we do seem to love our swag. Despite some laudable efforts to reduce waste (Munro 2009; Butcher 2008), conferences still commonly supply each participant with a new bag full of memorabilia, as well as other opportunities to pick up "goodies" on the expo floor. Indeed, while in library school a few years back, one of the first stories I heard about our annual regional library conference was that it was not uncommon for attendees to bring additional empty trolley cases to the expo floor to load up on giveaways (a sight that I have witnessed in the years since). It seems to me that the "greening" of swag does little to address the entrenched dynamics of ecologically destructive overconsumption that such practices exemplify. Our conference bags may be composed of recycled materials (and our name-tag holders biodegradable); and I may derive some personal comfort in the practicality of the (recycled newspaper) pencils I ordered (I've never had a student ask for a [solar-powered] pedometer during a reference desk shift, after all). Indeed, I remain convinced that genuinely useful items like recycled newspaper pencils and reusable recycled-fiber tote bags can, if consistently used as replacements for their conventional alternatives, represent a relative reduction in environmental impact. Still, as Gamerman (2008) reports, those near-ubiquitous recycled-fiber bags handed out year after year are accumulating in drawers and closets, eventually making their way into landfills (and staying there quite a bit longer than the average paper or plastic bag); apparently, folks are forgetting to reuse them—or, in other cases, purposefully avoiding doing so because they are "too nice to load up with diapers or dripping chicken breasts" (W1). And yet it is their near-talismanic status as cheap-yet-chic, instant environmental responsibility that fosters such accumulation while tending to inhibit critical consideration of the hidden environmental impacts of their lifecycles—the energy-intensive fiber production process (Gamerman 2008), for instance, or the emissions involved in shipping them from China to our local promotional product supplier in Canada.

But it is less a pointed, intricately woven analysis of recycled pencils and bags as individual "eco-solutions" that concerns me. The broader point here is that it is precisely the wider cultural context of quick-fix, cornucopian consumerism within which "green" swag operates—and by which it is enabled—that both limits its ability to even incrementally reduce environmental impact and discourages deeper questions about the problems of overconsumption in the first place. It seems to me that the process of greening libraries, in turn, must address not only the content of swag, but also its very logic. Inexpensive promotional items may indeed work as efficient vehicles for relationship building, with "green" swag providing a conduit for the quick communication of eco-consciousness. However, these moves flow with such ease precisely because they follow mainstream cultural currents, aligning with extant practices of consumption that privilege immediate material gain and short term efficiencies over environmental cost. A practice of greening libraries must confront the very need for those acts of consumption in which we engage: it is a matter not simply of handing out progressively less destructive bags each year at conferences, but of considering ways in which the need for bags itself might be reduced, if not eliminated. The greenest swag is that which does not exist at all.

Of course, this may sound both idealistic and dire—a call to immediately "go without." While I stand firmly by an understanding of ideals as both powerful and practical, it is worth emphasizing that the process of greening libraries need not simply be about joyless sacrifice. To this end, we might draw productively on the concept of "green pleasures" as outlined by Richard Kerridge (2009), whom I have chosen to cite at some length here:

> A "green" pleasure is one that follows the logic of environmentalism—by using less carbon, deepening one's love of things already at hand, appreciating cycles of growth and renewal in the local and global ecosystems, understanding and taking delight in interdependency. This logic might point, for example, to taking joy in family and friendship, rather than working long hours (if you get the choice). It points to holistic care for the body rather than binges, addictions and quick fixes for symptoms. With this goes affection for one's naturally formed and naturally ageing body, and resistance to the commercialised "beauty myth". And there should be "green" pleasure in craft rather than mass production; making things rather than buying them; knowing and repairing them, treating them even with a kind of loyalty, rather than discarding them as soon as they are old or impaired. (131)

In drawing on such sentiments, the process of greening libraries embraces not only a confrontation of crises, but also the pleasures of crafting alternatives. While few would argue with the idea that we should, for example, buy recycled conference bags where they are needed (and where their lessened impact is genuine), we might also focus our efforts on developing appreciation for measures that encourage attendees to bring those from previous years; indeed, there is some suggestion that library conference participants would take pride in such reuse, overwhelmed as they are with closets full of bags and other giveaways

(StevenB 2009). In other cases, we might simply choose to de-emphasize promotional trinkets, channeling our marketing efforts instead into creative outreach and publicity activities, such as flash mobs (University of Guelph 2009b) or rock shows (see, for instance, the well-established Rock & Roll Library Tour, www.rockandrolllibrarytour.com); or redoubling efforts to foster an organizational culture that emphasizes interactions with library users not simply as service provision, but as relationship building—the same sort of memorable connection one might make through a recycled newspaper pencil.

There is, of course, no prescription for such creativity. Indeed, in keeping with the insights of "green" consumerism critics, we might observe here that such creative responses cannot be bought as premade, individual "eco solutions": since their shaping requires a critical confrontation of deeply entrenched cultural logics of consumerism, those more substantive solutions—those that foster deliberate cultural devaluing of swag in favor of joy in creative alternatives—are necessarily collective. Just as the practice of greening libraries more broadly cannot be achieved without engaging those outside the library world as part of larger sociocultural movements and conversations, so too must such work within the world of libraries itself necessarily be founded on meaningful critical dialogue and collaboration for collective solutions—a practice with which we are, in many senses, well acquainted (and of which this anthology provides an example).

Moving beyond swag as an expression of greening libraries might take as its basis another well-established tradition within libraries: our practiced professional commitment to intergenerational sustainability. Here, we draw less on the role of libraries as storehouses of stuff—the more books, the more resources, the more content, the better—and more on our practice as facilitators of knowledge between and across generations. In the recirculation of resources across checkout desks and through bibliographies, we place implicit value not only on the resources we share, nor even simply on the (crucial) act of sharing itself: consciously or not, our very practice locates knowledge itself as something that lives only ecologically, only in the inseparability of that which has come before us, that which surrounds us, and that which will come after us. Within the world of libraries, there is thus a basis for valuing that which extends well beyond us, for the long term—for a conception of progress that eschews the logic of constant, linear upgrades that rejects the culture of new-as-trump-to-old. Where such values of ecology are acknowledged and practiced, they stand in stark contrast, in other words, to the immediate, ethereal character of swag, no matter how "green" such swag may be, and provide the grounds, in turn, from which to foster collective, creative alternatives.

References

4imprint Inc. 2010. Promotional Environmentally Friendly at 4imprint. 4imprint Canada. http://www.4imprint.ca/group/1106/Environmentally-Friendly (accessed January 28, 2010).

Advertising Speciality Institute. 2008. *Advertising Specialties Impressions Study: A Cost Analysis of Promotional Products Versus Other Advertising Media.* Advertising Speciality Institute, http://www.asicentral.com/html/open/EducationandEvents/powersummit08/Impressions_Study.pdf (accessed January 28, 2010).

Alam, Shahidul. 2008. Majority world: Challenging the West's rhetoric of democracy. *Amerasia Journal* 34, no. 1: 89–98.

Amsterdam Products, Ltd. 2010. Amsterdam Canada. http://www.amsterdamproducts.ca (accessed January 28, 2010).

Apple. 2010. Apple launches iPad. Apple. http://www.apple.com/pr/library/2010/01/27ipad.html (accessed February 1, 2010).

ASI. *See* Advertising Speciality Institute.

Backcountry.com. 2009. The North Face Hayden shoe—Men's. Backcountry.com. http://www.backcountry.com/outdoorgear/The-North-Face-Hayden-Shoe-Mens/TNF2887M.html (accessed January 28, 2010).

Blumenstein, Lynn. 2008. SLA Goes Green, Faces Changes. *Library Journal*, August 15. http://www.proquest.com (accessed January 28, 2010).

Bockman, Shel, Nabil Y. Razzouk, and Barbara Sirotnik. 2009. Going green—from left to center stage: An empirical perspective. *Journal of American Academy of Business, Cambridge* 14, no. 2: 8–16. http://www.proquest.com (accessed January 28, 2010).

Butcher, Don. 2008. Going green. *Feliciter* 54, no. 2: 47. http://www.proquest.com (accessed January 28, 2010).

Community Environmental Council. Shop green. 2009. Community Environmental Council. http://www.cecsb.org/index.php?option=com_content&task=view&id=32&Itemid=82 (accessed January 26, 2010).

Cone. 2008. Cone releases 2008 green gap survey. *Cone.* http://www.coneinc.com/content1136 (accessed January 28, 2010).

———. 2009. Cone releases 2009 consumer environmental survey. *Cone.* http://www.coneinc.com/content2032 (accessed January 28, 2010).

Dauvergne, Peter. 2008. *The Shadows of Consumption: Consequences for the Global Environment.* Cambridge, Mass.: MIT Press.

De Graaf, John, David Wann, and Thomas H. Naylor. 2005. *Affluenza: The All-consuming Epidemic*. 2nd ed. San Francisco, CA: Berrett-Koehler.

Ecoteriors [Beath, Alicia]. 2008. Eco-friendly bathroom renovation tips. Home Renovation Guide. http://www.homerenovationguide.com/articles/eco-friendly-bathroom-renovation-tips (accessed January 26, 2010).

Erdman, Brian. 2008. Is green really your color? *Brandweek*, February 4. http://www.proquest.com/ (accessed January 28, 2010).

Fairware. 2009. Fairware. http://www.fairware.ca (accessed January 28, 2010).

Gamerman, Ellen. 2008. An inconvenient bag. *Wall Street Journal*, Sep 26, Weekend Journal, eastern edition. http://www.proquest.com (accessed January 28, 2010).

Gates, Bill. 1999. *Business @ the Speed of Thought: Using a Digital Nervous System*. New York: Warner Books.

IEA. *See* International Energy Agency.

International Energy Agency. 2009. *World Energy Outlook 2009 Fact Sheet*. http://www.worldenergyoutlook.org/docs/weo2009/fact_sheets_WEO_2009.pdf (accessed January 26, 2010).

Kahn, Richard. 2009. Producing crisis: Green consumerism as an ecopedagogical issue. In *Critical Pedagogies of Consumption: Living and Learning in the Shadow of the "Shopocalypse,"* ed. Jennifer A. Sandlin and Peter McLaren, 47–57. New York: Routledge.

Kerridge, Richard. 2009. Green pleasures. In *The Politics and Pleasures of Consuming Differently*, ed. Kate Soper, Martin H. Ryle, and Lyn Thomas, 130–153. Basingstoke: Palgrave Macmillan.

Kitzes, Justin, Mathis Wackernagel, Jonathan Loh, Audrey Peller, Steven Goldfinger, Deborah Cheng, and Kallin Tea. 2008. Shrink and share: humanity's present and future Ecological Footprint. *Philosophical Transactions of the Royal Society B* 363, no. 1491: 467–475. http://rstb.royalsocietypublishing.org/content/363/1491/467.full.pdf+html (accessed January 28, 2010).

Levine, Cynthia. 2006. *Not Buying It: My Year Without Shopping*. New York: Free Press.

Macedo, Donaldo. 1999. Decolonizing indigenous knowledge. In *What is Indigenous Knowledge? Voices from the Academy*, ed. Ladislaus M. Semali and Joe L. Kincheloe, xi–xvi. New York: Falmer Press.

Manget, Joe, Catherine Roche, and Felix Münnich. 2009. *Capturing the Green Advantage for Consumer Companies*. Boston: BCG Publications. http://www.bcg.com/documents/file15407.pdf (accessed January 28, 2010).

Maniates, Michael. 2002. Individualization: Plant a tree, buy a bike, save the world? In Princen, Maniates, and Conca, 43–66.

McKibben, Bill. 1992. *The Age of Missing Information*. New York: Random House.

Muldoon, Annie. 2006. Where the green is: Examining the paradox of environmentally conscious consumption. *Electronic Green Journal* 1, no. 23, http://www.escholarship.org/uc/item/00t326gx (accessed January 28, 2010).

Munro, Karen. 2009. Going green. *College & Research Libraries News* 70, no. 6: 331. http://crln.acrl.org/content/70/6/330.full.pdf+html (accessed January 28, 2010).

National Geographic and GlobeScan. 2009. *Greendex 2009: Consumer Choice and the Environment—A Worldwide Tracking Survey—Highlights Report*. National Geographic, http://www.nationalgeographic.com/greendex/assets/Greendex_Highlights_Report_May09.pdf

Pencils. 2008. *World Watch*. September–October, 1. *Academic OneFile, Gage Cengage Learning* (accessed January 28, 2010).

Pitman, Teresa. 2009. A healthy, reliable, sustainable energy future. *At Guelph*, April 22. http://www.uoguelph.ca/atguelph/09-04-22/featuresfuture.shtml (accessed January 28, 2010).

Poudre River Public Library District. 2009. Case study: Your council tree library is designed for sustainability. Poudre River Public Library District. http://www.poudrelibraries.org/news/pdf/leeds.pdf (accessed January 28, 2010).

PPAI Research. 2009. *Effectiveness of Promotional Products as an Advertising Medium*. Promotional Products Association International, http://www.ppa.org/NR/rdonlyres/BA94A823-E0A8-4E32-A2BC-6D3912D4D45A/0/09EffectProProAsAdMed_PowerTool.pdf (accessed January 28, 2010).

Princen, Thomas, Michael Maniates, and Ken Conca, ed. 2002a. *Confronting Consumption*. Cambridge, Mass.: MIT Press.

———. 2002b. Confronting consumption. In Princen, Maniates, and Conca, 1–20.

Salvador, Michael, and Jack Samosky. 1991. Is doing something better than doing nothing? Environmentalism and the paradox of green consumerism. In *Conference Proceedings—National Communication Association/American Forensic Association (Alta Conference on Argumentation)*, 325–329. Washington, D.C.: National Communication Association. Communication & Mass Media Complete, EBSCOhost (accessed January 28, 2010).

Self, Donald R. 2001. Promotional products: Adding tangibility to your non-profit promotions. *Journal of Nonprofit & Public Sector Marketing* 9, no. 1/2: 205–213. http://www.informaworld.com/10.1300/J054v09n01_13 (accessed 28 January 2010).

Seyfang, Gill. 2005. Shopping for sustainability: Can sustainable consumption promote ecological citizenship? *Environmental Politics* 14, no. 2: 290–306. http://www.informaworld.com/10.1080/09644010500055209 (accessed 28 January 2010).

Soper, Kate, Martin H. Ryle, and Lyn Thomas, ed. 2009. *The Politics and Pleasures of Consuming Differently*. Basingstoke: Palgrave Macmillan.

StevenB [Bell, Steven]. 2009. Green conference bag is a letdown. *ACRLog*, March 21. http://acrlog.org/2009/03/21/green-conference-bag-is-a-letdown.

University of Guelph. 2008. Completed energy projects. University of Guelph. http://www.pr.uoguelph.ca/sustain/energy/pastenergyprojects.htm (accessed January 28, 2010).

University of Guelph Library. 2009a. Library goes green. University of Guelph Library, October 1. http://www.lib.uoguelph.ca/about/news/dsp_viewArticle.cfm?src=Library%20Goes%20Green (accessed January 28, 2010).

———. 2009b. *The University of Guelph Library & Friends Read*. Online video. http://www.youtube.com/watch?v=Is1obG5UcfM (accessed January 28, 2010).

University of Western Australia. 2009. Printing and copying. University of Western Australia Library. http://www.library.uwa.edu.au/students/computers/printing (accessed January 28, 2010).

Wapner, Paul, and John Willoughby. 2005. The irony of environmentalism: The ecological futility but political necessity of lifestyle change. *Ethics & International Affairs* 19, no. 3: 77–89. Academic Search Premier, EBSCOhost (accessed January 28, 2010).

Wood, John. 2002. (Un)managing the butterfly: Co-sustainment and the grammar of self. *International Review of Sociology* 12, no. 2: 295–307. http://www.informaworld.com/10.1080/0390670022000012512 (accessed 28 January 2010).

Worldwatch Institute. 2008. *2008 State of the World: Innovations for a Sustainable Economy*. New York: W.W. Norton & Company.

WWF International, Global Footprint Network, and Zoological Society of London. 2008. *Living Planet Report 2008*. Gland, Switzerland: WWF International. http://www.footprintnetwork.org/download.php?id=505 (accessed 28 January 2010).

Environmental Programs and Green Practices: An American Library Association Timeline from 1989-2010

Maria J. Jankowska

The concept of sustainable development, advocating a balance between economic growth, social equity, and ecology, "that meets the needs of the present without compromising the ability of future generations to meet their own needs"[1] has moved from theory into practice after the United Nations Conference on Environment and Development in Rio de Janeiro in 1992. Libraries' operations had the basic characteristics of sustainable practices long before the concept of sustainability gained a wider acceptance. The economic model of library operations has been characterized by frequent borrowing instead of constant buying of information materials, and by sharing resources rather than unnecessary duplication. Social equity values have been practiced in libraries by collecting, archiving, preserving, and providing public access to collections for all current and future users. Environmental values have been expressed by developing collections focused on environmental topics, teaching environmental literacy, disseminating environmental information, building green libraries, and green practices and sustainable solutions taking place in libraries.

Recently, green practices and sustainable solutions in public and academic libraries have grown considerably. The American Library Association (ALA) has played an important role in shaping the history of environmental activities in librarianship and providing a platform for action. This timeline presents the last 21 years of ALA's green units, programs, practices, initiatives, and actions, and acknowledges librarians involved in these activities. Many of the programs and actions included in the timeline were organized by the Task Force on the Environment (TFOE) and its members, as one group of the Social Responsibilities Round Table (SRRT). The TFOE was a prominent, but not the only entity in the ALA to present program, concerns, and action about environmental sustainability. Other groups that actively promoted the concept of environmental sustainability in libraries included: SRRT, Library Leadership and Management Association (LLAMA), Association of College and Research (ACRL), Government Documents Round Table (GODORT), Library and Information Technology (LITA), Public Library Association (PLA), and Business Reference & Services Section (BRASS).

The intent of this retrospective is to provide a starting point for a more comprehensive assessment of the ALA's and individual libraries' progress towards environmental sustainability, and to contribute to a discourse on pathways that can enable sustainable development of libraries in the future.

1989: Creation of the TFOE as One of the SRRT Round Tables During the ALA Annual Conference in Dallas

In 1989, the year of the Exxon Valdez oil spill in the Gulf of Alaska, Elizabeth Morrissett, a librarian from the Alaska Pacific University, received an approval from the ALA's Action Council to form the Environmental Information Task Force. As Elizabeth stated, "such a task force is long overdue within SRRT and ALA, especially given the current governmental situation in the U.S."[2] The TFOE was the first official venue for ALA librarians interested in environmental issues following the lead of librarians in the Special Library Association (SLA), who by the late 1970s already worked on and discussed issues related to the dissemination of environmental information, management of natural resources, and libraries' roles in supporting environmental research. The first TFOE organizational meeting took place in Dallas.

1990: Environmental Events During the ALA Annual Conference in Chicago

From the beginning until today the TFOE's objectives have been to:

- "Promote awareness of environmental issues within ALA;
- Unite librarians and information professionals for mutual benefit and support;
- Provide TFOE members with opportunities for career development, skills enhancement, and leadership experiences;

- Facilitate networking among peers and professional associates;
- Provide services, programs and publications that assist TFOE members and others in their careers, workplaces, homes and communities."[3]

Terry Link, an information/reference librarian from Michigan State University Library took over TFOE's helm after Elizabeth Morrissett. During the Chicago conference the members of the task force met four times to discuss its role in the ALA, programs for future conferences, and related projects. The same year the *Library Journal* published an article by Terry Link and the TFOE members titled "Sources for a Small Planet: Environmental Bibliographies Reflect a Question of Values." In the article, the founding members of TFOE compiled sources pertaining to green consumerism, biodiversity, pesticides, periodicals, books for parents and children on the environment, online information, and sources of environmental information with a listing of first electronic forums on BITNET, Biosphere, Ecology Discussion List, Conslink, Econet, and Usenet news groups.[4] In October 1990, the *Canadian Library Journal* published the winning Student Article Contest by Susan A. Safyan titled "Access to Information for Environmentalists: A Library Perspectives."

1991: Environmental Programs and Events During the ALA Annual Conference in Atlanta

In Atlanta the first TFOE program was titled "How Green is Your Library: Environmentalists at Work," where Laurie Sabol, Elaine Clark, Terry Link, and John Sams focused on environmental issues concerns all libraries, and various green initiatives in libraries. TFOE also co-sponsored two other sessions. The first session on "Empowering the Public: Information Literacy for Environmental Issues," was organized in collaboration with the ACRL's Law and Political Science Section and provided an overview of legal environmental issues that people confront at the local, state, and national level. The second session on "Environmental Information Resources" was organized in collaboration with the Public Library Association Metropolitan Libraries Section. During the TFOE's two business meetings, librarians discussed issues related to greening the ALA conferences, sick building syndromes, race, poverty and an environmental award for publishers, and topics for future conference programs.

The TFOE members also decided to support publishing of the *Green Library Journal: Environmental Topics in the Information World* by the University of Idaho. The journal's goal was to disseminate information on international environmental resources to places and countries where accesses to these resources were limited.

1992: Environmental Programs and Events During the ALA Annual Conference in San Francisco

In San Francisco, David Brower, a chairman of the Earth Island Institute and a former chair of the Sierra Club, was the main speaker for TFOE's program on "Poverty, Development and the Environment: Information Challenges for Libraries." Brower and other presenters discussed how governments and citizens were working to address poverty and the environment and how libraries and librarians could help societies deal with these problems. The second TFOE program, "Tools of the Trade or Poisons for the Planet: the Environmental Impact of Paper, Computers, and Microfilm," was focused on environmental concerns with production and the use of various media in the workplace. During two TFOE business meetings, members concentrated on issues related to a green award for publisher, a proposal for publishing "Environmental Information Sources: a Guide for Citizens and Libraries," and a program for the New Orleans conference. Nancy Pope and Trish Cruise were appointed as the new co-chairs of TFOE.

1993: Environmental Programs and Events During the ALA Annual Conference in New Orleans

The 1993 ALA conference was marked by TFOE's resolution on the use of chlorine-free papers by the ALA. In New Orleans, the Task Force's program on "Tracing the Ecological History of Louisiana's Coast through Special Collections and Technology" featured Richard Condrey, Dwain Zack, and Nancy Pope discussing research on coastal ecology using the special collections of the Louisiana State University Libraries and a scanning project of the 19th century French monograph. TFOE held two business meetings devoted to the environmental bibliography book project, the resolution on the use of chlorine-free papers, programming for the Miami conference, and election of a new chair, Maria A. Jankowska from the University of Idaho, Moscow.

1994: Environmental Programs and Events During and After the ALA Annual Conference in Miami

In Miami, TFOE presented "Libraries in the Balance: Bridges to Environmental Information" with David Fisher, Gayle Alston, Laura Powers, and Millicent Gaskell as invited speakers. *Library Journal* categorized this program as a valuable source of current environmental information. During two business meetings, TFOE worked on a dialogue with the Exhibits Round Table concerning ALA's environmental impact on exhibitors, and a letter to endorse the concept of the National Institute for the Environment. Other activities included a discussion on the "Environmental Information Access Project" with a nonprofit organization Libraries in the Future from New York, creation of the TFOE newsletter, and the presentation of the resolution on the use of chlorine-free papers. Maria A. Jankowska was elected as co-chair of the Task Force, with Millicent Gaskell from the South Jersey Environmental Information Center, West Deptford Public Library, New Jersey.

In June 1994, the first issue of the *Electronic Green Journal* (*EGJ*) was published by the University of Idaho Library with the support of TFOE members. *EGJ* was the first peer-reviewed digitally born journal that provided open access to scholarly international environmental information via gopher and FTP. The journal was edited by librarians and published by the academic library.

1995: Environmental Programs and Events During the ALA Annual Conference in Chicago

In Chicago, TFOE presented the program titled "Global Change Data and Information Systems: Roles of the Libraries," with Robert Rand, Linda Hill, Gerald Barton, Patty Owen, and Fred Stoss as speakers. The session was focused on libraries participating in the U.S. Global Change Data and Information System (GCDIS) that provided the full spectrum of information services for the worldwide dissemination of environmental information. During two Task Force business meetings, Harriet DeCeunynck presented an update on the Clinton administration and the environment. Also, the final version of the resolution on chlorine-free papers used by ALA was presented. Fred Stoss from Carbon Dioxide Information Analysis Center, Oak Ridge National Laboratory, in Tennessee was elected as the new TFOE chair.

1996: Environmental Programs and Events During the ALA Annual Conference in New York

In New York, TFOE's program focused on "Environmentally and Socially Responsible Business: Finding the Information to Make the Decision to Buy or Invest" with Albert Wilson, TIAA–CREF; Alice Tepper Marlin, Council on Economic Priorities; Steven Lydenberg, Strategic Vision for Domini Social Investment; and Terry Link, Michigan State University Library . The program examined how companies, corporations, or pension funds could operate in an environmentally and socially responsible manner. Members of TFOE also visited the U.S Environmental Protection Agency's (EPA) Region 2 Library. The open house provided an opportunity for TFOE members to meet EPA library staff and to establish networking and communication links to the environmental resources community. During two business meetings, TFOE members concentrated on an award for outstanding environmental children's books, bringing the resolution on the use of chlorine-free papers to the floor for discussion and discussion of the final presentation to SRRT members at the 1997 midwinter meeting in Washington, DC. Fred Stoss from the State University of New York, Buffalo was re-elected as the TFOE chair.

1997: Environmental Programs and Events Before and During the ALA Annual Conference in San Francisco

TFOE held two programs in San Francisco. "The Need for an Environmental Information Infrastructure," and "Environmental Education Resources for the 21st Century." TFOE members concentrated on the ALA Budget Analysis and Review Committee's answer to the resolution on use of the free papers, which stated that moving to chlorine-free printing would increase ALA expenses from $70,000 to $120,000 annually. The resolution recommended that ALA for its publications and correspondence use only chlorine-free papers. Maria A. Jankowska was re-elected as chair of TFOE with Fred Stoss as co-chair. In order to improve communication with both members and non-members of the American Library Association, TFOE's web page was created with links to valuable information sources, a TFOE's mailing list, and an electronic newsletter, *GreeNotes* were established.

1998: Environmental Programs and Events During the ALA Annual Conference in Washington, DC

Going Green @ ALA was a theme for the 1998 conference in Washington, DC. TFOE sponsored a program on "Chemical Facts—Essential Resources for Your Library Collection" that presented two significant resources on hazardous substances: *Chemical Fact Sheets* published by the EPA and *Chemical Scorecard* published by Environmental Defense Fund. During the DC conference the members of TFOE participated in programs entitled "Social Research and GIS: Applications for the Library," "National Library for the Environment—An Update," and "Global Reach Local Touch: The Environmental Protection Agency Headquarters Libraries." This last program was an open house held at the EPA Head Quarters Information Resources Center in Washington, DC. Another conference program devoted to environmental issues was titled "It Isn't Easy to be Green: Environmentally Friendly Libraries Sustaining Our Resources" which was organized by the LLAMA Safety and Security of Library Buildings Committee. During two business meetings, the members of TFOE endorsed the creation of a digital National Library for the Environment, discussed a resolution for environmentally responsible papers, and planned a program for the New Orleans conference. Maria A. Jankowska remained the TFOE chair.

1999: Environmental Programs and Actions During the ALA Annual Conference in New Orleans

In New Orleans, TFOE presented "Environmental Resources for Public, School, and Academic Libraries: Making Environmental Information Relevant" with Carolyn Offutt, Richard Huffine, Fred Stoss, and Maria A. Jankowska as speakers. The program concentrated on the essentials of the EPA Superfund Program, navigating the EPA in cyberspace, resources for Earth Day, and presentation of the *Electronic Green Journal*. The second program, "GIS as a Tool for Collaborative Spatial Decision Making (CSDM): Libraries Perspective," was co-sponsored by LITA Geographic Information Systems Interest Group. The program, presented by Piotr Jankowski, a geography professor from the University of Idaho, focused on collaborative spatial decision making, an emerging field combining GIS and a group approach to decision-making, and its application to an environmental restoration plan for the Duwamish Waterway in Seattle. The program also presented the Idaho Geospatial Data Center, known today as Interactive Numeric & Spatial Information Data Engine (INSIDE Idaho), as an example of online geographical data repository responding to public needs for spatial information. Two business meetings concentrated on questions of the relevancy of TFOE activities to librarians' interests and needs, and steps aimed at attracting more members. Maria A. Jankowska and Fred Stoss were elected as co-chairs of TFOE.

2000: Environmental Programs and Actions During the ALA Annual Conference in Chicago

The ALA president, Sarah A. Long, focused her 1999–2000 term on the theme "Libraries Build Community." In her presidential address, she stated, "Libraries in the United States have a unique opportunity to show their concern about the environment."[5] One of her initiatives was support for a special pre-conference workshop held at the ALA Conference in Chicago on July 6, 2000. The main goal of the workshop was to teach librarians community-building skills in order to promote sustainable development in their localities. TFOE program demonstrated on how libraries could sustain the momentum of Earth Day throughout the year with "Libraries Making Earth Day Every Day" with

Jeffrey L. Brown, Executive Director, Global Learning Inc., Fred Stoss, SRRT Coordinator, Maria A. Jankowska, chair of the TFOE and general editor of the *Electronic Green Journal*, and Irwin Weintraub, Life Sciences Specialist from the City University of New York, Brooklyn. Maria A. Jankowska and Irwin Weintraub were elected as co-chairs of TFOE.

2001: Environmental Programs and Events During the ALA Annual Conference in Chicago

"Sustaining Communities: Deciding Tomorrow Today" was the theme for the workshops at the ALA Annual Conference in 2001. Workshop participants enjoyed an interactive activity called "Postcards from Home." The postcards addressed issues related to auto traffic and parking lot space in a small suburban town, the damaging effects of coal mining on mountain ranges, unplanned development, urban sprawl, and maintaining clean drinking water resources. As part of the workshop, the participants enjoyed the Community Inventory Role Playing activity. This exercise demonstrated how public libraries could be involved in local communities in many domains including: economic development, air quality, land use, job training, health care, civic participation, literacy, and quality education. The ALA theme on "Libraries Build Community" brought important sustainability values into the profession, and presented ways to change the library's image as an active partner in building local sustainable communities.[6] "Libraries Build Sustainable Communities" was a major program for the Association in 1999–2001. All training for 1,900 librarians expanded their knowledge and outreach efforts towards sustainability. In Chicago TFOE organized a program on "Earth Day in the 21st century: Environmental Activism," with Denis Hayes, one of the co-founders of the first Earth Day in 1970. The second program, "Sustaining Libraries for the Future: Energy Efficiency, Friendly Buildings, and Libraries' Sustainability," had three speakers: Donald Wulfinghoff from Wulfinghoff Energy Services explained how libraries could have more funds to buy library materials by savings energy expenses; James Weiner offered practical guidelines on how to plan, design, and operate library buildings that are energy efficient and conserve resources; and Cate Gable from Axion Communications International focused on how information technology and the global ecological crises could impact the sustainability of libraries. Maria A. Jankowska, University of Idaho Library, and Irwin Weintraub, Rutgers University Library, were elected as the co-chairs of TFOE.

2002: Environmental Programs During the ALA Annual Conference in Atlanta

In Atlanta, TFOE program "Promoting Public Health and Community Protection: Can Libraries Help?" was presented by speakers from government, Mary Hudak, the Federal Emergency Management Agency (FEMA), academia, Marlena Wald, Emory University School of Medicine, and a consulting firm, Amy Vickers, Amy Vickers and Associates. The speakers educated the public about disaster relief communication, community health, water conservation, and sustainable living resources and practices. The second TFOE program, organized with LLAMA, "Going Green without Going Broke: High Impact, Low Cost" highlighted environmentally responsible products and solutions adopted in the building of Multnomah County Library. Speakers included the library director, Ginnie Cooper, the architect, Ralph DiNola, and Alan Locke, both from the consulting engineering firm involved in the building's design. Maria A. Jankowska and Irwin Weintraub remained the co-chairs of TFOE.

2003: Environmental Programs and Events During the ALA Annual Conference in Toronto

Ralph Nader, the 2000 Green Party presidential candidate, was the keynote speaker for Maurice J. Freedman's ALA President's Program. "Clear the Air and Water—Environmental Selections for Children, the Public and Academic Libraries" presented a selection of environmental resources for children, academic researchers, and the general public. The program speakers included Judy Halpern, from The Magic Suitcase in Kitchener, Ontario, Canada; Maria A. Latyszewskyj, Environment Canada Library in Toronto; and Tim Grant, Co-Editor, *Green Teacher* in Canada. Speakers discussed and demonstrated various outreach initiatives going beyond library walls to educate the public about the environment. Maria A. Jankowska and Jonathan Betz-Zall, Branch Librarian, City University, Everett, Washington became the co-chairs of TFOE.

2004: Environmental Program During the ALA Annual Conference in Orlando

For the conference in Orlando TFOE sponsored a program on the environment and intellectual freedom resources, "Are You Missing Any Information? Speaking and Publishing Freely on the Environment." Maria A. Jankowska and Jonathan Betz-Zall remained the co-chairs of TFOE.

2005: Environmental Programs and Events During the ALA Annual Conference in Chicago

For the first time, the ALA conference attendees enjoyed discounted rates on bicycle rentals ($10 per day, which included the use of a helmet and lock) to help them get around Chicago without having to burn petroleum fuel. The TFOE program "Get the Lead (Information) Out!" presented access to timely information helping to identify children at risk in urban, suburban, and rural communities. Speakers from federal, state, and local lead poisoning prevention programs described the extent of the lead poisoning and efforts to prevent lead exposure, and addressed the issue of community involvement in preventing lead poisoning. TFOE also organized an open house at the EPA library in Chicago and joined the ALA Conference Services in discussing how ALA's conferences could best observe green practices. Fred Stoss and Jonathan Betz-Zall were elected as the co-chairs of TFOE.

2006: Environmental Programs and Activities During and After the ALA Annual Conference in Orlando

After the tragedy following hurricanes Katrina and Rita, the need for more effective emergency preparedness and greater collaboration at all levels of society became apparent. "Preparedness Matters: Planning for Disaster," a half-day workshop organized by TFOE, addressed the role of libraries in helping the communities they serve to develop community disaster and emergency preparedness programs, and assisting in recovery plans and operations in response to an emergency or disaster. Gayle Alston, from the Department of Homeland Security/FEMA Region 4 in Atlanta, and Fred Stoss, a librarian from the State University of New York, Buffalo, led the workshop. ALA took strong action in saving the EPA libraries: ALA President Leslie Burger spoke on EPA Library Closings at the National Advisory Council Meeting and the ALA passed Resolution on EPA Libraries[7] and Resolution on Protecting the Toxics Release Inventory Program. Fred Stoss and Jonathan Betz-Zall were elected as the co-chairs of TFOE.

2007: Environmental Programs During the ALA Annual Conference in Washington, DC and Beyond

The ALA program, "A Contract with our Future" presented by Robert Kennedy, Jr. focused on environmental policy and sustainable development. "Finding Environmental Information in the New Millennium: Continuing the Dialogue" was sponsored by the GODORT, Federal and Armed Forces Libraries

Roundtable, and TFOE hosted a dialogue on access to environmental information. Speakers included Bernadine Abbott Hoduski, Government Information Advisor and the founder of the ALA Government Documents Round Table; Jonathan Betz-Zall, Reference Librarian for Highline Community College in Des Moines, Washington; Emma J. McNamara, Information Access Division of Information Analysis and Access in the Office of Environmental Information of the US EPA; Jeff Ruch, Public Employees for Environmental Responsibility. Fred Stoss, University of New York at Buffalo, Arts & Sciences Libraries, was the moderator. In the program "The Data and Information Behind "Truth:" A Librarian's Perspective on Global Warming" Fred Stoss, trained by Al Gore and The Climate Project staff, reviewed data and resources used in Gore's Oscar-winning documentary film and *New York Times* bestselling book, *An Inconvenient Truth.* The ALA President Leslie Burger testified on EPA Library Closings to Senate Environment and Public Works Committee.[8] Outside the ALA "Eco-Libris: Plant a Tree for Every Book You Read" blog was founded[9] and the wiki Guide for Architects and Librarians was created by the ACRL/LAMA Designing Spaces for Higher Education Task Force. Fred Stoss and Jonathan Betz-Zall were elected as the co-chairs of TFOE.

2008: Environmental Programs and Activities During the Midwinter Conference in Philadelphia, the ALA Annual Conference in Anaheim, and After Conferences

During the midwinter conference in Philadelphia, Monika Antonelli from the Minnesota State University, Mankato, Elaine Harger from SRRT, and Fred Stoss from TFOE organized the "Cup by Cup for a Greener ALA" a drive which encouraged librarians to bring their own cups to the conference instead of using expendable drinking utensils. The drive was considered a successful environmental campaign.[10] TFOE also organized a program on "Nature and the Environment @ your library: Nature Journals as a Tool for Children's Library Program," which presented the use of nature journaling to enhance children's environmental literacy programs in libraries. Speakers included Doug Wechsler, Director, The Academy of Natural Sciences; Mark Baldwin, Director of Education; Roger Tory Peterson, Institute of Natural History; and Andy Boyles, Science Editor, Boyds Mill Press and *Highlights for Children* magazine.

In Anaheim, TFOE presented two programs. "Earth Wind and Fire @ Your Library: Changing Climate and Changing Lives" focused on the consequences of global warming in our homes, places of work, and recreation. The program emphasized the world-wide aspects of global climate change while discussing energy-smart and environmentally friendly behaviors needed to address the climate crisis. The main speaker was Fred Stoss, who was among the first 500 people to present Al Gore's *Inconvenient Truth* slide show on climate change. The second program, "Greening of the Presses," presented speakers from the Green Press Initiative, the Book Industry Study Group, and New Society Press. They discussed the environmental impact of book publishing and printing and the need for environmental stewardship within the publishing world. Also during the ALA conference in Anaheim, LLAMA presented preconference tours of green designs room the Santa Monica and Cerritos, California libraries. Two other conference programs were "Sustainable Libraries: Shades of Green," devoted to green library buildings presented by Peter Magnani and Greg Mullen, and "Security & Preservation of Rare Materials: Planning an Environmental Building Model" with Caryn J. Carr, Director of Pennsylvania State Library; Larry Nesbit, Chair, Rare Books Room Committee; Cornelius Rusnov, Project Architect; and William Joyce, Head of Special Collections, Pennsylvania State University. After the ALA conferences the ACRL lead OnPoint live chat session engaging librarians in discussion on Green Libraries. The *Electronic Green Journal* changed its publisher from the University of Idaho Library to the University of California Los Angeles (UCLA) Library and has been published via the University of California eScholarship. In 2008 also *Going Green @ your library* website on environmentally friendly practices for libraries and beyond was created by Beth Filar Williams from the University of North Carolina Greensboro and the *Green Library* blog on green activities, events, literature, and project that focused on libraries was started by Gerry McKiernan from the Library of Iowa State University. Fred Stoss and Jonathan Betz-Zall remained the co-chairs of TFOE.

2009: Environmental Programs During the National Meeting of the ACRL Conference in Seattle, ALA Midwinter in Denver, and the ALA Annual Conference in Chicago

In Seattle, the ACRL's conference attendees signed Green Pledge to put ecological ideas into practice. The conference featured bags made of recycled materials and the lack of tangible handouts at program sessions. The conference was called "the most eco-friendly major event ever held by an ALA division."[11] After the conference the ACRL continued OnPoint chat on Seattle Green: Lessons Learned from greening the ACRL 14th National Conference.

During ALA midwinter conference in Denver, the TFOE discussion focused on "Kermit, It Is Easy Being Green! Librarians' Perspectives and Ideas." In Chicago Wanda Urbanska "urged the crowd to make green choices in their libraries and their lives. Reclaim your role as eco-role models and exemplars in your community," she said. "Change is happening rapidly. Let libraries continue to be at the center of it."[12] The TFOE program, "Grassroots Greening / Greening Libraries from the Inside," examined green activities in public and academic libraries. The ALA publishing went greener. "Each year, approximately 30 million trees are used to make books sold in the United States 1,153 times the number of trees in New York City's Central Park, according the Green Press Initiative (GPI). This statement, among other issues and concerns, has prompted ALAs Publishing Committee to examine ALAs green publishing practices, with the goal of making them as environmentally friendly as possible,"[13] The *CLS Newsletter,* a semiannual publication of the College Libraries Section of the Association of College and Research also switched to electronic format. "Advantages to an e-only publication are obvious: unlimited page count, color vs. black/white, environmentally friendly, and it saves the association about $12,600!"[14]

Also the Green Libraries website for information about green and sustainable libraries in North America was created by Monika Antonelli and the Green Libraries Community wiki was stated by Fred Stoss, who remained the chair of TFOE.

2010: Environmental Programs During the ALA Annual Conference in Washington, DC and Beyond

In Washington, DC ALA's Business Reference & Services Section presented a program titled "Clean, Green, and Not so Mean: Can Business Help Save the World?" This program revealed the trends that help transform business from the boardroom to the grassroots level. Speakers included: Timothy Fort from George Washington University School of Business; Lisa Hall, CEO and Founder of Community IT Innovators, and Michael Matos, Business and Economics Librarian at the American University, Washington DC. The TFOE co-sponsored a program with the new ACRL Interest Group on Health Science entitled, "Is It Safe to Go Outside? Health Effects of Climate Change and Global Warming," was cancelled. Librarians Lise Van Susteren and Fred Stoss travelled to Nashville for training session with Al Gore on climate change. The ALA made a decision to hold an online green election for the first time.

The ALA edition of Kathryn Miller's *Public Libraries Going Green* was published by the American Library Association, and also Sam McBane Mulford and Ned A. Himmel published *How Green is My Library?* by Libraries Unlimited. Maria A. Jankowska from the Charles E. Young Research Library, UCLA became a chair of TFOE.

For more than twenty years, ALA librarians have worked on many environmental resolutions, programs, actions, campaigns, activities, and operations.

TFOE together with SRRT, LLAMA, ACRL, GODOR, LITA, BRASS, and PLA, introduced the use of chlorine-free papers in publishing and their communication operations, recycling practices and greening conferences. Green library proponents participated in environmental initiatives aimed at book publishing,[15] disseminated environmental information, participated in environmental scholarly communication by publishing the *Electronic Green Journal*, saved the EPA libraries, and contributed to building sustainable communities , as well as designing and building green libraries.

This timeline presents the diversity of actions covering many facets of environmental programs and practices in libraries and librarianship. An assessment of these actions might lead the ALA and its members to take proactive steps to guarantee the future development of sustainable libraries not only in regard of environment but also social and economic components. Such steps could include exercising environmental stewardship in collaboration with the publishing industry, further greening of the ALA conferences, requiring green practices and products from vendors, and developing the Association's guidelines for environmental sustainability as part of strategic planning for public and academic libraries.

Endnotes

1. World Commission on Environment and Development (WCED). Our Common Future. Oxford: Oxford University Press, 1987 p. 43.

2. New SRRT Task Force to Form. SRRT Newsletter: A Publication of the Social Responsibility Round Table of the American Library Association 91, (March 1989):3. http://libr.org/srrt/news/srrt091.pdf.

3. American Library Association. Task Force on the Environment. http://www.ala.org/ala/mgrps/rts/srrt/tfoe/taskforceenvironment.cfm.

4. Maria A. Jankowska, "The Need for Environmental Information Quality," *Issues in Science and Technology Librarianship*, Spring 2000. http://www.library.ucsb.edu/istl/00-spring/article5.html.

5. Sarah A. Long, "Libraries Can Help Build Sustainable Communities," American Libraries, June/July 2000, p. 7.

6. Maria A. Jankowska, "Can the ALA interest in sustainable development be continued?" (2001). *Public Libraries* 40 (1): 22–23.

7. ALA. EPA Library Closings http://www.ala.org/ala/issuesadvocacy/advocacy/federallegislation/govinfo/fedlibs/epalibraries/index.cfm.

8.   American Library Association. Testimony before the U.S. Senate. Environment and Public Works Committee. February 6, 2007. Available at: http://www.ala.org/ala/issuesadvocacy/advocacy/federallegislation/govinfo/fedlibs/epalibraries/EPA_Testimony_burger_Final.pdf.

9.   Eco-Libris as a member of the Sustainable Business Network of Greater Philadelphia started campaign "Every book you read was once a tree. Now you can plant a tree for every book you read." http://www.ecolibris.net/.

10. Cup by Cup: Librarians Raise their Cups for Planet Earth. http://wikis.ala.org/midwinter2008/index.php/Cup_by_Cup.

11. ALA. Campus libraries continue to thrive in age of Google, FaceBook, Twitter. (March 3, 2009) http://www.ala.org/ala/newspresscenter/news/pressreleases2009/march2009/acrlcampuslibsthrive.cfm.

12 . Greg Landgraf, Urbanska Sees Positive Signs for Green Libraries. AL *Inside Scoop* (July 2009) http://www.al.ala.org/insidescoop/2009/07/12/urbanska-sees-positive-signs-for-green-libraries/.

13. ALA Publishing Goes Greener. Cognotes 3 (January 25, 2009):3 http://www.ala.org/ala/aboutala/offices/conference/confservices/Cognotes%20Sun%20Jan%2025%20.pdf.

14. Last print edition –Goin' Green. *CLS Newsletter* 25 issue 2 (Fall 2009):4 http://www.ala.org/ala/mgrps/divs/acrl/about/sections/cls/newsletters/clsnewsfall09.pdf.

15. Fred Stoss, "How and Why We Got Here Today: A History of the ALA Task Force on the Environment," *SRRT Newsletter* 168, (September 2009). http://libr.org/srrt/news/srrt168.html#6.1.

Building on Green: Sustainable Thinking Goes Beyond Green to Unite Library Space and Community

Audrey Barbakoff & Brett Barbakoff

When we green a library building, what do we really want to accomplish? Of course we like the immediate environmental brownie points, and a reduced energy bill doesn't hurt, either. But aren't we also thinking about the great publicity and increased library use the upgrade is sure to bring, at least temporarily? We recognize that a green space has a significant impact on our community as well as on our environment. However, we often fail to articulate for ourselves the relationship between green building and sustainable community. After all, green buildings are ostensibly proof that we in the library profession have embraced our stewardship over the earth's resources and the well-being of the communities we serve. Yet even as we celebrate the installation of photovoltaic panels or the construction of a new, energy-efficient building, we may be betraying the very values we support. These buildings are no doubt green, but are they—and are we—sustainable?

Green is Not a Synonym for Sustainable

The terms green and sustainable have become functionally synonymous in common usage; however, their actual meanings are distinct. Green means simply environmentally friendly. Whether referring to something as large as the construction of a new, state-of-the-art library building or as small as encouraging patrons to carry books in reusable bags, a green decision is "of, pertaining to, or supporting environmentalism."[1] There are many wonderful digital and print resources for information on how to green your library,[2] so I will not focus on that here.

Sustainability, on the other hand, has a temporal constraint. By definition, something sustainable must be, well, . . . sustained. It must "be capable of being maintained at a certain rate or level"; its effects must be for the "long-term."[3] This is the key distinction we must consider when making choices for the library. It is wonderful to be green, of course, but the positive effects of a green decision may be fleeting. Those high-tech gadgets will not be cutting-edge forever; in a few years they will be supplanted by newer, more effective technologies. Today's photovoltaic panel is tomorrow's coal stove. Worse, our gadgetry may actually have negative unintended consequences on our ability to build community.

A recent study from the University of Toronto demonstrated that making a "green" purchase, such as organic produce, can lead people to act unethically. The authors conclude that "behaviors are figured into an implicit calculation of self-perception where virtuous behaviors boost moral self-image while transgressions dampen it. . . . [Thus, people] are least likely to scrutinize moral implications and regulate their behaviors right after their moral self experienced a boost from a good deed. This implies that virtuous acts can license subsequent asocial and unethical behaviors."[4] If we encourage our communities to purchase a green library with their tax dollars but do not require citizen involvement, it is possible that we are discouraging individuals from the positive social interactions sustainable communities require.

The larger conclusion we must draw is that sustainability is not about piecemeal changes, such as buying organic produce or even a new library. We cannot simply plug in a new green building where the old library once stood and expect

---

1. Green, *The Oxford English Dictionary Online*, http://dictionary.oed.com (accessed January 18 2010).

2. For more on this topic, see Monika Antonelli, "The Green Library Movement: An Overview of Green Library Literature and Actions from 1979 to the Future of Green Libraries" *EGJ* 27 (2008), http://escholarship.org/uc/item/39d3v236.; or Johanna Sands and Libris Design Project, *Sustainable Library Design* (San Francisco: C.M Salter Associates, 2000). A few digital resources, though there are many others: Green Libraries' "Resource" page, http://www.greenlibraries.org/resources, and http://thegreenlibraryblog.blogspot.com.

3. Sustainable, *The Oxford English Dictionary Online*, http://dictionary.oed.com (accessed January 18 2010).

4. Nina Mazar Chen-Bo Zhong, "Do Green Products Make Us Better People?" *Psychological Science* 21 (4), (2010): 494–498.

a profound, permanent, and systemic change. If our choices are merely green, this burst of environmental responsibility will be reduced to a blip in the long history of the public library when the new eco-toy proves too expensive to install or maintain. If, however, we cultivate an attitude of sustainability in ourselves and our communities, we will build long-term solutions that maintain the gains for which we have worked and offer benefits we have not even imagined.

The Library as Place Fosters Environmental and Community Sustainability

Though we often hear about sustainability in the context of buildings, the library profession has long recognized its role in community as well. The American Library Association sponsored a "Libraries Build Sustainable Community" project from 1999–2001, and the resulting web resources are still maintained by its Social Responsibilities Round Table.[5] Connections between libraries and sustainable communities have been drawn by Frederick W. Stoss,[6] past ALA President Sarah Ann Long,[7] Don Sager[8] and Jonathan Betz-Zall,[9] among others. But what does sustainable community mean, and how does that relate to our understanding of sustainable building?

Jeffrey L. Brown, director of Global Learning Inc., answers that "a sustainable community not only lasts over time, but also takes care of the environment and the community's natural resource base, provides opportunities for ample livelihoods, and treats all its members fairly."[10] To me, however, this reads more like a description of what the sustainable community does than of what it is. The "Libraries Build Sustainable Communities" page never really offers a concrete explanation. It discusses three elements of sustainable communities: economy, ecology, and equity. It mentions, in various prominent places, attributes such

---

5. ALA, "Libraries Build Sustainable Communities," American Library Association, http://www.ala.org/ala/mgrps/rts/srrt/tfoe/lbsc/librariesbuild.cfm.

6. F.W. Stoss, "Sustainable Communities and the Roles Libraries and Librarians Play," *Reference and User Services Quarterly* 42, no. 3 (2003): 206–210.

7. Sarah Ann Long, "Libraries Can Help Build Sustainable Communities," *American Libraries*, 31, no. 26 (2001): 7.

8. Don Sager, "Public Libraries and the Sustainable Communities Movement," *Public Libraries* 40 (2001): 22.

9. Jonathan Betz-Zall, "Libraries Build Sustainable Communities at PNLA," *PNLA Q* 67, no. 1 (2002): 5.

10. Jeffrey L. Brown, "Making a Huge Difference in So Many Little Ways," *Public Libraries* 40 (2001): 22.

as long-term resource planning, environmental responsibility, money, diversity, technology, and community decision-making.[11] Librarians seem to have jumped straight into how to create sustainable community before identifying clearly what it is. This is tremendously dangerous. Without a definition, we cannot hope to capitalize on the relationship between sustainable communities and sustainable buildings to the maximum benefit of the environment, our users, and ourselves.

The definition I offer is simple and widely applicable. Sustainability, whether applied to cities, communities, buildings or individuals, is about the recognition and strengthening of connections. A sustainable design recognizes and enhances its relationship with its surroundings and resources; a sustainable community forges enduring bonds between people and institutions. A green building alone does not necessarily promote sustainable community, nor is it any guarantee that the library will continue environmentally-friendly practices in the future, because it does not inherently build important human connections. However, when we design the library space to intentionally situate the library within its human and environmental ecosystem, each can enhance the other. Librarians and architects must understand and consciously mold the dynamic between the library space and the community in order to maximize the sustainability of both.

When space is well-designed there is often no distinction between environmental and community sustainability. Consider, for example, a community that makes a simple decision to locate its library in a busy part of town. Environmentally this is sustainable, as it encourages residents to walk, bike or take public transit rather than drive. However, it is equally beneficial in terms of sustainable community. More people will gather more frequently at the library, because it is convenient, highly visible, and because, without a car, they are likely to check out fewer items per trip. The hope is that this results in more interactions between diverse users and a strong positive association with the physical library, enhancing residents' sense of community.[12]

Studies support this common-sense connection between space and a feeling of community. Environmental psychologist Terri Mannarini noted that "residents who provided positive descriptions of places, accordingly proved to have a more marked sense of belonging to the human and physical community; . . . on the contrary, those who associated it with negative traits were characterized by

---

11. ALA, "Libraries Build Sustainable Communities," American Library Association, http://www.ala.org/ala/mgrps/rts/srrt/tfoe/lbsc/librariesbuild.cfm.

12. The Storefront Library in Boston is an interesting example of the possible community impact of a well-situated library. See http://www.storefrontlibrary.org for details.

a weaker emotional bond with their neighborhood."[13] Residents' sense of community is tied to positive associations with place. The library, as a public space, is uniquely positioned to create a healthy, environmentally responsible, and inviting building with the power to reinforce a sense of community for all residents.

In turn, a strong community directly affects the environmental sustainability and general flourishing of the library. An involved and supportive community is more likely to agree to any future green developments the library would like to make. In this way, a sustainable community becomes the difference between a library structure that is green for now and one that will continue to be sustainable for the future. The community needs the library's communal space in order to develop the network of deep and casual bonds which make it sustainable ("bonding" and "bridging" social capital),[14] but the library also depends profoundly on the community to support its environmental initiatives. Through conscious use of space, library and community recognize and reinforce their interconnectedness; both are made more sustainable.

With this acknowledgment of interdependency, the library no longer serves the community as a benevolent outsider; it is part of the community. Thus, when a library considers a green building, it should ask itself not only the impact its choices will have on the environment, but also and even primarily on the people it serves. What message does the grand, gaping Central Library set apart from the rest of the city landscape send about our commitment to integration, community, and sustainability?

Library as Place Affects the Library's Mission

Professional literature has begun to emphasize that space is not some secondary aesthetic consideration but an essential factor in how we experience the library.[15] The example of a library being located in a busy section of town is only

---

13. Terri Mannarini et al., "Image of Neighborhood, Self-Image and Sense of Community," *Journal of Environmental Psychology* 26 (2006): 211.

14. Robert Putnam, *Bowling Alone: The Collapse and Revival of American Community*. (New York: Simon & Schuster, 2000): 23.

15. Karen Fisher et al., "Seattle Public Library as Place: Reconceptualizing Space, Community, and Information at the Central Library," in *The Library as Place: History, Community, and Culture*, ed. John E. Buschman and Gloria J. Leckie (Westport, CT: Libraries Unlimited, 2007): 134–160; Emily Ranseen, "The Library as Place: Changing Perspectives," *Libr Adm Manage* 16, no. 4 (2002): 203–207.; Council on Library and Information Resources, *Library as Place: Rethinking Roles, Rethinking Space*, (Washington, D.C.: Council on Library and Information Resources, 2005).

one small and obvious way that space can be manipulated for the benefit of all. When many design decisions work in tandem to shape that space, their impact on the community can be extremely powerful. The way patrons interact with the library space affects the library's core missions as information provider, builder of social capital and democratic symbol.

Many consider providing information to the community to be the central mission of libraries. Without changing the formal services offered, altering the library space can profoundly enhance the information-seeking environment. It is intuitive that a hidden, inaccessible, or intimidating reference desk will draw fewer patrons than an approachable one. It is less intuitive but equally important to recognize and facilitate the ways people seek information not from librarians or Google, but from each other. By creating comfortable spaces for certain types of interaction and activity, the library can encourage its use as a low intensive meeting place[16] or even an "information ground", a place where people gather for a life activity but find themselves seeking and sharing information.[17] Consider, for example, a playground, where mothers come to let their children play but end up exchanging information on childcare needs.

It is easy to see how the community's social capital[18] will be increased through these more frequent and substantive interactions between diverse people.[19] They can be instrumental in cultivating the increasingly elusive bridging social capital or "weak ties"[20] which unite acquaintances. Since these networks are inclusionary and may connect people of many different demographics and life experiences, they encourage diversity. They have tangible benefits for patrons especially at a time of high unemployment, as most people find their jobs through weak ties, not from cold applications or even close friends.[21] The di-

---

16. Ragnar Audunson et al., "Public Libraries, Social Capital and Low Intensive Meeting Places," *Information Research* 12, no. 4 (2007), http://informationr.net/ir/12-4/colis/colis20.html.

17. Karen Fisher et al., "Social Spaces, Casual Interactions, Meaningful Exchanges: 'Information Ground' Characteristics Based on the College Student Experience," *Information Research* 12, no. 2 (2006): 2.

18. "Whereas physical capital refers to physical objects and human capital refers to properties of individuals, social capital refers to connections among individuals—social networks and the norms of reciprocity and trustworthiness that arise from them" (Putnam, 2000, 19).

19. Andreas Varheim, "Do Libraries Matter? Public Libraries and the Creation of Social Capital," *Journal of Documentation* 64, no. 6 (2008): 889–890.

20. Mark Granovetter, "The Strength of Weak Ties," *American Journal of Sociology* 78 no. 6 (1973): 1362.

21. Ibid, 1373.

versity, robust and free exchange of information, and social and economic opportunity which are so enhanced by a library space which encourages use as an information ground speak to the American vision of democracy.

Do our current library spaces promote such use? Fisher, Saxton, Edwards and Mai examined The Seattle Public Library's central building (SPL) as place. The modernist glass-and-metal building, stuffed to the gills with green systems and complete with coffee shop, retail space, and auditorium, is a perfect example of the direction modern libraries have taken. The authors acknowledge that "the new SPL building was designed with the express purpose of bringing people together via its meeting rooms, collaborative work spaces, coffee stand, atria, use of color, lighting and furniture. Indeed, the third floor of SPL is called the 'Living Room.' But . . . how effective are these efforts?"[22]

The modern mega-library's good intentions are only partially successful. While many people enjoy and use the library, others find it cold or intimidating. Fisher, et al. also concludes that the central library has never reached the status of Oldenburg's "third place,"[23] like the neighborhood bar or even the bookstore, which invites conversation and a sense of community. Emily Ranseen recognizes the role of the library space in combating "a world of incredible fragmentation"[24] by offering a multitude of spaces to appeal to a diverse population, which SPL does. However, she doubts that this function must be tied to coffee shops, theatres, and other trappings of the modern library building. Does the library even need to be an independent, freestanding structure to serve these needs?

The Urban Planning Perspective and the Boston Model

While librarians have just begun to study the library as place, architects have been examining the relationship between space and human interaction since William Hollingsworth Whyte's revolutionary 1980 *The Social Life of Small Urban Spaces*, in which he observed and analyzed several thriving public spaces in New York City for the elements which affected human interaction.[25] Many oth-

22. Karen Fisher et al., "Seattle Public Library as Place: Reconceptualizing Space, Community, and Information at the Central Library," in *The Library as Place: History, Community, and Culture*, ed. John E. Buschman and Gloria J. Leckie (Westport, CT: Libraries Unlimited, 2007): 145.

23. Ray Oldenburg, *The Great Good Place: Cafes, Coffee Shops, Bookstores, Bars, Hair Salons, and Other Hangouts at the Heart of a Community* (New York: Marlowe, 1999): 16.

24. Emily Ranseen, "The Library as Place: Changing Perspectives," *Libr Adm Manage* 16, no. 4 (2002): 203.

25. William H. Whyte, *The social life of small urban spaces.* (Washington, D.C.: Conservation Foundation, 1980).

ers followed suit,[26] and their general analyses of public places are often directly applicable to libraries. The City of Boston distilled these theories into a plan for developing "21st century streets" which established 11 criteria for a "Great Street." Because the goal of this plan is to increase interaction, interest, and information flow in a public space, it is also well-suited for discussing the success of a library. The criteria of the Boston model are: pedestrian comfort, flexibility, art and activity, inviting to everyone, understandability, long-term & sustainable, 21st century Boston image, utilizes technology, partnership, wayfinding, and seamlessness.[27]

Pedestrian comfort includes both comfort and safety. Flexibility means that a public space can be a "marketplace, promenade, performance space, [and/or] formal venue." Art and activity is about creating a vibrant cultural space. Inviting to everyone, defined as "equal quality and accessibility to all people" resonates with the library's staunch commitment to accessibility and diversity. These criteria are enhanced by partnership, as we cultivate "relationships . . . to sustain programming."

Understandability, or visual cues that help a person navigate the space, and wayfinding, or the people's knowledge of "where they are [and] what's around them" in order to find what they need, are equally relevant in any large space. Long-term and sustainable is self-explanatory, but Boston's succinct description of "longevity, equity, and participation" is appealing because it clearly unites environmental choices like longevity with community concerns like equity. Seamlessness is related to participation as well; it is free and active flow of people into and around the space.

Obviously the 21st century Boston image is specific to one area, but the idea of a space which clearly reflects both a modern sensibility and the traditional values of its community is universally applicable. Since no space will accommodate all criteria equally, we must make spatial decisions based on those which are most important to our communities. The most effective choice does not need to resemble a traditional or modern library building. In fact, it is unlikely to do so, as the library structure was not pioneered with sustainability in mind. If a library is to be truly sustainable, it must be willing to radically reconceptualize its space if necessary. Architects recognize the inadequacies of our current paradigm

---

26. "The Human Setting," *Architectural Association Quarterly* Special Edition ed. Dennis Sharp.; 1 no. 3 (1969).; David M. Callejo Pérez, et al., "Pedagogy of Place: Seeing Space as Cultural Education." (New York: P. Lang, 2004).

27. Mayor Thomas M. Merino and the City of Boston. *Crossroads Initiative.* (Boston: City of Boston, 2005): 11.

and its attendant assumptions. "The 20ᵗʰ century city is over," said SPL architect Rem Koolhaus. "It has nothing to teach us anymore."[28]

Questioning Our Paradigm

Our idea of how a library should look and function is rooted in a set of assumptions based on the way we perceive library history. We have tended to follow the Carnegie model of large, independent, iconic buildings (albeit with evolving aesthetics) when designing new libraries. As a result, when American libraries became aware that they needed to integrate with other community institutions,[29] they stayed true to this precedent and absorbed elements of those entities into their own buildings. The product is the modern mega-library, much like SPL's central building.

Yet a single, centralized library may not be the most sustainable solution, especially as other sustainability efforts have reached a different conclusion. The EVI ecovillage at Ithaca[30] will serve as an example of a different paradigm of consciously-designed sustainable space. The development recognizes that physical proximity is closely tied to sustainability. Though the ecovillage cooperative owns 176 acres, residents use only 20% for homes, offices, and recreational spaces, maintaining the rest as wilderness preserves. Through proximity, the ecovillage encourages seamless flow (recall that seamlessness is one criterion of the Boston model) between many daily activities. The arrangement reduces gasoline consumption, promotes green space, supports the local economy, and encourages social relationships.

A central library may be far from many of its users, especially the poor who rely most heavily on its services. Rather than seamlessness, distance encourages dedicated trips to the library. Its size and aesthetic further promote a consciousness that the library is distinct. Even branch libraries are usually discreet destinations, if somewhat more convenient ones. They may reduce travel, but do not really promote seamlessness. As most library systems lack the immense resources that would be required to maintain a comprehensive network of branches, some residents may still travel significant distances. Clearly, sustainability requires that we develop a new way to consider location.

28. Nicolai Ouroussoff, "The New, New City" *New York Times*, June 8, 2008, http://www.nytimes.com/2008/06/08/magazine/08shenzhen-t.html?_r=2.

29. Cathryn Harris, "Libraries with Lattes: The New Third Place," *Australas Public Libr Inf Serv* 20 no. 4 (2007): 145.

30. Andy Kirby, "Redefining Social and Environmental Relations at the Ecovillage at Ithaca: A Case Study," *Journal of Environmental Psychology* 23 (2003): 323–332.

A second issue with our current paradigm is the demand for immediacy. Most environmentally sustainable choices require a greater investment of time than our productivity-obsessed culture generally allows. Walking takes longer than biking; mending something takes longer than replacing it; waiting for a bestseller on hold at the library takes longer than buying one new. Yet the modern centralized library emphasizes convenience. It's a one-stop shop. Though this may seem appealing on the surface, it is ultimately unsustainable. Time-consuming eco-friendly activities are vital for building sustainable community and fostering diversity. Ranseen defines diversity not as ethnic or cultural variety, but as "the differences in the ways individuals feel and act."[31] When we can't accomplish everything ourselves and instantaneously, we are forced to recognize and rely on each other's unique skills and perspective.

The library as place has the power to bring diverse people together if it prioritizes diversity and community over immediacy. This is a core principle of the EVI ecovillage. For example, members who enjoy cooking do the cooking for all, while those who prefer childcare supervise their children.[32] As they share work, the residents also build social ties. Researchers observed that, "(t)his easy sociability replaces the effort traditionally required to invite someone to dinner, organize baby-sitters, etc., and serves to keep people in touch with each other in a natural and informal way."[33] When we take the time required to be environmentally sustainable, we build sustainable community.

Of course there is no value for libraries in delivering the same service we already offer more slowly, just as there would be no value in waiting a few minutes longer in your car for your fast-food burger, and I am not suggesting that we intentionally inconvenience people. However, if we can develop a model of space which emphasizes community, collaboration, and diversity first, and convenience only secondarily, we will be adhering much more closely to our professional values.

A Different Paradigm is Possible

The current paradigm of distance and haste, embodied by the centralized and all-encompassing building, is to integrate ourselves into the web of the community by sucking other resources *in*. I hold that we must do the opposite,

---

31. Emily Ranseen, "The Library as Place: Changing Perspectives," *Libr Adm Manage* 16, no. 4 (2002): 203.

32. Andy Kirby, "Redefining Social and Environmental Relations at the Ecovillage at Ithaca: A Case Study," *Journal of Environmental Psychology* 23 (2003): 326.

33. Ibid.

and *turn the library inside out.* We must put the library, or at least pieces of it, where people already are. Of course, it is generally large, central buildings, not branches, which follow this consumptive model; however, as it is usually these central showpieces that we are so keen to "green," it is here that I am most concerned about ensuring that we are not merely green but truly sustainable. Branch libraries are a step towards turning the library inside out, but they may lack some of the qualities of a third place.[34] The branch is just that—a branch, a limb, an extremity. A useful tool to be sure, yet our goal is to be the heart. If we abandon the idea that the library must first and always be its own building, and instead recognize and capitalize on the important spatial relationships already extant in the community, we can be truly integrated and sustainable.

There are many possible realizations of this idea, which libraries are only beginning to explore. Why not check out library books, or even talk to a librarian, at an existing local third place, like a coffee shop or park? Street Lab's Uni Project, which will place modular structures that house library materials and services in public spaces, is an excellent example of this type of innovation.[35] We should continue to think creatively along these lines. Why not have a library at a transit station, for example? Commuters could pick up the latest thriller just before stepping onto the train or bus, get recommendations from a librarian, or participate in a program during a long wait. The library could even offer a reloadable card which could simultaneous check out a book, cover bus fare, pay a fine, and serve as a visual reminder of the library's presence. The proximity is absolute; the library is located in a place the user already visits on a twice-daily basis. By seeing the librarian and other regular users with such frequency, and by occasionally taking a few moments out of his rushed morning routine to chat about a book, the user is sure to develop and deepen social connections. The fact that some immediacy is compromised—a user who wants a particular book may have to wait a few days, and talking with a librarian and other users consumes a few minutes—is a small loss considering what has been gained in terms of environmental and community sustainability.

This can also be applied to place-dependent resources other than books. Consider free access to a computer and library-only databases in popular community locations. Librarians, of course, are the library's most powerful resources. Readers' advisory in a shopping mall? Facilitated book groups at a popular

34. Karen Fisher et al., "Seattle Public Library as Place: Reconceptualizing Space, Community, and Information at the Central Library," in *The Library as Place: History, Community, and Culture,* ed. John E. Buschman and Gloria J. Leckie (Westport, CT: Libraries Unlimited, 2007): 152–153.

35. Kelley, Michael, "Using the Cube to Bring Back the Book," Library Journal (2011): http://www.libraryjournal.com/lj/home/891436-264/using__the_cube_to.html.csp.

restaurant? Book talks at open mic night? Librarians at the theatre to answer historical questions after a Shakespeare play? Libraries and librarians could create many opportunities to integrate themselves into their communities, increasing their engagement with all users but also creating new ways to reach currently underserved populations. Consider how many more immigrants, who may distrust government institutions, might participate in conversation groups or citizenship classes if they took place on more familiar and comfortable ground. Think of how many teens might talk to a librarian at a trendy hangout, even if they never set foot in the library. What are the popular places in your community? If appropriate aspects of the library are there (graphic novels at a teen hangout, perhaps, or fiction bestsellers for the morning commute), people who would never have considered the special trip to the downtown library will make the library part of their daily lives.

This model requires a sizeable and knowledgeable librarian team, a significant expense. However, that is exactly the kind of expense we want. It will exponentially increase the number and quality of interactions people have with their library. It will make access to knowledge and resources truly available to all residents in a way previously unimaginable. It may be tempting for libraries to meet staffing needs for libraries out in the community by turning to the increasingly popular model of rotating a bare-bones staff through multiple locations. However, staffing inconsistency interferes with developing sustainable community because it prevents individuals from forming an ongoing connection with a librarian. Each location in the community should offer a familiar face as well as materials and services.

It's time to acknowledge that sustainable community requires connections, and connections mean relationships with human beings. Librarians are an essential human part of the community, and cannot simply be shuffled around like identical copies of a book. Both the community and the library staff themselves will experience greater satisfaction and sense of community with this arrangement. Wouldn't we rather use our money to support people than enormous and costly buildings and gadgets that will break or become obsolete in a few short years? I think a community willing to sanction money for a building would be even happier to devote it to a cause that will directly impact their daily lives in addition to offering increased sustainability. This will also offset the potentially anti-social effects of simply "buying" a green building[36] by enhancing social interaction and community ties.

That said, a central building is not necessarily incompatible with this kind of networked outreach. There may be a place for one in your community. You

36. Nina Mazar Chen-Bo Zhong, "Do Green Products Make Us Better People?" *Psychological Science* 21 (4), (2010): 494–498.

may have a community of researchers who need a large body of printed work on hand, or you may have a special collection which needs to be safely stored. If your town is small enough, the library may already be a fully integrated space. A large, showy building might be appropriate if you are trying to attract tourists. My argument is only that there is no reason to assume that this is necessary without considering the dynamics of your community.

Evaluating with the Boston Model

The Boston model can be a useful tool for deciding which spatial decisions will be best for your community. As an example, I will analyze the general concept of "turning the library inside out," or putting library resources where people already go, but your library should conduct its own analysis based in local context.

Some criteria are essentially unaffected by the proposed change. "Pedestrian comfort" is a concern no matter the location. Some people will be comforted by the traditional library setting; others will enjoy seeking information in their most familiar surroundings. Safety remains a concern of unchanged importance, and, as in libraries now, will be handled differently depending on the community's needs. "21st century image" is also a matter of opinion. Which building has aesthetics more in keeping with your town's image is entirely subjective. "Utilizing technology" also is largely unaffected. Web-based catalogs, downloadable and mobile resources, and library websites will not be significantly altered by even a radical alteration in physical design. At most, a few computers or databases will be available at different locations than before; the services offered need not change. Finally, "understandability" will continue to be dependent on interior organization and signage, which is not dependent on external location.

However, some criteria will be monumentally strengthened. "Flexibility" will be heightened enormously. The library will not be limited to including features and locations it can accommodate within its existing bulky structure; it will be able to incorporate itself into as many different types of environments as the community can imagine. Along these lines, the connections between the library and its partners ("partnership") will be amplified. With financial resources ever more limited, many libraries have already come to rely on community partners. Sharing a physical location will pave the way for even more sustainable and vibrant long-term relationships, while reducing the overhead for both groups and increasing the number of possible partners. Art and activity will also be improved through such relationships with cultural institutions. As the lines are blurred between the library, other community institutions and businesses, work, transit, and entertainment, the library will begin to take on the "seamlessness" of the ecovillage.

Most important, perhaps, is the major gain in the realm of being "inviting to everyone." Defined by the Boston model as "equal quality and accessibility to all people," in the library context this takes on the connotation of equal access and intellectual freedom. While a looming central building might intimidate or alienate some people, passively limiting their access, bringing resources to environments they find welcoming will actively include them. All of these criteria working together result in a library, community, and environment that is "long-term and sustainable," engaged heavily in "longevity, equity, and participation."

The only criteria which will likely be compromised is wayfinding. Signage to the library from the street might be lost, and the library would have to advertise its new locations. Libraries located inside other community institutions, like coffee shops or train stations, would be dependent on their host institutions to make the library space visible and easily navigable. However, these concerns can be mitigated by advance planning. Furthermore, this criterion is not always realized in an ideal fashion in existing central libraries. In nearly all ways important to environmental and community sustainability, an inside-out model of library development is equal or potentially superior to the modern gobble-it-all-up mentality.

Conclusion

It is good for a library building to be green, but it is far from enough. If we acknowledge a responsibility to our earth and our communities, we must focus on being sustainable for the long-term. Sustainability means recognizing and strengthening the connections between the indivisible elements of the built library, the environment, and the community. Architects and urban planners have developed solutions for articulating and reinforcing these connections in other contexts which can be applied to libraries. These solutions translate into a new era in sustainable design, in which the library focuses on integrating itself into existing community spaces rather than pulling services into an expensive and technology-dependent library building. Proof of the robustness of this concept is provided through an urban planning framework, the Boston model. However, this concept by nature requires local context; therefore specific innovations will need to be developed and analyzed at the local level.

References

American Library Association. "Libraries Build Sustainable Communities." American Library Association, http://www.ala.org/ala/mgrps/rts/srrt/tfoe/lbsc/librariesbuild.cfm (accessed January 18, 2010).

Antonelli, Monika. "The Green Library Movement: An Overview of Green Library Literature and Actions from 1979 to the Future of Green Libraries." *Electronic Green Journal* 27 (Fall 2008), http://escholarship.org/uc/item/39d3v236.

Audunson, Ragnar, Andreas Varheim, Svanhild Abo, and Erling Dokk Holm."Public Libraries, Social Capital and Low Intensive Meeting Places." *Information Research* 12, no. 4 (2007), http://informationr.net/ir/12-4/colis/colis20.html.

Betz-Zall, Jonathan. "Libraries Build Sustainable Communities at PNLA." *PNLA Quarterly* 67, no. 1 (2002): 5.

Boston Street Lab, Inc. "Storefront Library." (2010) http://www.storefrontlibrary.org.

Brown, Jeffrey L. "Making a Huge Difference in So Many Little Ways." *Public Libraries* 40 (2001): 22.

Council on Library and Information Resources. *Library as Place: Rethinking Roles, Rethinking Space.* Washington, D.C.: Council on Library and Information Resources, 2005.

Fisher, Karen E., Carol F. Landry, and Charles Naumer. "Social Spaces, Casual Interactions, Meaningful Exchanges: 'Information Ground' Characteristics Based on the College Student Experience." *Information Research* 12, no. 2 (2006), http://InformationR.net/ir/12-1/paper291.html.

Fisher, Karen, Matthew Saxon, Phillip Edwards, and Jens-Erik Mai. "Seattle Public Library as Place: Reconceptualizing Space, Community, and Information at the Central Library." In *The Library as Place: History, Community, and Culture,* edited by John E. Buschman and Gloria J. Leckie. Westport, CT: Libraries Unlimited, 2007.

Goldberg, Martin. "Books, Billiards, and Bowling: Joint-Use According to Carnegie." *American Libraries* December (1999): 50–53.

Granovetter, Mark . "The Strength of Weak Ties." *American Journal of Sociology* 78, no. 6 (1973): 1360–1380.

Harris, Cathryn. "Libraries with Lattes: The New Third Place." *Australasian Public Libraries and Information Services* 20, no. 4 (2007): 145–52.

Kelley, Michael, "Using the Cube to Bring Back the Book," *Library Journal*, July 28, 2011, http://www.libraryjournal.com/lj/home/891436-264/ using__the_cube_to.html.csp.

Kirby, Andy. "Redefining Social and Environmental Relations at the Ecovillage at Ithaca: A Case Study." *Journal of Environmental Psychology* 23 (2003): 323–332.

Long, Sarah Ann. "Libraries Can Help Build Sustainable Communities," *American Libraries* 31, no. 26 (2001): 7.

Mannarini, Terri, Stefano Tartaglia, Angela Fedi, and Katiuscia Greganti. "Image of Neighborhood, Self-Image and Sense of Community." *Journal of Environmental Psychology* 26 (2006): 202–214.

Mazar, Nina and Chen-Bo Zhong. "Do Green Products Make Us Better People?" *Psychological Science*, 21 (4), (2010): 494–498 http://pss.sagepub.com/content/21/4/494.full.pdf+html?ijkey=NN141Y SvYeuC6&keytype=ref&siteid=sppss&utm_source=eNewsletter&utm_medium=email&utm_campaign=1J22.

Merino, Thomas M., Mayor and the City of Boston. *Crossroads Initiative*. Boston: City of Boston, 2005.

Oldenburg, Ray. The Great Good Place: Cafes, Coffee Shops, Bookstores, Bars, Hair Salons, and Other Hangouts at the Heart of a Community. New York: Marlowe, 1999.

Ouroussoff, Nicolai. "The New, New City." *New York Times*, June 8, 2008, http://www.nytimes.com/2008/06/08/magazine/08shenzhen-t.html?_r=2.

Putnam, Robert. *Bowling Alone: The Collapse and Revival of American Community*. New York: Simon & Schuster, 2000.

Ranseen, Emily. "The Library as Place: Changing Perspectives." *Library Administration and Management* 16, no. 4 (2002): 203–207.

The Oxford English Dictionary Online. http://dictionary.oed.com.

Sager, Don. "Public Libraries and the Sustainable Communities Movement." *Public Libraries* 40, no. 1 (2001): 22.

Sands, Johanna and Libris Design Project, *Sustainable Library Design*. San Francisco: C.M Salter Associates, 2000.

Stoss, F.W. "Sustainable Communities and the Roles Libraries and Librarians Play." *Reference and User Services Quarterly* 42, no. 3 (2003): 206–210.

Varheim, Andreas, Sven Steinmo, and Eisaku Ide. "Do Libraries Matter? Public Libraries and the Creation of Social Capital." *Journal of Documentation* 64, no. 6 (2008): 877–892.

Whyte, William Hollingsworth. *The social life of small urban spaces*. Washington, D.C.: Conservation Foundation, 1980.

The Public Library's Role in the Transition Towns Movement

Monika Antonelli

Throughout the United States, public libraries play an important role in supporting the quality of life in their local communities. But in a world facing increasing instability due to economic, energy and environmental challenges, public libraries could find themselves functioning as lifeboats for community revival and survival.

In his book, *The Long Emergency*, James Howard Kunstler analyzes a world facing the end of cheap fossil fuels. This event, frequently known as peak oil, refers to the point at which oil production begins to decline worldwide and energy prices begin to continuously rise. Since modern living depends on the availability of cheap oil to provide the necessities of everyday life—from computers to electric lights and from cars to air conditioning—this situation is predicted to cause severe economic disruption leading to recession and possibly a global depression.[1]

Author David Korten in his book, *The Great Turning*, also describes the looming crisis facing the United States and the Western world. Korten depicts this situation as a crisis of choice between two different organizing models, the choice between Empire and Earth Community. Korten describes the path of Empire as the road society is currently moving down. It is a path of continuous

---

1. James Howard Kunstler, *The Long Emergency: Surviving the Converging Catastrophes of the Twenty-first Century* (New York: Atlantic Monthly Press, 2005).

economic growth, which ends in the collapse of modern civilization. Empire's collapse is harnessed to a troika composed of energy shortages, global climate change, and economic meltdown. In contrast, Earth Community uses cooperation organized through community partnerships to establish a new societal model that shares resources for the benefit of all members.[2]

One need only to open a newspaper to find examples of energy, environmental and economic stresses being played out on the local level. In the wake of Enron the availability of affordable and reliable electricity can no longer be considered a given. Throughout the United States chronic power outages have demonstrated the vulnerability of the power grid infrastructure. In 2005 the destructive effect of climate change was experienced through Hurricane Katrina. Rising gasoline prices have strained wallets and led to an increase in the percentage of household income being spent on transportation costs.

Throughout these events public libraries have been available to assist people and their communities weather the disruptions these economic and environmental challenges bring. By embracing their role as an educator for the community, libraries can also play a part in transitioning their communities to more positive societal outcomes. To help their communities cope with economic, energy and environmental challenges, libraries will need to look to the past as well as to the future. There are lessons to be learned from the 1970s from the back to the land movement, and from the 1980s on providing services for the homeless and the unemployed. But new initiatives like the Transition Towns movement can be employed to revolutionize the public library and prepare it for a central and expanded role in society.

In March 2008, *Library Journal* published the article, "After Oil: Public Libraries will have an Important Role to Play in our Post-Peak-Oil Society" by Professor Debra Slone from the School of Information at the University of South Florida. In the article Dr. Slone explained how oil is a finite resource and that society will need to adjust to new ways of doing everyday things. She also goes on to state her opinion that public libraries will be havens for community members.[3]

In 2008 the cost of gasoline rose above $4.00 a gallon and in 2012 there are many who forecast that gas will go beyond $5.00 a gallon. The rise in oil prices has affected the cost of many manufactured goods. Food costs have risen

2. David C. Korten, *The Great Turning: From Empire to Earth Community* (San Francisco: Berrett-Koehler, 2006).

3. Debra J. Slone, "After Oil: Public Libraries will have an Important Role to Play in our Post-Peak-Oil Society," *Library Journal* 133, no. 5 (March 15, 2008): 28–31, Academic Search Premier (31320894).

dramatically over the last few years and products made out of petroleum also continue to rise in price. At the same time the economy continues to be stuck in a recession. Because of the economic downturn public libraries have become a place where many people turn to get free online access, to use resources to look for work and to apply for jobs. Libraries have again become a place where many people and families are turning for recreation, be it library programs or the borrowing of recreational materials like DVDs and picture books.

In January 2009, before the ALA Midwinter Meeting, the Denver Public Library hosted a daylong event called *Transition Libraries: Resources for a Green Future*. The purpose of the event was to begin a conversation about what was at stake for communities, what were pathways of transition, and what was the role of libraries in the process.[4]

If people are to respond to peak oil and climate change by moving to a lower energy future and by relocalizing their communities, then citizens will need many of the skills that older Americans took for granted. Unfortunately, here in the United States many people have forgotten or never learned how to cook, sew, knit, repair things, grow food, build soil and live thriftily. In the future relearning these skills will be vital to the welfare of the populace, and communities will need public libraries to help people acquire these skills.

The Transition Towns movement is a grassroots initiative focused on building community resilience in the face of the challenges brought about by peak oil, climate change, and economic recession. The Transition concept emerged from work that permaculture designer Rob Hopkins did with his students at Kinsale Further Education College in County Cork, Ireland. While at Kinsale, Hopkins wrote an "Energy Descent Action Plan."[5] The idea was adapted and expanded in Hopkins hometown of Totnes, England and Totnes became the first Transition Town.[6]

The Transition process begins when a small group of community members come together to discuss their concerns about the challenges of peak oil, climate change and economic collapse. This small group then seeks to involve the larger community in creating a Transition Initiative to address the need to increase community resilience, reduce carbon emissions, and look for ways to strengthen the local economy. Transition Initiatives do not claim to have all of the answers

---

4. "Conference: Transition Libraries: Resources for a Green Future," *The Green Library*, accessed March 12, 2012. http://thegreenlibraryblog.blogspot.com/2009/01/conference-transition-libraries.html.

5. Rob Hopkins. The Transition Handbook: From Oil Dependency to Local Resilience (Totnes [England]: Green, 2008) 122–130.

6. Ibid, 177–183, 187–193.

for their community. Instead they use traditional wisdom and skills, combined with the creativity, determination, and knowledge of group members to produce solutions for local situations.[7]

As of March 2012, there were over 400 communities recognized as official Transition Towns in the world and nearly 100 official Transition Towns in the United States. Boulder City, Colorado, has the distinction of being the first U.S. city to become a Transition Town.[8]

The Transition movement has seven guiding principles which are used to empower and motivate communities. They include: 1) *positive visioning*; 2) *help people access good information and trust them to make good decisions*; 3) *inclusion and openness*; 4) *enable sharing and networking*; 5) *build resilience*; 6) *inner and outer transition*; and 7) *subsidiarity: self-organization and decision making at the appropriate level.*[9]

As can be discerned, the Transition movement's seven principles and the American Library Association's *Library Bill of Rights*[10] share several points in common. For example, the first half of the Transition principle 2 states: *help people access good information.* Most people are aware that the main mission of public libraries is to assist people in connecting to good information, not just information people want but the information they need. The Library Bill of Rights states, "*Books and other library resources should be provided for the interest, information, and enlightenment of all people of the community the library serves.*"[11] With these similar goals public libraries and Transition Towns have a common foundation for collaboration.

Libraries are also in sync with the Transition movements' third principle, "*inclusion and openness.*" The *Library Bill of Rights* states, "*A person's right to use a library should not be denied or abridged because of origin, age, background, or views.*"[12] Libraries are also supportive of the Transition movements' fourth principle, "*enable sharing and networking.*" Public libraries are leaders when it comes to sharing resources and networking with other libraries. The late Donella

---

7. "The Transition Town Movement," *Transition United States*, accessed March 15, 2012. http://transitionus.org/transition-town-movement.

8. "Transition Initiatives Directory," *Transition Network*, accessed March 15, 2012. http://www.transitionnetwork.org/initiatives.

9. "The 7 Guiding Principles of Transition," *Transition United States*, accessed March 15, 2012. http://transitionus.org/initiatives/7-principles.

10. "Library Bill of Rights," American Library Association, accessed March 16, 2012. http://www.ala.org/advocacy/intfreedom/librarybill.

11. Ibid.

12. Ibid.

Meadows described the public library as one of the "seven-plus wonders of sustainability" because of its ability to share resources.[13] It could be said that sharing resources is public libraries' brand identity.

While not stated in the *Library Bill of Rights* one could argue that public libraries are supportive of principle 5, "*inner and outer transition.*" One of the reasons libraries provide information resources is so that people can use them to improve their lives, be it by learning a new skill, getting a job, succeeding in school, or overcoming a personal challenge. Libraries are also familiar with principle 1, *positive visioning.* They are known to employ positive visioning whenever they engage in brainstorming type activities.

Unique to the Transition Towns movement are principles 5, *build resilience* and 6, *subsidiarity: self-organization and decision making at the appropriate level.* However these are two principles that could be employed by public libraries. For example, if libraries were able to improve their resilience, they would be better able to deal with economic downturns or even devastating acts of nature. In turn libraries could offer programs that teach patrons how to be more resilient and how to make their communities more resilient. By incorporating subsidiarity into the organization it would allow public libraries to function more efficiently. One way libraries already do this is by giving patrons the ability to purchase books on demand. Another way is by empowering library employees to respond to situations at the appropriate level of engagement. If a library clerk can solve a patron's problem, give the clerk the authority to solve the problem at that level.

Because public libraries serve as a community space it makes them an ideal education location, and many Transition Town Initiatives already host programs and events at their public libraries. Examples of libraries hosting Transition Town programs include the Missoula Public Library in Missoula, Montana which hosted the Transition Town Missoula's book discussion of *The Transition Handbook,* and film showings of *End of Suburbia* and *A Crude Awakening.*[14] On March 3, 2012, the Canton Public Library in Collinsville, Connecticut hosted the *Sustainable Living, Community Resilience and Transition Towns* program presented by Tina Clarke, a popular Transition Town trainer.[15]

---

13. Donella Meadows, "Seven-Plus Wonders of Sustainability," *Grist,* accessed March 12, 2012. http://grist.org/living/of4/.

14. "Transition Town Missoula," accessed March 11, 2012. http://sites.google.com/site/transitiontownmissoula/.

15. "Transition Towns Talk on March by Tina Clark, Transition Towns Trainer, at Clinton Public Library," *Connecticut Climate Change,* last modified February 23, 2012. http://ctclimatechange.com/index.php/transition-towns-talk-on-march-by-tina-clark-transition-towns-trainer-at-canton-public-library/.

Frequently public libraries will host Transition Town kick-off events like the one held on April 22, 2009 by the Newburyport Public Library in Newburyport, Massachusetts, which promised an introduction to the Transition Town Initiative, peak oil, climate change, economic instability and the International Transition Movement[16]. In April 2011 the Wayland Free Public Library hosted a talk to introduce the Transition Town model and how it could be used to impact the town of Wayland, Massachusetts.[17]

Another common information activity provided by Transition Town groups is the hosting of reskilling events. Reskilling events offer programs where people can rediscover older or more traditional ways of doing things, often by combining these traditional skills with 21st century knowledge. These reskilling abilities can include everything from how to darn a sock to how to cook with a solar oven; from how to raise bees to how to create a hoop tunnel. Again with their commitment and ongoing mission to providing community programs, libraries make ideal institutions to host and provide reskilling workshops.

Guest speakers for reskilling events can be found throughout a community. Some good places to find speakers are with the slow food movement, the urban farming movement, the DIY movement, and the permaculture movement as well as the Transition Towns movement itself. An example of a library hosting a reskilling event occurred on November 10, 2010 at the Berea Kentucky Library in Berea, Kentucky presented a *Reskilling Workshop on Clothes Mending*. At this program patrons were shown how to mend tears and sew on buttons.[18]

While not called reskilling workshops, many libraries currently offer programs that teach reskilling skills. The Lodi Public Library in Lodi, California held on October 18, 2010 a program called "Raising Chickens 101" where participants were taught how to raise backyard chickens.[19] Santa Barbara Public Library offered its 4th Annual Community Seed Swap on January 29, 2012. Participants were encouraged to bring seeds, plants and cuttings as well as gar-

16. Lynne Hendricks, "Local Residents Preparing Transition for Life after Oil," *Daily News*, April 13, 2009, http://www.newburyportnews.com/local/x845859435/ Local-residents-preparing-transition-for-life-after-oil/print.

17. Brooklyn Lowery, "Q&A with Transition Town Initiator Kaat Vander Straeten," *WaylandPatch*, April 2, 2011, http://wayland.patch.com/articles/ qa-with-transition-town-initiator-kaat-vander-straeten.

18. "Re-SKilling Workshop on Clothes Mending," *kyGREENtv*, accessed March 19, 2012, http://www.kygreen.tv/2010/07/re-skilling-workshop-on-clothes-mending/.

19. Pam Bauserman, "4-H leader Cherie Sintes-Glover Offers Tips for Raising Chickens," *Lodi News-Sentinel*, September 20, 2010, http://www.lodinews.com/features/ article_3aa025a8-0db2-5596-aa06-d4bc0034538e.html.

den knowledge to swap. Activities were offered on how to make seed balls, seed envelopes, as well as how to save seeds.[20]

When planning transition programs libraries should ask their patrons what they want to learn. Answers to this question can come from observing or by surveying the community. Programming can be made easy by reaching out to groups that are doing this work already. Librarians can bring their targeted audience to the library or they could also take their programs to their audience. Most importantly public libraries should not be afraid to be bold and have fun. This is easy to do by saying "yes" to new ideas, allowing enthusiastic energy to lead the direction of the programming, and by celebrating new achievements.

By building and strengthening relationships with local Transition Town Initiatives, libraries can look to Transition Town members for support. People engaged in the Transition Town movement care deeply about their communities and are committed to having a positive effect on the world. This means Transition Town members are also frequently politically engaged and, most if not all, can be assumed to be strong supporters of public libraries.

Public libraries and Transition Towns share common objectives and have much to gain from working together. By collaborating, both institutions can synergize their efforts. Having a community partner to assist in providing desired programming can be a valuable asset to public libraries. Public libraries can play an important role in the Transition Towns movement by offering groups places to host programs. In turn, by working with their local Transition Initiatives, public libraries can create loyal library supporters. Most importantly community members will be able to acquire the new skills they need to deal with economic, energy and environmental challenges facing society. Having public libraries and Transition Towns work together is a beneficial situation for all involved.

---

20. "4th Annual Santa Barbara Community Seed Swap," *Transition California*, accessed March 19, 2012, http://www.transitiontownsca.org/events/4th-annual-santa-barbara-community-seed-swap.

Author Information

Samantha Alberts received her MLS from Queens College in 2009. She earned a Masters in Public Policy from SUNY Stony Brook. She currently works at the Suffolk Cooperative Library System as the Technology and New Initiatives Librarian. She can be reached at samantha@suffolknet.org

Rebekkah Smith Aldrich, MLS, is the Coordinator for Library Growth & Sustainability at the Mid-Hudson Library System in New York where she has assisted 66 public libraries in the areas of governance, management, funding and facilities since 1998. Rebekkah is a certified Sustainable Building Advisor (NaSBA), Leadership in Energy & Environmental Design Accredited Professional (LEED AP). Rebekkah is the author of the Handbook for New Public Library Directors in New York State, a 2010 Library Journal Mover &Shaker and an active member of the New York Library Association. Rebekkah is a frequent presenter at conferences and runs her own consulting business, Sustainable Libraries, to help libraries find sustainable funding and facility options. You can connect with Rebekkah at http://www.facebook.com/SustainableLibraries or Rebekkah@SustainableLibraries.org

Christine Andresen is a Liaison Librarian for the College of Allied Health Sciences, Laupus Library, East Carolina University. Her research interests include information literacy instruction and outreach services for the allied health sciences. She can be reached at andresenc@ecu.edu

Monika Antonelli serves as an Outreach / Reference Librarian at Minnesota State University in Mankato, Minnesota. She received her MLS from the University of North Texas. In 2005 she received her Permaculture Certification. She currently serves on the MSU Environmental Committee. Monika can be reached at monika.antonelli@mnsu.edu

After working at a variety of public and academic libraries in BC and Alberta, **Julie Backer** has worked as a librarian in both public and technical services at West Vancouver Memorial Library since 2000. In June 2011 WVML received LEED Canada Existing Building: Operations and Maintenance Silver certification, the first LEED Canada EB: O&M certified building in British Columbia and the first library in Canada to receive the award. Julie belongs to a Vancouver car-sharing co-op and has two worm composters on her balcony. She can be reached at jbacker@westvanlibrary.ca

Audrey Barbakoff is an Adult Services Librarian at Kitsap Regional Library in Bainbridge Island, WA. Her passion for sustainability grew through Adamah, a farming and intentional community fellowship, in 2007. She continues to seek out ways to craft a more sustainable life for herself and her community through her library work. Her articles on public librarianship have appeared in American Libraries, Public Libraries, Library Philosophy and Practice, and In the Library with the Lead Pipe. She received her MLIS from the iSchool at the University of Washington in 2010. She can be reached at audrey.barbakoff@gmail.com

Brett Barbakoff is a sustainable designer running his own design services consulting company in the Pacific Northwest. He studied architectural design at the University of Illinois Urbana–Champaign for his Masters of Architecture and the University of Wisconsin–Milwaukee for his Bachelors of Architecture Studies. Brett has worked for several professional architecture firms, and is especially committed to creating affordable, sustainable built environments that promote design excellence and quality of life. Brett is a LEED Green Associate and pending BPI Building Analyst + Envelope professional, furthering his commitment to sustainable energy efficient design. He can be reached at barbakoffdesign@gmail.com

Laura L. Barnes is a Librarian with the Prairie Research Institute, embedded in the Illinois Sustainable Technology Center's Emerging Technology and Assistance Program. In addition to her day-to-day responsibilities as a librarian, she teaches businesses and organizations, including libraries, how to go green; serves as an information consultant to the Great Lakes Regional Pollution Prevention Roundtable (GLRPPR) and the Pollution Prevention

Resource Exchange (P2Rx); and authors the Environmental News Bits blog (http://envnewsbits.wordpress.com). Ms. Barnes earned a B.A. in History and an M.S. in Library and Information Science from the University of Illinois at Urbana–Champaign. She can be reached at l-barnes@illinois.edu

Nancy Bender is a librarian at Santa Monica Public Library. After earning her Master's in Library and Information Science from UCLA in 2004, she joined the Public Services department, responsible for adult programming at SMPL, and quickly established a niche in sustainable programs and marketing. Through programs such as the Sustainable Cinema series; panel discussions and author talks; collaborations with City of Santa Monica departments such as the Office of Sustainability and the Environment and the hugely popular Santa Monica Farmers Market; and the annual Green Prize for Sustainable Literature Awards, Nancy has provides the community with information and resources on the continually evolving sustainability movement. She is a member of the ALA and PLA, and chairs both the Green Prize for Sustainable Literature and Sustainability Committees at Santa Monica Public Library. She can be reached at nancy.bender@smgov.net

Greta Bever holds a BA from the College of the University of Chicago and an MA from the Graduate Library School of the University of Chicago. She began her professional career at the Chicago Public Library as a Children's Librarian in 1986. She worked in neighborhood branches in positions of increasing responsibility until 2001, when she was promoted to the position of Director of the Sulzer Regional Library. She has served as the Assistant Commissioner for Central Library Services of the Chicago Public Library since 2003. Greta can be reached at gbever@chipublib.org

Charles Forrest has more than thirty years of experience in academic and research libraries. After nearly a decade with the University of Illinois libraries, he moved to Emory University in 1988 where he has held a series of administrative positions in the Emory Libraries, including director of instructional support services and director of planning and budget. Currently director of library facilities, Charles has served as library project manager for numerous library construction and renovation projects, including the Center for Library and Information Resources, a major addition to Emory's main library. A member of the Committee on the Environment of Emory's University Senate, Charles served as library project manager for the renovation of Emory's original main library, the first LEED-certified renovation project on campus. With Karen Munro, Charles co-chaired the 2009 ACRL Conference Planning Green Component Committee. He can be reached at charles.forrest@emory.edu

As the Special Projects Librarian at the Calgary Public Library, **Rosemary Griebel,** chairs the Library's Eco-Action Committee, and is an active eco blogger. She is also involved in additional green library projects including the building of a sustainable new Central Library and the creation of library community gardens. Rosemary has always had a deep love and respect of the land, having grown up on the prairies. This passion for nature is reflected in her creative writing and in the off-hours she is a published poet and performer. She can be reached at rosemary.griebel@calgarypubliclibrary.com

Amy Gustavson is Coordinator of Instructional Services at Joyner Library, East Carolina University, Greenville, North Carolina. Her research interests include information literacy instruction and assessment. She can be contacted at gustavsona@ecu.edu

David Hisle is currently the Reference and Instruction Librarian at the Carteret County Community College Library, Morehead City, North Carolina. He was the Joyner Library Fellow at East Carolina University's Joyner Library from 2008–2010. He can be contacted at hisled@carteret.edu

Dave Hudson is a librarian at the University of Guelph in Guelph, Ontario, Canada. His efforts in support of environmental justice these days include providing research education to student and community activist organizations, as well as performance and other creative work as a spoken word artist (YouTube channel: davidjameshudson). Dave can be reached at davidjameshudson@gmail.com

Maria Anna Jankowska (majankowska@libray.ucla.edu) is the Social Sciences Librarian at the UCLA Charles E. Young Research Library. She holds a Ph.D. in economics from Poznan University of Economics in Poland and an M.L.I.S. from the University of California at Berkeley. She is the founding editor of *Electronic Green Journal* (http://escholarship.org/uc/uclalib_egj), the first peer-reviewed open access journal devoted to environmental information sources. Since 1994, the journal provides platform for scholarly communications in the area of national and international environmental information sources and environmental sustainability. Maria for many years has chaired the American Library Association's (ALA) Social Responsibility Round Table Task Force on the Environment. She was working on the ALA adoption of non-chlorine paper policy, greening ALA conferences and exhibits, and many environmental programs organized by the Task Force. In 2002, *Library Journal* named her as one of fifty "Movers and Shakers" in American librarianship. Maria was recognized for her scholarship in libraries, work on synthesizing information for Web access, promotion of environmental ethics and information, and national and international activities. In 2004/05 she was awarded a Senior Fulbright Fellowship. In 2010, she co-authored an article in *College & Research Libraries* entitled "Sustainability Challenges for Academic Libraries: Planning for the Future." The article is available at: http://crl.acrl.org/content/71/2/160.full.pdf+html

Susan Kendall, PhD, MS (LIS), is the Health Sciences Coordinator and Biology Librarian at the Michigan State University Libraries. She has been a member of the MSU Libraries Environmental Committee since 2006. With a degree in biology, she has a special interest in ecology, biodiversity, and wildlife habitat conservation and has done library exhibits on these themes. In her free time she is interested in native plant gardening for wildlife. She lives in a retrofit cohousing community in downtown Lansing, Michigan, where she shares resources, environmental values, and grows organic vegetables with neighbors. E-mail: skendall@msu.edu

Kate Lawrence is a recently retired librarian and author of The Practical Peacemaker: How Simple Living Makes Peace Possible (Lantern Books, 2009). She encourages sustainability through her blog "A Practical Peacemaker Ponders . . ." at practicalpeacemaker.com, and through vegetarian/vegan outreach activities. She welcomes reader comments at kate@practicalpeacemaker.com

Mark McCullough is the Reference Services Coordinator at Minnesota State University in Mankato, Minnesota. He received his MLS from Indiana University. He can be reached at mark.mccullough@mnsu.edu

Karen Munro is Head of the University of Oregon Portland Library & Learning Commons. She has also served as E-Learning Librarian at the University of California, Berkeley, and as Literature Librarian at the University of Oregon. She's interested in learning spaces, new models for publication and scholarly communication, and transformative user services in academic libraries. She co-chaired the 2009 ACRL Conference Planning Green Component Committee, helping to set new sustainability standards for ACRL and ALA conferences. Karen can be reached at kmunro@uoregon.edu

Kriss Ostrom is the Head of Circulation Services in the Michigan State University Libraries. She was one of four library staff members who began personally recycling library newspapers around 1982, was an early member of the MSU Libraries Recycling Committee in the late 1980s, and continued as a member from the late 1980s (when the committee became the Library Environmental Committee) until now. She has been the library liaison to the MSU

Campus Recyclers and the MSU Surplus Store since 2000. Kriss served as the Board President of the East Lansing Food Co-op from 2005 to early 2011, during which time the co-op moved from near insolvency to thriving. She has also coordinated ticket sales for the East Lansing Film Festival since 2005. E-mail: kriss@mail.lib.msu.edu

Dri Ralph is an urban planner working for the King County Library System as the Facilities Design Coordinator. Since 2005 Dri has helped KCLS design and build more than 20 buildings, all have been sited and built using the best available practices regarding sustainable design and construction. Prior to her time at KCLS, Dri worked for the City of Bremerton as an environmental planner. Dri got her master's degree from Tufts University's department of Urban and Environmental Policy and Planning. She can be reached at driralph@gmail.com

Krista Reynolds, MLIS, serves as the science librarian at Concordia University in Portland, Oregon. She earned her MLIS from the University of Washington and her B.S. in biology from Willamette University, where she first became passionate about environmental issues. Krista enjoys exploring the outdoors with her husband, Rick, and helping him to create a series of environmental education books for children starring "The EverGreen Twins." Email: kmreynolds@cu-portland.edu

Matt Reynolds is the Public Services Librarian for the Verona Joyner Langford North Carolina Collection at East Carolina University. His research interests include bibliographic instruction in special collections settings and the impact of the digitization of rare materials on the same. He can be reached at reynoldsm@ecu.edu

Robbie Sittel works for the Tulsa City-County Library as a Government Documents and Reference Librarian. She is a founding member of the Library's Green Team. When she's not working as a reference librarian, Robbie attempts to be a small scale urban homesteader through rainwater harvesting, composting, and edible gardening. She can be reached at rsittel@tulsalibrary.org

Kathryn Totten is manager of outreach services for Anythink libraries in Adams County Colorado. She has held leadership positions in the American Library Association Office of Literacy and Outreach Services Bookmobiles Committee and the Association of Bookmobiles and Outreach Services. She has been instrumental in planning local and national outreach and bookmobile programing and staff training. She has been a speaker at ALA Annual Conference and ABOS Conference. She can be contacted at this email address: ktotten@anythinklibraries.org

Michael Unsworth is the American History and Canadian Studies Librarian at the Michigan State University Libraries. Since 2005, he has been a member of the MSU Libraries Environmental Committee, most notably in coordinating the Libraries' participation in the annual Smart Commute Challenge. As Assistant Director of the MSU Canadian Studies Center, he followed the controversy over Canadian trash exports to Michigan. He maintained a website on the issue and spoke to numerous groups. He is active in bicycling advocacy, serving as the moderator of the Mid-Michigan Active Transportation Coalition and as an instructor in bicycling commuting. Email: unsworth@msu.edu

Beth Filar Williams has served as the Coordinator of Library Services for Distance Learning at the University of North Carolina at Greensboro since 2008. She has Masters of Library and Information Science from the University of Maryland and BA in Geography from the Johns Hopkins University. She was previously a library consultant serving all types of libraries through the Colorado Library Consortium, a Map/GIS Librarian at the University of Colorado at Boulder and a middle school librarian in Howard County Maryland. She has been blogging at Going Green @ your library for several years, presented for various libraries and consortiums, and published articles and a couple book chapters on the topic. Visit her blog http://greeningyourlibrary.wordpress.com/ , follow her on Twitter @greenyourlib, or email her at greeningyourlibrary@gmail.com

Kate Zoellner is the instruction and reference liaison librarian to the College of Education and Human Sciences and the Department of Psychology at The University of Montana's Maureen and Mike Mansfield Library. In addition to her role as a liaison, Zoellner develops collections, coordinates outreach to regional high schools, and serves as chair of the Library's Assessment Committee, working with colleagues across departments to gather and analyze quantitative and qualitative library and user data. Zoellner received her Masters of Science in Information from the University of Michigan's School of Information. She is an active member of the Association of College and Research Libraries' Education and Behavioral Sciences Section. She can be reached at kate.zoellner@umontana.edu

Index